THE POORHOUSE
STATE

THE AMERICAN WAY OF LIFE ON
PUBLIC ASSISTANCE

THE
POORHOUSE
STATE

THE AMERICAN WAY OF LIFE ON
PUBLIC ASSISTANCE

by

RICHARD M. ELMAN

Pantheon Books · A Division of Random House

NEW YORK

Give money me, take friendship who so list,
For friends are gone, come once adversity,
When money yet remaineth safe in chest
That quickly can thee bring from misery;
Fair face show friends, when riches do abound,
Come time of proof, farewell they must away;
Believe me well, they are not to be found,
If God but send thee once a lowering day.
Gold never starts aside, but in distress,
Finds ways enough to ease thine heaviness.

Barnabe Googe
Sixteenth century English poet

Merely responding with a "relief check" to complicated
social or personal problems—such as ill health, faulty education, domestic discord, racial discrimination, or inadequate skills—is not likely to provide a lasting solution.
Such a check must be supplemented, *or in some cases made
unnecessary* [emphasis added] by positive services and solu-
tions, offering the total resources of the community to
meet the total needs of the family to help our less fortunate
citizens help themselves.

John F. Kennedy, Special message to
Congress, 1962

Food	$15.86
Clothing	2.55
Electricity	1.55
Gas	.80
Laundry	1.80
Wash and dry	2.35
Personal care	.95
Household supplies	.50
Total needs semimonthly	**$26.36**
Plus shelter	24.10
Relief budget for a single man in New York, 1965	**$50.46**

AUTHOR'S NOTE

• I have disguised—whenever possible—the identities of the functionaries and their clients who appear here, and also some of the settings, but I have not invented anything. Beyond formal interviews and research, I spent two years talking with people on and off public welfare. Let this then be an acknowledgment to the many who told me where to look and helped me to see. To R.C., S.B., F.P., C.E., J.K., and B.L., I owe much, but they should not bear the blame for my errors. Their commitment has been an inspiration to me. To my editor, Sara Blackburn of Pantheon Books, I extend special thanks for advice and encouragement; and of course I am, as usual, indebted to my wife Emily for putting up with my wanderings, missed dinners and appointments, and all too many long-winded conversations about poverty.

CONTENTS

PART ONE

ix

PART TWO

x

PART
ONE

1

THE POORHOUSE STATE

• Fascism "at its very best," wrote George Orwell, "is socialism with the virtues taken out." Precisely the same relationship exists between the Poorhouse State and the Welfare State to which an increasing number of Americans now belong and from which we can now "claim" a variety of benefits.

The Welfare State subsidizes the farmer; the Poorhouse State distributes his surplus product.

The Welfare State insures against old age; the Poorhouse State discourages dependency.

The Welfare State provides loans for small businessmen; the Poorhouse State provides retraining for the poor.

The Welfare State subsidizes the slumlord; the Poorhouse State subsidizes the tenant.

Not only are benefits under any given Welfare State program apt to be more generous and uniform than under a similar program of the Poorhouse State, but they do not customarily demand humiliation of the recipient. It is not the aim of the Welfare State to make its beneficiaries forfeit liberty and justice. By applying for assistance from the Poorhouse State, however, you must expect to forgo such privileges, for you will be treated as a social problem.

In the watery environs of New York City there are many small islands, nearly all of which serve this Poorhouse State. Hart's, Riker's, North Brother, and Welfare Island, among others, minister to individualized deprivations which have manifested themselves through misdemeanors and felonies, insane and addictive behavior, chronic illnesses, but for our largest category of deprivation—poverty itself—the City has created islands within its own precincts, racial and class ghettos in which one out of every fifteen New Yorkers lives on public assistance. In a period of unsurpassed national prosperity, their numbers are still increasing by an average of 5,200 persons a month. Even as the unemployment percentages drop, the relief rolls increase. In October, 1965, the Department of Welfare estimated that there were 512,497 such dependents in New York City. Out of narrow accommodation to—or perhaps self-protection from—the majority's problematical diagnosis of their indigence, they are often forced to lead lives as distinctively covert and habitual as those of drug addicts or any other members of the underworld.

The presence of so many public assistance clients has never been allowed to go unnoticed. They have been studied and lamented, analyzed and counseled. Occasionally, it has seemed as if their problems were distinctively urban or occupational in character, determined by their race, or their sex, or their uncertain family circumstances; but, like nearly all the eight million Americans presently living on public assistance, these half a million New Yorkers could also be characterized as frustrated consumers. As such, their situation is unique. Their desires to consume

4

have been overly stimulated, but their economic capabili-
ties are underdeveloped. Moreover, they have to abide by
a set of rules that tries to enforce their prudence. Enjoined
to consume by some, they are subsidized to a bare necessity by others. When a corporation reaches such an im-
passe, it floats stock or obtains a defense contract; for
people, there is only welfare. And whether they live in the
Borough of Manhattan or in an agricultural village in
Kansas, they may have to face suspicion, enforcement,
and victimization; in return for the minimum subsidies
they can expect to receive for food, rent, clothing, and
personal care, these eight million dependents are regularly
policed, punished, and rehabilitated, often with a complete disregard for their constitutionally guaranteed rights,
which, in some cases, they are expected to forfeit in advance as conditions of assistance. Threats of ultimate insti-
tutionalization are made, and they are forced to live under
constant suspicion of fraud. Applying for assistance, they
are often greeted by an armed policeman. They also become
acquainted with more subtle symbols of coercion throughout their dependencies. They are a target population in
the War on Poverty, which as often as not seems to view
them as the enemy.

Most of us can rationalize our behavior as consumers
through a variety of harmless gambits. Either we say it is
our pleasure, or our responsibility, or our compulsion, and
we usually feel little guilt about the waste we are helping
to perpetrate. But this presumption of competence is never
extended to the consuming clients who are too young, too
old, too sick, too unskilled, or too burdened down with

5

dependents to earn the wages that would allow them to be full-fledged consumers; and there are few among the approximately 190 million Americans not presently in need of public assistance who would argue that it should be. What we do for these people we say we are doing in their own best interests, reasonably certain that their consumption must be limited because we are sure that we shall never be in their situation. Stigmatized historically as paupers, indigents, and vagabonds but more recently as AFDC, TADC, OAA, MAI, or HR,[1] their bureaucratically alphabetized miseries are deemed suitable for the pre-added budget and the as-needed grant (in administering which, the social service worker must function as a detective) because it is assumed that their dependencies must be short-lived. And because the original programs of public assistance were created during the great depression for a caseload of skilled laborers (European immigrants and their descendants) who had been thrown temporarily out of work, the new clients—many of them dark-skinned, disadvantaged, perhaps unemployable under present circumstances—often find themselves at odds with this increasingly middle-class American polity because of their tendency to consume and still be dependent, which is considered alarming and which must, therefore, be controlled, suppressed, rehabilitated, even quarantined.

Dark-skinned people are only a minority in America. The dark-skinned welfare poor are a minority within that mi-

---

[1] Aid for Dependent Children, Temporary Aid for Dependent Children, Old Age Assistance, Medical Aid to the Indigent, and Home Relief are among the chief public assistance programs. County Welfare departments also offer aid to the blind and the disabled and assistance to veterans.

nority, lacking even the solidarity of its numbers, for the same majority that continues to make and administer the rules governing economic dependency commonly regards them as socially or morally, as well as economically, dubious; and the clients have been urged to agree with this diagnosis. It is, in fact, so prevalent that the Office of Economic Opportunity's insistence that it will not operate a "handout" program, when combined with its demands for the "maximum feasible participation" of the poor in all antipoverty programs, may prove out to be a cruel self-deception based on contradictory assertions. In what are these harassed unmarried mothers, children without fathers, old and disabled people, or men without futures expected to participate? They might, of course, begin to participate in a higher standard of living, commensurate with the general national affluence, if it were not so generally upheld by nearly the entire population that such people should not be coddled or everybody might aspire to the same deprivations.

There is no other group in America whose rights have been so often impugned and trampled upon as the citizenry of our Poorhouse State. In those states where racism has been official, Negro indigents have had to contend with racially, as well as morally, punitive statutes and policies that even now bar large numbers from minimum grants of public assistance. In general, the defenders of the working-class poor have not been shy, but the defenders of this *workless, shirking class* have been, responding only to the most blatant outrages. When Louisiana struck some 22,000 illegitimate Negro children from the welfare roles in 1960 to spite their parents, liberals and professionals had a difficult

7

time arousing any meaningful indignation from the federal establishment against such policies. Even now, in New York City, where as many as one thousand cases of Home Relief are closed every month for unspecified reasons, such behavior on the part of public welfare officials is regarded as routine.

These officials point out with some truth that they are under constant pressure at the state and local levels to keep costs down, but the indignities they must then administer become routine as well as pervasive. Women with illegitimate children can be examined in humiliating detail about the paternity of their offspring before being granted aid. Although "separate but equal" schemes of public education have been termed inherently unfair by the Supreme Court, all the state laws governing the economically dependent would appear to be, in this manner, discriminatory. The costs of such a dependency can be charged off against the applicant's legally responsible relatives (i.e., parents, grandparents, children, wives, and husbands), who must also pay income taxes for the support of these same applicants. To obtain assistance, the applicant must be prepared to sue his relatives in court. If he balks at doing so, assistance will be withheld. If, moreover, the legally responsible relative is declared a "putative" father and he defaults at acknowledging his paternity, he can be cited for contempt, tracked down, convicted, and sentenced, perhaps, to a penal institution such as Hart's Island.

Historians of American welfare legislation are fond of tracing its peculiarly punitive thrust to puritanical borrowings from the Elizabethan poor laws, but such a purposeful vindictiveness seems equally in keeping with our propensity for measuring success or failure in terms of economic mobility, of lauding the success, despising the failure, and rating the course of every human life in a kind of fever chart where a man is shown as either one or the other. Many of our poor have never been allowed to be either. They have been required to consume without ever being given the means to participate in the presumptive competence of those who consume in order to create the incentives for more consumption. Elsewhere consumption is maximized, but they remain marginal men. Being so far behind, it is sometimes difficult for them to envisage how they can begin to participate in the consumer paradise, to which they so aspire, through mere labor.

But the majority of us do labor. We work hard. Despite machines, far too many of us are forced to gain our comforts through drudgery. It may not be physical labor. Increasingly it may be only the wretchedness of office work that consumes our lives so that we often feel deprived when we do not work. Faced, therefore, with a new leisure class that has never, apparently, earned the right to that leisure that we detest, we tend to become abusive of those who are not even sharing in the daily ordeal of work. Somehow, we think, they must be taught the value of work and the need to rise as a consequence of their own efforts, perhaps so we may begin to share in their leisure with a clearer conscience. It is not that we do not wish these "poor" to share our aspirations; we say we are only too willing to help them if they prove to us that that is their intention. But we want them to go the hard route, to be our taxi drivers, restaurant employees, secretaries, and factory hands so that they can support their families and thus improve their lives. We want them to believe in our values—and they do! But when they still seem dependent we become angry and abusive, and not always in the old, obvious ways. We know, in fact, that the leisure of the poor can be a misery, so we no longer try to chastise them for it but to uplift them from it. We tell those who deal with our poor not to pamper their weaknesses but to encourage their strengths. Yet our jargon seems curiously prone to images of violence; we describe this process as an effort to "break the circle of dependency."

If you regard taking money from others as a bad habit and you wish to "break" somebody of that habit, you usually do not encourage him to ask for more of the same. Thus Nathan Glazer[2] recommends that birth control can break the circle of dependency of New York's Puerto Ricans on the theory that "the job at $50 a week, which manages to support such a small family in the Bronx and which, compared with the $12 a week income that was left behind on the island, represents real advancement, is completely inadequate to support five children or more . . ." And Edgar May, Inspector General of the Office of Economic Opportunity, would like social workers to become "the turnstile guardians of relief."[3] Lamenting over the period he spent as a case investigator in Buffalo, May writes: "I was now part of the system . . . a system where help was measured by what it

[2] Nathan Glazer and Daniel Moynihan, *Beyond the Melting Pot* (MIT-Harvard, 1963), page 120.

[3] Edgar May, *The Wasted Americans, Cost of Our Welfare Dilemma* (Harper & Row, 1964).

bought at the grocery and gave to the landlord. I had become a dispenser of checks and very little else."

As the administration of our Poorhouse laws has become more professionalized, the invidious character of much of our earlier vocabulary toward the poor has undergone some modifications; but we tend to want to be just as harsh in our judgments and just as niggardly in our allowances. Federal assistance programs provide only meager incentives for those to whom the word "job" has long been empty of meaning. Many training programs still "cream off" the worthy and allow the unworthy to go untrained. If no American now starves, many do go hungry supporting those who are still not eligible for assistance on their own niggardly assistance budgets, which have been devised by Pecksniffs with professional degrees on the theory that the poor man must be given the incentive to eat better by earning more. We ask the poor to consume along with us, but then we turn and ask only them to justify their consumption. If social service workers no longer divide their caseloads into the wise and the wasteful, they now tend to lay the blame for waste on "emotional disturbance," the "multiproblem family," the "female-centered family," or the poor man's propensity toward schizophrenia, which reduces our common human squalor to an exotic psychological squalor defined by class.[4] In his own best interests the person on public assistance is no longer threatened with the workhouse or the prison hulks, but he can be forced to accept "counseling" as a con-

[4] One New York City Department of Welfare survey in 1962 diagnosed more than sixty percent of the caseload for one health area as "emotionally disturbed."

dition of eligibility, or he may be asked to place his children in a home as another condition, or he may himself be committed to a mental institution. Throughout his dependency, his alleged character deficiencies will be used to explain why he is unable to obtain better service from the bureaucracy; and his defects of personality will come to justify his continuing squalor. He will be urged, cajoled, coerced, and exhorted to seek help, or to restore himself to productive citizenship, or to break the circle of dependency—a condition that may be problematical to everyone but himself— and when he asks for more help (i.e., more cash) he may be accused of being "manipulative," and he will be punished, perhaps by the withholding of that same help.

Too often, what is most problematical to the recipient is his demonstrated lack of resources. Through the scrupulously administered "means test" his lack of work or other resources has been certified so that he has been given a professional status—that of Welfare recipient—and, as the constant reinvestigation of his need continues, he is still willing to cling to this profession as tenaciously and with as much energy and commitment as if he were some aspiring employee in the mail room of a large firm. But although he must operate within the Welfare system with as much aggressiveness as the clerk seeking to rise above his fellows, the Welfare system will invariably punish him whenever he shows too much aggressiveness as a consumer. If he seeks to move out of his slum into a decent neighborhood, his apartment security may be withheld. If he asks for more money, his need may be reinvestigated. If he shows a taste for beefsteak, he will be reminded that he should use surplus foods. Dinned into his ears are the new federal slogans stressing "Rehabilitation instead of Relief." The pervasiveness of our highly advertised consumer culture is such that even he, in his aggrieved state and with his limited prospects, understands that no one would be so obsessed with his joblessness or lack of skills or with the fact that he was a school dropout, or came from a broken family, or was mildly schizophrenic if he could boast a Diners' Club card, an M.A. degree in English Literature, or 5,000 shares of American Telephone and Telegraph. But it is usually impossible for him to convince the functionaries that the priority of his needs calls for money before any other form of assistance. Too often the functionary has been given a mandate to define the person as defective simply by his application for assistance and to justify his invasions of privacy in the same way. Just as often it has been made organizationally feasible for the functionary to combine a great deal of advice with a minimal amount of assistance. In New York City, for example, the more senior caseworkers are always placed on "intake" because it is assumed that they will be more discerning in rejecting Welfare applicants. Such rejections are, of course, thought to be rehabilitative, since they return the applicant to the job market.

For the rejected applicant, rejection creates the necessity for poorly paid work, which, in turn, creates poverty; but for the successful applicant the situation is apt to grow just as nightmarish as he becomes more deeply involved in the Poorhouse State apparatus. Confronted continually by hierarchies of functionaries who have been endowed with extraordinary discretionary powers, the recipient will learn to accept the "social plan" by which he is to live out his dependency, take himself off Welfare, or be punished for failing to comply with a set of regulations that are sometimes at variance with state and federal policies. If he chooses compliance, he must get used to a continual interrogation about his resources, his friends, his family relationships. Rarely will he be given any record of these transactions. Although all the information he gives is to be regarded by regulation as confidential, so as to insure his privacy, this is usually used as a device to insure the privacy of the functionary and to conceal his activities. He can still judge and punish his client whenever he fails to act in accordance with a given policy. Thus, the woman who tells her investigator that she has parents in South Carolina, for example, may find that she must remove herself to South Carolina if she is to receive assistance.

If only we could guarantee stable and rewarding jobs for everyone who needs to work, the daily perjuries that take place at any Welfare office might be illegitimate, and such extensive scrutiny might make sense; but the increase in jobs has not kept up with the influx of people into the job market. Moreover, government economists seem to get the inflation jitters whenever the employment rate dips below four percent. If we can no longer hope to guarantee employment for all, the problem will be especially crucial among Negroes, which—along with a gradual lessening in discrimination against them when they apply for Welfare—accounts for their increasing access to Welfare. The Negro comes to Welfare cynical and bitter, a defeated man. Often he does not come at all but sends his family. Through what is believed to be the temporary application of Public Assistance payments, the assumption is that such "families" will be able to restore in six months or a year what has been taken from them over generations. Our impatience grows when we see that they fail to perform as we had hoped on subsistence incomes and substandard living conditions. But, if we are now sufficiently appalled with their performance to disguise some of our most angry impatience in a psychiatric or social scientific *newspeak*, this has little save a punishing effect, finally, on the lives of our newest class of dependents. Even when finally "rehabilitated," many may not be more than a few pennies better off. Lacking money or real political and social organization to uphold their rights as the recipients of public assistance, they are still held in the residual thralls of that older Poorhouse system, which rewarded virtue and punished vice and which regarded the continuing prospect of a person's economic dependency as the *prima facie* evidence of his improvidence, incompetency, and illegitimacy.

Thus, although all Americans are free to cross state boundaries and choose their residences to their liking, special residency laws are always being enacted—in one form or another—by nearly all the states denying this guarantee to the person who applies for public assistance after coming from another state.

(In California a one-year residency is required of women with children; three years is demanded of single persons. In New York State a modified residency law, or Welfare Abuses Act, was passed in 1962, allowing the functionary to decide whether a person has come to New York for the purpose of collecting Welfare and to reject him if he can be shown to have done so.)

15

Although Americans need not fear illegal searches and seizures or the arbitrary violation of their privacy, the person on Public Assistance (or living in a low-income public housing project) can protect himself against such actions only at the risk of disqualification (or eviction).

For more than a hundred years all Americans have been protected against "involuntary servitude," but the functionaries who are engaged in city and state offices of "employment rehabilitation" do not interpret this to mean that their clients have the freedom to accept or reject work.

Violations of constitutional guarantees are endemic to many aspects of our Public Welfare programs. Some localities maintain work relief programs that verge on "peonage." In the 1960s many states passed "suitable home" laws, which denied assistance—in violation of the equal protection clause of the Fourteenth Amendment—to women with illegitimate children. Still other states adopted "substitute father" provisions, which give the states the right to cut off assistance to unmarried mothers—in violation of both due process and equal protection—if they have a relationship with any male who could be considered a substitute father. In 1961 the Department of Health, Education and Welfare ruled that states would have to abandon their "suitable home" laws unless other means were provided to support the children. At present the NAACP is also attempting to bring an action against the states of Arkansas and Georgia so that HEW will rule similarly in the case of "substitute father" provisions.[5]

[5] For a good discussion of these two issues in particular, see Winifred Bell's *Aid to Dependent Children* (Columbia University Press, 1965).

· The American Way of Life on Public Assistance ·

When the beneficiary of a Poorhouse State program appeals some violation of his rights, some new affront to his dignity, he is not guaranteed an impartial trial by a jury of his peers but is made to come before an administrative tribunal that can function with only the most perfunctory regard for due process of law.

Within recent years the rapid growth of the Welfare State has been the cause of some alarm, particularly among political conservatives, whose ultimate fear seems to be that they will be treated as subjects of the Poorhouse State; but these fears have little basis in reality. Only for women who mother illegitimate children while on Welfare have our legislators ever proposed involuntary sterilization. Only for such families has Congress ever contemplated making child desertion a federal offense. These are also the only Americans for whom it has been recently suggested that corporal punishment be reintroduced as a possible deterrent to welfare recidivism.

At present, therefore, citizenship in the Poorhouse State —unlike enrollment under a program such as social security—still manages to be rigidly restrictive and subject to the power fantasies of other humans. Whenever efforts are made to eliminate the distinction between claiming benefits and applying for assistance, even responsible organs of public opinion are likely to express great outrage. Vermont Senator Winston Prouty's recent bill to extend social security benefits to recipients of old-age assistance (who are among the 1.8 million persons over seventy presently ineligible) was greeted editorially by the *New York Times* as a "hare-brained idea" and a "share-the-wealth scheme."[6] "Mr. Prouty's prodigal measure is not limited to proffering relief to those who need it . . . the proposal offers blank coverage to everyone reaching three score and ten."

The paradox of such reasoning is that only eight million Americans of any age have thus far been certified for assistance, although some believe that two to three times as many may be eligible. Not only do the various federal statutes by which people qualify for public assistance echo with contaminations of the "deserving poor" categories (and even some of the humiliations) of the pre-New Deal local poor laws, but they have also been made operative under state welfare codes, which tend to be even more restrictive in attempting to define and determine need; and then they have been placed—along with the usual emphasis on rehabilitation—under the administration of state and local functionaries who are jealous of their prerogatives, anxious to use discretion, and subject to greater political pressures from their local communities than from the generally benign federal establishment.[7] A veteran Welfare worker gave me

6 *New York Times* editorial, March 10, 1966, "Perverting Social Security." At this writing, the Prouty bill narrowly has gotten through the Senate, but stiffer opposition is expected from the usually more conservative House.

7 Legislators, professionals, and administrators of an earlier generation rewrote the Public Assistance sections of the New Deal Social Security Act of 1936 so there were no nationwide incomes policies established. It was felt in the South that a uniform federal income subsidy would destroy already depressed low-wage-paying industries such as agriculture. The result has been a crazy quilt of benefits whereby New York was recently paying out $41.38 per dependent child per month and Mississippi paying out

as a rule of thumb of Welfare administration that "the Feds propose, the states oppose, and the localities dispose" of new programs. In the matter of eligibility, however, the applicant usually finds himself at the combined mercies of these three interest groups, each of whom is equally interested in conserving funds. No two counties are likely to have the same eligibility requirements, but residence laws will penalize the person who "shops" for benefits. Since all three levels of government participate in welfare funding on a matching basis, all are subjected to the same widening circle of indifference or active hostility, which means that disagreement at any level may immobilize a given program. The matching formula was initially devised to preserve local autonomy and federalism, but its chief appeal has been to further exaggerate our selfish individualism by assuring prosperous farmers that they are not bearing the costs of urban improvidence and vice versa.

Administratively the Welfare system is cumbersome and grants a great deal of local discretion where it can be easily abused; but it also places obstacles before the well-intentioned functionary. Recently, for example, a liberal New York City Welfare Commissioner announced that his department was considering eliminating the means test in favor of "relief by affadavit." He also announced at the same time that he was hoping to increase the amount of money a man could earn and still collect assistance. "Just Sign Up,

---

$8.91. As Schneider and Deutsch pointed out at the conclusion of *The History of Public Welfare in New York State* (University of Chicago, 1941, p. 355): "The Social Security Act of 1936 was essentially a compromise measure embodying several contradictory principles as a result of amendments forced by conflicting interests."

Collect Relief While on Job," a *Herald Tribune* headline blared; but the Commissioner had tried to anticipate such criticism by stating that his new policy would not cost the City any more money, "at least at first." If, as he pointed out, applicants would no longer be subjected to the lengthy means test interview, workers would be free to focus on their clients' rehabilitation, he asserted, and no longer would there be the need for checking and cross-checking every request of the clients. Assistance would be granted on the client's testimony, and the caseload would then be subjected only occasionally to "spot checks" to attest to their veracity. The Commissioner stressed that what he was considering initially was a "pilot program" at only one Welfare center. He also made it clear that he would have to seek federal and state approval for funding such a program. But whereas the federal bureaucracy has vaguely put itself on record as endorsing simplified eligibility requirements but has not yet provided any incentives, the state has been far less generous. Even as the Commissioner was announcing his proposals, the State Department of Social Welfare was recalling retired welfare workers to serve as "quality control" experts within local welfare departments. These people were to read and study the case records of all those declared eligible and report back any ineligibles directly to the state, which could then hold up its matching fund reimbursements on the basis of such reports.

In general, the federal-state-locality nexus maximizes administrative discretion at the expense of clients' rights. In some states only so much money is appropriated by the Welfare system through this arrangement, only so many clients can be granted benefits. Federal law stipulates that aid can be given to the dependent child and mother, the aged person, the disabled, the veteran, or the blind person,[8] if a state so chooses, but uniformly, and according to a plan devised by each state. But, though rights are vaguely articulated for the recipient in nearly all these state programs, they continue to be vested most clearly in the state and county (or city) size bodies choosing those programs they will consent to administer. Even after a program is adopted, with need as the chief criterion for eligibility, the people who administer our Poorhouse laws are often not able to adjudicate need to their satisfaction through the present means test; they protect themselves against criticism from the press and other generally conservative groups by superimposing further bureaucratic criteria, which are even more selective, so that they can arrive at a satisfactorily restrictive definition of who is needy and who is not.

Suppose we say that the needy are those who present no extraneous behavioral problems to the functionary. It becomes, then, a very simple matter of moral arithmetic to subtract from the candidates' lists those who, for one reason or another, can be described as troublesome, or potentially troublesome, or troubled, and, therefore, undeserving, or to make their eligibility for a particular benefit contingent upon their good behavior. Thus applicants for public

---

[8] There are also deserving poor among the deserving poor, to judge from annual reports of New York City's Department of Welfare. In 1962 New York City spent more than $50 million on some 32,000 old persons while 212,000 mothers and their dependent children received approximately $121 million. Least deserving of all were the better than 37,000 on Home Relief, who were given only a little more than $17 million.

21

welfare in New York are regularly rejected for such reasons as "obnoxious behavior" or because they are deemed employable (by whom?); and applicants for any of the scarce units of low-cost public housing in the city may be denied admittance if they have ever been evicted from private housing, if they show irregular work histories, if there are out-of-wedlock children, if the husband and wife have been separated two or more times in the past five years, or if any members of the family are mentally retarded. They can also be admitted conditionally upon their acceptance of counseling, and once they become residents they can be evicted for poor housekeeping or if any members of their family are arrested. At the hearings to review these charges they can be asked about anything that reflects to their discredit. In a memo to its supervisors, the New York City Housing Authority recognizes that there just is not enough public housing for everybody, for it states that its major objective in making these seemingly arbitrary discriminations against those who have been defined as in need is to "create for its tenants an environment conducive to healthful living, family stability, sound family and community relations and proper upbringing of children." But a prime result of such policies is that while New York State voters continually defeat propositions to increase the number of units of low-income public housing, public housing authorities become increasingly defensive and discriminatory in the selection of tenants, so that many poor find it impossible to be admitted or, once admitted, difficult to maintain their residence. In New York City they must reside in the blocks of deteriorating tenements[9] which, in many instances, are owned by the city in receivership or are wholly subsidized by the Poorhouse State through its Department of Welfare.

Welfare is a way of life for some. It is all the mobility they have. In New York a Negro woman can collect more from Welfare than she could earn by doing housework in Alabama or Georgia; but living standards tend to make such comparisons meaningless. If, by nationwide standards, New York is considered such a liberal branch of the Poorhouse State that it tends to attract the indigent from other states, they do not fare any better once they get here. In Syracuse they can be issued food vouchers instead of cash. In Albany they are encouraged to use surplus foods by pegging cash benefits below the minimal living standards; in Buffalo they are not allowed to use their food vouchers to purchase beer or cigarettes; and within New York City, they have difficulties getting special grants, even for such things as carfare reimbursements (30¢). None of New York's social welfare policies toward the dependent consumer is deliberately biased, but they are all unfair because they do not acknowledge the poor as consumers and because they are subject to unchallenged interpretation by local administrators. "Liberal" New York State has two legislative committees on public welfare and many hundreds of interested community and voluntary groups. It will expend nearly $500

[9] In 1964 there were 43,000 tenements erected before 1900, which housed approximately 900,000 persons—nearly twice as many as those presently living in public low-income housing.

million in 1966 on public assistance alone, of which more than half will go to New York City. Augmented by its share of federal and local funds, the city's welfare budget will be larger[10] than the state's, which is not surprising if one realizes that there is a city of paupers the size of Buffalo within the crowded 319.1 square miles of the five boroughs. The largest group of dependents is children under eighteen. They are among the clients about whom the New York City Department of Welfare, in its official manuals, advises its employees that it is dangerous to manifest "an exaggerated solicitude and over-willingness—even anxiety—to 'do things.'" The state also has some rather niggardly attitudes toward these clients which it wishes to see enforced. It is because of its insistence upon proper and frequent investigation of the caseload that New York City welfare employees were until recently told during their training sessions that the applicant for public assistance must forfeit his right to privacy and choice.[11]

A fifteen-minute subway ride from Times Square will take you to Manhattan's Lower East Side, a welfare ghetto. Officially more than ten thousand paupers and their dependents now occupy this congested area, but there are probably even more.

Once almost exclusively a system of overlapping ethnic ghettos from which the Jewish, Irish, Italian, Hungarian, Polish, Greek, and other immigrant groups struggled for

[10] In January, 1966, the then Acting Welfare Commissioner asked for $663,607,986, approximately a third of it to come from each level—federal, state, and city.

[11] Federal law stipulates one investigation a year. In New York four are considered mandatory for all categories of public assistance but Old Age and Veterans Assistance. The department visits those they deem untrustworthy even more regularly and without notice.

economic mobility and assimilation, achieved through their
own sweated labor, the Lower East Side (with its socialist
past and high-camp bohemian present) has in large part
become a dependency ghetto, a kind of seedy familial ex-
tension of the nearby Bowery. The new influx consists of
highly visible recent immigrants from Puerto Rico and
Negro migrants from the rural South; most arrived with
many of the same ambitions as earlier generations to find
themselves increasingly superfluous or redundant in an economy that no longer needs their unskilled labor. If many
of these people have remained resourceful, others have
revealed all the weaknesses resulting from generations of
poverty. There is a good deal of what we choose to define
as antisocial behavior (i.e., high rates of drug addiction,
illegitimacy, alcoholism, felonious assault) and a pervasive system of credit bilking, consumer frauds, and other
forms of mercantile corruption. For more than four
years an ambitious federally funded social work program
called Mobilization for Youth has been in the area, attempting to give the newcomers "a stake in conformity"
by helping them to organize themselves and by providing their children with skills and opportunities. Of all
"colonialist" operations among the poor this has probably been one of the most benign, the most willing to yield
some of its sovereignty to its constituents; the extent of its
success has varied from program to program. If it has en-
hanced the reading skills of some youngsters or the job
prospects of others, it has not been given the resources to
create any of the vitally needed public services (housing,
health, and child care), and it has not yet been able to
change any of the prevailing power relationships of the

area. When it attempted to do so there were denunciations in the press and attacks on its personnel.

Still largely powerless, the new residents of the Lower East Side have become increasingly dependent on public largess which claims to view their dependency as a social pathology but which, through its procedures of scrutiny, confidentiality and rehabilitation, treats it more often than not as if it were a psychological aberration. As one woman on public assistance told me: "When I am in arrears (to the landlord), you should see how angry they get at the Welfare. When I want a pair of eyeglasses for my daughter, hell can freeze over."

In comparatively liberal New York the Poorhouse State functions differently than it does in thrifty New Hampshire or racist Mississippi; its procedures differ from the city of Newburgh to the Borough of Manhattan and, in some of its behavior, from welfare center to welfare center.

In New York some 5,000 social investigators, augmented by a special grand investigations bureau, serve the requests of such clients. Many of the investigators are so new to the department that they have not had time to learn the multiplicity of regulations under which they are said to be operating. Among residents of the Lower East Side, they are known simply as the Welfare, DW, or the man from *Bienestar* (Welfare); and they help to account for the many thousands of Welfare disqualifications within the city every month.[12] In addition, an average of two out

[12] The ratio of Welfare workers to Welfare clients is greater than the ratio of police to the citizenry of New York at large. In 1962 the Department spent nearly four times as much for salaries (approximately $48 million) as it gave out in grants to persons on Home Relief. Welfare job

of five applicants for public assistance are rejected when they appear at the intake desk to apply; and every day, in nearly every center, injustices are recorded for which there is apparently no redress. In fact, in the entire city of New York there are only about fifteen formal appeals (or Fair Hearings) made from Welfare decisions every year. These injustices are, in the main, so petty and routinized that the caseworker may not even regard his conduct as problematical; and the recipient, ever mindful of his precarious status, will not be likely to jeopardize it by taking the caseworker to task. To the citizen of the Poorhouse State, the need to consume is so unsatisfied and the possibility of punishment always so imminent that he is not likely to complain about the daily degradations, the violations of his privacy, the errors that are buried and made unremediable, the arbitrary handling of his problems. He may not even complain when he has a toothache because he will not wish to travel all the way to Queens for his dental care; and he may be afraid to ask his caseworker to make other arrangements. Despite well-meaning programs of legal advocacy on behalf of such people, the intimidation of the poor remains pervasive, in part because the Poorhouse State apparatus still reserves the right to see its clients unencumbered by the presence of lawyers, translators, or social workers, in a sanctity that is policed only by the discretion

classifications are under civil service except for the unclassified and more highly paid fraud investigators. In general, Welfare salaries are considered low. Starting pay for a social investigator (case worker I) is $5,750 per annum, approximately three times as much as he can give out in a year to a family of four on public assistance; but I was told that a major problem of the Department is petty theft among employees.

and good intentions of the caseworker and in part because services are so scarce that those on welfare must always beg for whatever they get. Thus the responsibility rests with the caseworker to discern worthy and unworthy petitioners. If many workers use this discretion judiciously and well while others are so preoccupied with petty paper work that they use it only sporadically (if at all), it is in the nature of his dependency for the client to regard his worker as an enemy who can deny him what he needs. But most cannot afford to act upon this recognition. When at any moment after such a meeting, a determination can be made affecting your destiny—during the process of which you will normally be consulted only to incriminate yourself—prudence dictates that you "sit back and just take it." More often than not, the bad news will later arrive by mail.

2

WHERE IS JESÚS ESCOBOSA?

THE CITY OF NEW YORK

•

DEPARTMENT OF WELFARE

Notice of Discontinuance of Public Assistance

Mrs. Nestor Escobosa   ADC, 228 6747
160 West 80 Street
New York City

Our investigation shows that effective immediately you are
not eligible to receive (*Public Assistance*) for the following
reasons: *Refusal to comply with Department of Welfare
Policy.*
You may wish to review the pamphlet which was given to
you at the time of your application. It explains the provisions under which this type of public assistance is granted
and your rights with respect to review of this decision.

B. *Brudig*   7/9/65   35-5
Unit Supervision   Date   Caseload Number

On the day the above letter arrived at the fourth-floor
redstone apartment of Mrs. Nestor Escobosa, Mrs. Nilde,

who lives three floors below, was shaking out her dustmop in the stairwell when she heard screams:

"BY MY MOTHER I SWEAR YOU SONS BITCHES WILL BE SORRY FOR THIS! I WILL KILL THE CHILDREN! I WILL KILL ALL THE SONS BITCHES! . . . THE CHILDREN! . . . THE MAYOR WITH HIS WHORE OF A WIFE! . . . I WILL KILL ALL THESE LITTLE BASTARDS!"

It was one of the hottest days of a hot summer in a depressing, drought-filled year. Apparently all the occupants had their doors open, for Mrs. Nilde's neighbor, Mrs. Serrano, also heard the voice and rushed out to join her on the landing. The lamentation increased:

"SONS BITCHES! . . . I WILL GIVE THEM RATS TO EAT! . . . I WILL PUT THEM OUT OF THE HOUSE! . . . I WILL PUT THEM IN THE HOSPITAL! . . . I WILL KILL THEM! . . . WHO WILL BLAME ME?"

Both women started up the stairs.

"Get away from me you filthy whores," screamed Nestor Escobosa from the doorway, where she was standing with a torn envelope in her hands. Her blouse was scratched open at the neck. Tears were streaming down her face. Mrs. Nilde said she hardly knew this woman. She said she personally doubted that any woman would actually want to kill her children, but she had heard of stranger things happening in New York. "What can be so wrong?" she asked.

"They tell you the money is for the children and that you must take care of the children," Nestor Escobosa explained. "And then they do this to me. How can I do what they wish me to do? How can I feed these children now?

Listen, you whores, I will kill them all before they become orphans..."

Mrs. Nilde said, "It's bad enough, this heat. You'll get an attack if you're not careful."

"Woman, calm down," Mrs. Serrano added. "What good are you doing for yourself by crying?"

"Yes," Mrs. Nilde said, "she's right. Here we don't cry. It doesn't do any good at all."

"They want to take away my children!"

"How do you know that?" Mrs. Nilde asked.

"Because they wish to punish me," the younger woman explained. "They wish to make me sorry. But I will punish them. I will kill all the children, and it will be their fault. You think I won't do it, you whores? You think I need to beg anybody? I will hurt these children so badly that everybody will know..."

An hour later I was summoned as I crossed the street by Mrs. Nilde, an old friend, but she would not come upstairs with me again. With fat Mrs. Serrano standing silently by her side she said, "A woman like this—you can never tell. She knows my husband, but she doesn't like me. But you must tell her she mustn't hurt her children. You must be very familiar with her, you know, but *strick*. It would be a terrible thing if she should hurt her children. You must tell her that, too, because you must make her understand."

"But you must not be too *familiar*," Mrs. Serrano added.

I am not a social worker. In my neighborhood I was known, if at all, as one who asked far too many questions, who said he was a writer, who was always hanging around asking these questions; but, as repayment for some of the things I learned, I had subsequently brazened a few of the single men onto relief by personally escorting them to one of the local Welfare centers. My prime interest was the Lower East Side, but it seemed silly not to draw upon my own neighbors. Hired to describe some of the activities of MFY as part of a government-sponsored research project, my curiosity about extraneous matters kept getting the better of me. I also found myself wandering about the Welfare streets in my own Upper West Side at odd moments. I suspect that not every person I met trusted me because few let me into their homes, and I already knew enough not to visit people unannounced. In fact, although I had been walking about the City's slum areas nearly two months, this was my first visit to a Welfare apartment, my first contact of this sort with a Welfare mother. Mrs. Nilde thought she was educating me, but as I climbed the long flight of stairs up to the Escobosas', wondering what I would say to this angry woman, I was just a little annoyed with her for getting me into such a predicament. When I came to the heavy green metal door leading into the Escobosa apartment, I stood in front of it for a long while, hoping to hear some reassuring noises of familial activities; and it was the dead silence that finally compelled me to knock.

"Don't be alarmed," I said timidly, after knocking just a few times. "Don't be alarmed, Mrs. Escobosa. *Quiero ser amigo suyo.* Listen, Mrs. Escobosa, I am not from the Welfare, you understand. *Sabes? No soy de Bienestar!* . . . *y quiero estar su amigo . . . Sabes?*"

After a moment I heard the latch slip. The door creaked open a notch, revealing only opaque darkness.

"You must keep talking," Mrs. Nilde whispered up to me from the bottom of the stairs.

Speaking more rapidly to whoever was behind the door, I said that I could do nothing for Mrs. Escobosa if she did not let me in but that I might be able to find somebody who could help her if she did. "I even know people who can help you with the Welfare," I said.

The door opened a little wider, and I heard a woman's voice, "You will come and see for yourself . . ."

"What will I see?"

"You will see for yourself . . . you will listen . . . you will go away . . ."

"I will do as you wish, Mrs. Escobosa."

When she finally opened the door fully, four of her five children were standing in the entranceway, naked. The oldest, a boy nearing twelve, had a pot belly like his little brothers, but under his the first black tracings of pubic hair were visible. When he started to step behind the threshold, his mother placed a restraining hand lightly on the boy's shoulder, saying: "*Guardes!*" The boy blinked frightened brown eyes and retreated behind his mother's skirts to join his brothers. Then Nestor Escobosa stepped forward. Sticking out her own belly, once again enlarged, she passed both hands over her tightly drawn black hair. As she wiped her oily hands against her skirt, her tongue licked at her sweat mustache. She was one of those once-pretty, doll-faced Puerto Rican women whose eyes are now dull, entirely lifeless. She made futile gestures toward the flaking doorpost, where a *mezuzah* was hanging loosely off one rusty nail and a cockroach was crawling timidly along the edge of that nail as if on some frighteningly high promontory. Then she handed me the letter. When I had read through it, Mrs. Escobosa asked, "You are indeed not from the

Welfare?" I nodded. *"Mucho calor,"* she said, stepping aside then to invite me in.

The apartment was exploding with heat. It was so hot that one expected to see the thick paint bubbling against the moldings. I stood at the end of the long dark corridor of heat, in which the only sounds were of electric current and the quiet crackling of the paint. Here green flaked to yellow enamel, and yellow enamel yielded up a fine white plastery dust; the smell was a combination of urine and pork fat. As she escorted me down the hallway toward her sitting room, beyond which was a kitchen and two bedrooms, Mrs. Escobosa explained in a mixture of Spanish and English that others in the building had filed a complaint last year with the City Rent and Rehabilitation Administration when the building was on rent strike because there was no heat; now her landlord was getting even with her by refusing to turn off her valves, which he controlled from the cellar, even though it was midsummer.

I asked, "Why you? Why not the others?"

"They pay him off," she explained.

"Still," I added, "that's a pretty expensive way to get even."

"It happens only at night," Mrs. Escobosa said, "and not every night but often. You know. So last night he comes to ask me for something and I say no, so he forgets to turn it off again, and it is costing a little money but he is not unhappy." In a neutral voice, she added, "This man is very cruel . . ."

I entered her sitting room.

The first thing I saw was a fully dressed infant in a crib.

34

He or she—I could not tell which in the mess of soiled garments—seemed to be sleeping, and there was a big clot of sour milk on the sheets next to its face. When the other children entered behind me, Mrs. Escobosa peered over the top of the crib and then invited us all to take seats. But I dreaded sinking into either of her two larger upholstered chairs. They were covered with sheets of gray plastic, so I feared I might scald myself. Too timid to ask that the plastic be removed, I just stood in the middle of that boiling room. The only two small gray windows I saw were already wide open. The linoleum felt sticky underfoot. I put my hand against the plastic; it was like touching fire.

Mrs. Escobosa said, "They came from the Welfare to see me."

"Who are *they?*"

She shrugged: "*They* . . . how do I know where Escobosa is? *They* say it is only important if he wants the Welfare. But again I say I don't know. Then *they* go away and come back again. This time *they* say we think he gives you this new baby. That one in the crib. He must be found. Will you help us? But again I don't trust anybody and I say no, I don't know where Jesús is, because even if I did know and they found him, he would only come back and beat me for talking about him. I ask will *you* take my beating? But the man from the Welfare, he says no, but if Jesus beats me I can take him to this judge.

"I say, 'What this judge going to do for me?'

" 'Oh, he will punish Escobosa, so you must cooperate,' he says.

"Then he goes away and comes back again with the policeman . . . and this time I am angry and I will not open the door for this *particular* because I have nothing more to say to him. I tell him if I do something wrong you arrest me, but he says I don't wish to arrest you just because I wish to find this man who you say is your husband. Why should he question me like that, and why should I believe him? But you know what he says. He tells me I will be sorry. It is now two months. I hear nothing. I keep my door locked except when the boys must go to school. Now it is summer so there is no school, but I get all my *cheques*. Then I am given this letter. Now what do I do?"

"Do you know where Mr. Escobosa is?" I asked, spying a metal bridge chair under a third window, stuck fast with paint.

When I started to sit down, Mrs. Escobosa said, "You talk like the Welfare . . ."

"I'm sorry," I said, groping for a way to change the subject. Then I added, "Your furniture looks like new . . ."

The gray sweaty face smiled. "I take care," she explained. She said that her chairs and the end table between them were nearly ten years old. Usually she didn't let the *niños* sit here. Now that there was not sufficient summer clothing to take everybody to the park, she was not being so strict with them. "If the father found out," she said, rising, "he would be very angry. Very. He would say I was at fault. The father is a *strick* man. What you say—a Pentecostal? I was born *Católico* . . . and though we are *strick* about some things we are not so *strick* about others. I do not like these Holy Rollers, but I do not like the priests here equally. Truthfully, they are all *maricones,* and the sisters that time when my oldest turned crazy used to beat him with something because he wet the bed. But, you see, I am still religious..."

As if to prove her statement, she showed me to her bedroom, which was furnished in cheap blond wood. A long, low dresser with a glass top was cluttered with scent bottles and small unframed photographs. Next to it was the usual mirrored vanity doubling as a makeshift altar, its mirror plastered over with the decal images of saints and flanked by cheap red glass votive candles. The bed was unmade; its headboard, also of blond wood, was very grand. Against the only bare wall in the room stood a new TV on a shiny brass stand. A silvery clock-radio also peered up from that portion of the floor. The room looked as if hijackers had dropped their loot and then fled.

"You see the things I have," Mrs. Escobosa said. She started to cross herself in the doorway but then moved on to show me the only other bedroom with its stained mattresses on the dusty floor, where her children slept. Then she padded about in the heat toward her kitchen, showing me the darkened refrigerator, its door ajar because it no longer worked, the window box in which she kept a little food, the sweating copper pipe in the tin sink, which gushed cold running water over a half-filled bottle of milk. The kitchen was swarming with flies, which clung to the sweat on my face. I realized then how impatient I was to finish my visit, but although Mrs. Escobosa now seemed quite in control of herself, she also seemed in no hurry to talk again about Welfare. At last I said, "You try to do your best, I see . . ."

One of the children began to whimper, "*Mama, haga-lo
. . . Mamacita . . .*"

"It seems I never get away from them," Mrs. Escobosa
shrugged. She drew a long dirty rag out of her skirt pocket
and held it under the tap. Returning to her sitting room,
she threw it at the complaining child, who first sucked
some of the cold against his lips and then began to swab
his skinny body all over. "You see how I live. I live in hell,"
Mrs. Escobosa explained matter-of-factly. Thinking I must
be unimpressed, she added, "*Ratones y cucarachas hay
muchas . . .*"

Two of the children started to giggle, and she shouted,
"*Basta!*"

I asked whether she had been to a doctor about the new
baby, the one she was carrying. Startled, speaking English,
perhaps so the children would not understand, she told me
she thought she would be "*reed* of this . . . of this one . . ."
And she poked herself hard. I asked how. "*Las mujeres
tienen modas,*" she explained.

It was very difficult to think of Mrs. Escobosa as a grown
woman. Despite the swelling from her pregnancy, she had
remained tiny, dainty, childlike, slim, with large eyes and
an open, unlined face. If her white sleeveless blouse seemed
just a bit skimpy on her, her skirts were gay, almost opulent.
I asked her age, and she told me that she was twenty-six.
How long had she been married to Escobosa? "I was fourteen," she said. Was she, I asked, surprised by my questions?
No, she was used to these questions. She had many problems, and she did not mind talking about them if it would
help. I asked her why she had not answered Welfare's ques-

tions, but she smiled and immediately explained that they could "do things" to her. They wanted to know these things so they could do things to her. What sort of things?

"When they ask me the last man I sleep with, don't you think I know why they want to know?"

"Why?"

"You sound very much like the Welfare."

I asked her again about Escobosa. What had happened to him? Did she know where he had gone? Mrs. Escobosa shrugged her shoulders helplessly. Then, as if to make certain that I believed her, she swore to me that all of the children, "*Menos el niño en la cuna y eso*"—pointing to her belly—"were his." No, she had no relatives in New York who could help her except her mother, and even if she did she could not tell the Welfare or they would try to do things to them. What about her mother? Where was she? Escobosa knew, but he would not let her find out because the woman did not like him. Did she have relatives in Puerto Rico? Mrs. Escobosa's face turned blank. "*They* will do things to them too?"

I started to say no but instead asked what she would do if Escobosa came back.

"Maybe I will kill myself . . . But maybe I will kill myself anyway," she smiled. "Some of these women around here," she poked herself again. Then she added, "If I am big it is only my fourth month. It is much too early to know what I will do . . . it depends . . ."

I was sweating so profusely that I lacked even the will to argue perfunctorily. "Perhaps I can help," I said.

There was silence until the baby in the crib started to

cry, thrashing about. Mrs. Escobosa quickly went to him, grabbed him under his arms, pulled him out to her, and unbuttoned the top of her blouse. The child's head started to loll to one side as if his neck were broken. The other children gathered around their mother to help her. She propped the infant back against her forearm and then clamped him to her breast. Looking up, satisfied that the child was sucking noisily and well, Mrs. Escobosa waved the other children away with her free hand, brushed a wisp of her hair back demurely, and said, "What will you tell the Welfare about me?"

"I have nothing to do with the Welfare," I explained.

While the child cried and grabbed and sucked at her, I said it was not my interest to inform. I told her that I had come at the suggestion of Mrs. Nilde, who said she was desperate.

"*That* woman," she sneered.

I added, only half truthfully then, that I knew people who might be able to help her find new quarters and who could give her new clothing and perhaps some help with the children.

"What people?"

"From Mobilization for Youth, downtown."

"They are not for the Spanish. They are for the Negro."

"That isn't true," I said.

"But what shall I do about the *cheque* . . . and Escobosa?"

Her child cried out, and she pulled the infant from her breast with such violence that it occurred to me that she might try to dash its head against the sticky linoleum, but she switched him to her other breast and lightly kissed his brow. I looked at her other children to see how they responded to this, her first gesture of open affection. A boy of eight had lost control of himself. He was staring with a sad, silly smile at the puddle he had made on the linoleum.

Mrs. Escobosa abruptly asked, "Where is my husband?" Her voice sounded like barking. "*Where is my husband?*"

"Welfare can find him," I said. "They can find him if you tell them where to find him. Have you talked to the Welfare?"

"You said you were not from the Welfare . . ."

"I know what they can do."

"I know equally," she replied.

Mrs. Escobosa told me then that Welfare knew about the baby in the crib but not about her pregnancy. She said that was why she did not want them to come inside her flat. If they knew, they would punish her. They would find Jesús and make him pay for her, and if he would not pay they would send him away, as they had done in the past; if they did get more money from him, he would be very angry and would beat her. It was not good to have the extra money if they had to know, because for the money you had to be punished. Even the police could not keep Escobosa away, because he was her husband and had his rights, and it was not his fault that they were on the Welfare. They had been on the Welfare even when he was at home, even when he was working, but it had never been enough. "Now I have nothing . . . I am punished equally," she smiled.

Mrs. Escobosa said that after the trouble with the Rent and Rehabilitation Administration, Welfare had not come to see her for nearly a year because the building inspectors from the Welfare were angry with the tenants for causing so much trouble. Then *they* had heard about the baby in the crib from one of her neighbors and had started bothering her again. *They* said if she would give them the name of the baby's father, they would be able to add the baby to her budget.

"What they have to speak to my neighbors?" she demanded. "I had more expenses, but I was getting along. I knew that they were only after Jesús. So now *they* have taken away all my money, and to get it back I must tell a policeman who is the father." She was pointing at the crib. "To tell you the truth," she said, "I do not know. What does it matter? They will ask their questions. They will make these men come back who I do not even know and my husband too, and my husband will see these men. Yes, they will want to tell about the child, and he will be very angry with me. We Spanish cannot trust the Welfare," she smiled, "not even for the *cheques* . . ."

"Then what will you do without it?"

Again the little smile twisted Mrs. Escobosa's childlike face. "Maybe I will die," she said. "Maybe I will do as we know how . . ."

"And the heat," I asked, "Will you file another complaint?"

Mrs. Escobosa giggled harshly. She pushed the sleeping child away from her breast and touched her pinky lightly to one of his closed lids. Then she stowed him back in his crib. "You see," she said, rising as if with a sharp back pain and pointing to her bedroom furniture, "I have nice things. You see my things? I will tell you that there is much a

woman can do with such things. Men like to come here. If
I make another complaint, my landlord tells the police. I
leave. The men will not know where to find me. Escobosa
will surely look for me and be angry. We shall all surely
starve, for even if there were Welfare there would not be
enough. When I have gotten *reed* of this," again she poked
herself, "I will offer to be good to the Jew who is my landlord. Then he will give us the heat in the wintertime, too. I
know these Jews. It is better that the Welfare does not remember me. They will only cause trouble . . ."

"And the *niños?*" I asked, hoping that by using Spanish
I might provoke a response from the children themselves.
But they scarcely looked up from their passive squatting.

Mrs. Escobosa replied, "What do you know about these
children? They are the mother's problem. I take care of
them. These things I have for myself were gifts. The money
from the Welfare was for them and I used it for them, but
it was never enough. *This one,*" she smiled, pointing to the
oldest, "*they* wished him to go to a special school. He
must also be punished for his mother. Look, he has squinty
eyes, and they say he is a little crazy . . ."

The child did not even blink at his mother's accusation.

"*And this one,*" she went on, grabbing a small fat boy of
about five around the waist and passing the flat of her hand
across his genitals. "Does he look normal to you?"

The child began to whimper, but whether from fright or
excitation I could not be sure.

Suddenly the alarm in her bedroom sounded like a fire
bell, and Mrs. Escobosa shoved the child away from her
and raced to turn it off. Coming back she said, "If Jesús

were here . . ." Then she seemed to become angry again. "You tell that nosy whore downstairs that Jesús Escobosa is a man with dignity. He will do as he pleases and she and her *maricón* husband must mind their own business. You tell her that I don't want your help. If you call on the Welfare Escobosa will hear of it. You will make him punish me for nothing. You must not call the Welfare, please!" she said. "Look," pointing to a swarm of flies in the adjoining alcove that was her kitchen, "there is food. We have beds. The man from the store lives right next door, and he will trust me. If I need money, I have things to sell. I will send the boy, and he will get money for these things . . . so I will wait until this is finished," again poking herself, "and then I will be able to get money. The rent I have for another month. Do you wish to see the check? It arrived only Friday."

"But suppose," I asked, "just suppose that the Welfare comes back and they decide that you are not able to take care of the children? Suppose they say you are not a good mother?"

"How can they do that to me? These are my children. And even if they should come, my husband has his rights. Parents suffer for their children. They have their rights . . ."

"But your husband is not here."

"These are his children. He cannot be denied!"

"And your mother," I asked, "shall I get somebody to help you look for her?"

"She's a terrible big whore! She will teach my children terrible bad things!"

I told Mrs. Escobosa that I would see if I could bring her help, food, clothing, perhaps some money until she was on her feet again, and I said I hoped she would not hurt the children. I also said that I knew a lawyer who might be able to take her case against the Welfare. I said, "Tomorrow maybe you will feel better, and then we can talk again about the Welfare and what you should do. Maybe you will want to see a doctor."

"Lawyers, doctors," she mimicked as she started to show me to the door. "Don't you see," she said, "whatever I do, it is better that the Welfare forget about me."

Returning along the dark corridor, I could hear rats in the walls. "Do they bother the children?" I asked.

"The children laugh at them. They do not believe in them," she explained. "Only I hear them. I know of them. The landlord and the Welfare equally, and so they leave them here to punish me. Soon the landlord will come back because you know they always come back, and they will scratch at the door. It is worrying about the rats which has made me so ugly . . ."

"You are not ugly . . ."

"*You.* What do you know? You think *I* don't know? This man from the Welfare, he wishes to screw me," she replied, angrily.

I said, "Maybe he made a mistake."

"No," she insisted, "He wish to screw me. You know. *Makes love.*" She was blushing, "So these rats are my punishment. To everybody I give but him . . . He was such an unhappy looking man . . . Why do you wish to tell the Welfare about *this?*" she asked, again poking herself in the stomach. "There is no law against having men. That woman downstairs also has men . . ."

I swore again to Mrs. Escobosa that I wouldn't say a word

45

to anybody if she did not want me to. "I am simply worried about you and the children," I added.

She frowned. "If they knew about the rats, maybe they would love their mother. Now they hate everybody for sending away their father. I didn't do it. There was another woman. He said how can we all live when there is so little money? He tells everybody they don't wish me to live. He says a man cannot live on Welfare. It is for the women. He is a religious man, but he did not wish to take the children with him. He says the Welfare is after him, and they are going to get him. Everybody around here says such things. All his friends. You think it is true? It is like when you work in the factory and they tell you that if you ask the man for a raise that you will be fired. I never believed such things, but they are true. Jesús believed. Many times he would come to visit us, and I would be afraid to let him in because of the Welfare or the other tenants. They would say you are the father of these children, and you must stay and support them. So when he would come, I would have these boys go to him in the park, but then he would not come any more, and he told everybody that I was no longer his wife because I would not let him into the house, and the only money he would send was for the one with the squinty eyes. So now they all hate me, and you want to get me a lawyer . . . but if they knew about the Welfare and the father, what difference would it make? If I told them of the rats, they would know how I saved them from the Welfare . . . from being taken away but, you see, they have no friends. They do not talk. What difference does it make? Maybe it is for the best that they be sent away. But, you know, where will they put them? What will they do to them? They will learn bad things . . . I know, they will learn bad things . . . I will be very lonely . . . If I had the money I could make their rooms just like mine . . . then we would be happy without this Welfare. But I can see what you are thinking. You will call the Welfare anyway. It is very cruel of you . . ."

Nestor Escobosa had already started to bolt her door in my face. I made one final effort to offer her help. "Welfare will find out," I said. "Sooner or later they will review your case or a new supervisor will come on the job, and he will want to know what has happened with that Escobosa woman and her children. He may not understand unless you are prepared with a lawyer . . ."

"I will not open my door again," she replied. "Why should I? Only my husband can punish me. The Welfare? They do not care to know any more. This man from next door will not betray me if I ask him for help. To the Welfare I am nobody at this time. They have closed my case. Let it be. Let them not find out or they will do things . . . please . . . don't tell the Welfare. Don't send for the Welfare, and I will not hurt these children. Please . . . come again tomorrow when I am feeling good, and you will see these children will be just as today, but don't send for the Welfare . . ."

When the door closed hard on my face the silence was like a deadening sting, as if two hands had been clapped hard against my cheeks. My clothing was now as drenched as if I had been under a shower.

From behind the door the sound of sobbing gradually emerged. Mrs. Escobosa and her children were crying together. Mrs. Escobosa was crying for her children because they were not, and the children were crying for their mother because she was not; and they were all crying for the Welfare check because it was not. I stood on that dark, stifling landing, staring down at my scuffed shoes.

Minutes later I descended the stairs again, feeling sodden, unkempt. At Mrs. Nilde's door I knocked and said, "Don't worry. She isn't going to hurt her children." I saw a man's shadow appear in the frosted glass entrance to the building. As I started out along the dirty tiled corridor toward the fresh, hot summer air, I noticed a young man in a business suit with a black looseleaf notebook under one arm. He was staring at the tenants' registry in a little niche to one side of the concrete stoop. Seeing him, Mrs. Nilde emerged from her doorway, waved at me, and then scurried back inside. I started down the steps, but I could see from the way the children in the gutters had stopped playing that even they knew he was a Welfare worker; they were staring at us. Did they think I was one too?

"*Mira . . . mira . . .*" a child cried.

I breathed in the hot cindery air and turned to face the fellow again, hoping to discover whether we looked alike or dressed alike. "You live here?" he asked flatly, glancing away from the registry.

I explained that I was just visiting.

He said, "I am looking for a family named Acevedo. Puerto Ricans . . ."

"Do they live here?"

"I'm new," he explained, "and I'm not really so sure. In fact," he said, a little startled by his own admission, "none of us are . . ."

Relieved to learn that he was not after Mrs. Escobosa, I asked where he was from.

"Yorkville." He smiled. Then he added, "*What a mess!*"

"Really?"

"I shouldn't be telling you this," he said, "but you look like the type of guy . . . I mean, are you from the main office?"

I shook my head no.

"Well, anyway," the young man said, "somebody lost a bunch of files and we only have the old addresses. They won't do us any good over at the Post Office, so we don't know what to do about some of these people. Anyway, I thought if you knew you might be able to help. One of our staff thought the Acevedos had moved to Pitt Street, so I have been going into every house."

I asked, "What did they do? Are they in trouble?"

"Honestly, if they were I would tell you," the fellow said. "It just isn't anything like that." He smiled. "We just wanted to make sure that they have been getting their checks. I mean, it is only two checks that are unaccounted for. So I thought it would be a good idea to find out if they had been received."

He seemed like a nice, earnest young man; he had the beginnings of a tiny red beard along his chin. If I had known anything, I would have been happy to help him, but I had to tell him that I knew nothing; even if Mrs. Nilde knew, I did not think it would be right to bother her.

"Funny," he added then, with a nice, boyish smile, "I don't know anything about you, but I bet half of these people are working all the angles against us, and we never even know about them unless by accident. And this guy Acevedo is maybe owed some money, so I've got to go all the way out in this heat and find the son of a bitch. Well," he said, glancing forlornly at the registry one final time, "I'm glad I'm not in this business for the rest of my life. It can get pretty depressing, I tell you. I suppose we will hear from Mr. Acevedo when he gets a little hungrier."

I said, "I hope so."

"Oh, you can count on it," the young man said, scratching some prickly heat alongside his beard. "People don't go hungry if they can help it."

"But suppose he has something he is afraid to tell you about. Suppose he thinks you are mad at him because he hasn't heard from you in such a long time."

"Who? Acevedo? I never even met the guy," the young man said. "Why should I be mad at Acevedo? I've only been on the job three weeks."

"How does he know that?"

"Look," the fellow said, "if he has something he's hiding, don't you think they ought to find out about it?" Then he seemed chagrined by his own sudden ferocity. "I bet the little guy has a job or went back to Puerto Rico," he said. "You know they fly back and forth just like shuttlecocks."

"Not all of them . . . and besides," I added, "where would he get the money?" I had spoken a good deal more ominously than I had intended; the young man, having begun to walk away, now turned on me again, stopping short. "Say, are you a cop, or a social worker?" he demanded.

"I'm just a guy," I said.

"What do you mean 'just a guy'?"

"I'm a journalist."

"Oh, yeah?"

The fellow looked at me as if I had said I was an interior

decorator. Then he played with his little beard and smiled again. "Oh, sure, I know what you mean," he said. "Somebody ought to be writing something about these people. I've been on the job three weeks but I can tell you it is a mess . . ."

"What is?"

"The way we treat people. It is a joke."

I now expected to hear the customary obscene catechism about unwed mothers and was surprised: "Thank God I don't have to work here the rest of my life. It is so cruel. You don't know what this is like. You think anybody really cares whether I find Acevedo or not? They've got nothing better to do with me, so my case supervisor, who is really a nut, told me to take a walk. What a screwy thing this is. If I weren't in law school, I would go out of my head. We are supposed to pretend we are like social workers, but everybody knows what we are. We are just out to make people's life miserable. And don't you think they know it? Listen, if they wanted this Acevedo because they thought he had been overpaid, they'd find him soon enough or they'd send him a special delivery letter. Listen, they really couldn't care less. Somebody complained upstairs, so I've got to go out in all this heat. What people! Some of them have been in the Department forever, and they are pretty bitter. It's easy to get bitter. And what is the client going to do about it? You should see some of the creeps we have . . ."

"You want to tell me about them?"

"Say, listen," the young man said, sweating, "I am only here temporarily. I go to law school nights. Otherwise, I'd go out of my head . . ."

"Do you think they will find Acevedo?"

"Honestly," the young man smiled, "who gives a shit? Do you?"

Twenty-four hours later Nestor Escobosa was in the women's prison ward at Bellevue for assaulting her Welfare investigator, and her five silent children were scattered in various hospital wards and shelters provided by the Department of Welfare. I might have mentioned what happened to the Commissioner of Welfare, with whom I had an interview a day later, except that it became clear as we talked that he was about to submit his resignation. Two days later, he did.

3

AN OVERCOAT

• With the exception of social workers and official antipoverty propagandists, far too many people in a city like New York seem to believe that Welfare clients drive around in Cadillacs when the total annual sum allotted to a family of four on Public Assistance may just about equal the cost of a small Ford.

When the public reads how the national Welfare budget increases by $1 billion every three years, they are usually not willing to distinguish the soaring administrative costs of such a program from what eventually goes into the pocket of the consumer.[1] When taxpayers' groups clamor for residency laws to keep new applicants from coming to New York and consuming tax dollars, they do not usually point out that the federal share of assistance has risen from less than 15 percent in 1940 to as much as 75 percent of every Welfare-expended dollar, in some categories through various federal incentive programs and systems of matching funds. The cost of programs for dependent children goes up, but the cost of Home Relief programs drops absolutely when compared with the whopping $112 million disbursed

[1] According to the National Association of Social Workers there were 85,000 Welfare caseworkers in America in 1960. If each was paid $5,000 a year, that alone would account for nearly half a billion dollars annually in Welfare costs.

by the State of New York in 1940. Naturally, the $5.5 billion annually consumed by Welfare families purchases clothing, food, home furnishings, and other important employment and wealth-producing items, yet the expenditure is constantly viewed as a drain on the economy. And if ignorance about Welfare economics allows the irate local taxpayer to conclude that he is bearing a disproportionate share of the cost of supporting vice and ignorance, only ignorance about what such a family may actually receive allows him to think that it may be living well enough to merit his censure.

A typical Welfare budget is designed to deprive. It standardizes bare subsistence in a country in which luxuries have become necessities. The budget attempts to meet the family's needs economically, expeditiously, and efficiently, but it carefully defines these needs and expects the needy individual to abide by such definitions. In New York the system is known as budget deficit, which means that the family's supposed resources are subtracted from its supposed requirements, and the difference is supplied. In other states, even more deprivating budget "ceilings" have been established, which often penalize large families by not varying by one penny whether the family includes three or six children. In Arizona, for example, the maximum grant for any family is $220 a month, although some Mexican-American families have as many as a dozen dependents.

New York State budgets are more liberal because they are so highly individualized. Each person in the family has his own budget. Constantly under the revision of the Department's home economists, who base their allotments on a 50–50 weighting of current market prices in New York City as opposed to the rest of the State, the budget for a city per-

son will also determine the necessary but varied caloric in-
takes of each member of every family unit according to his
age, sex, and occupational status. Food budgets increase
as children reach their maximum growth periods of adoles-
cence and then dip as they grow into adulthood. Adult
males receive less than their children do with this arrangement, but there is so little fat on any budget that nobody in
the family is likely to get much of an edge on anybody else.
The Welfare budget will so conform to the frugal standards
for adequacy imposed by the State Department of Social
Welfare that it will clamor to be violated, either by buying
on credit or by misrepresenting the facts to the caseworker.
Such a budget cannot begin to supply the resources needed
to support middle-class standards. Consequently people on
Public Assistance are constantly vying among themselves to
see who can do better with the Welfare. Often they are given
no option but to duplicate middle-class acquisitiveness on
their somewhat pettier scales. Some may even invent dis-
abilities because they will be rewarded with more money on
the budget.

A modest budget for four people based on 1962 prices in
the City of New York was prepared in 1963 by the Community Council of New York. If that family consisted of a
husband and wife, a boy of thirteen and a girl of eight, the
Council believed that it would need to spend $36.26 a week
on food, exclusive of the working father's lunches away
from home. Since 1962 food prices have significantly increased. Eggs have risen from forty-five cents to approximately sixty cents a dozen, milk has increased two to three
cents a quart and bread by approximately the same amount,
and the price of fresh pork has nearly doubled. If the same

family were living on a Welfare budget at present, it would be expected to make do on $25.62 weekly for food, approximately $11 a week less than the Community Council thought was necessary for modest eating in 1962 but still $7.00 more than one nation-wide "economy standard" diet presently recommended for public assistance families by the U.S. Department of Health, Education and Welfare.[2]

To feed itself on $25.62 weekly a family will have to be sparing with fresh milk or butter; fresh eggs, fruits, and vegetables will also have to be considered luxuries. The average American is said to consume 160 pounds of meat annually, but this family would eat beans to supply its major protein dosages. They would learn to substitute peanut butter for chicken (as one manual that I read recommended) and government surplus cornstarch for potatoes. Rice and the various cereals would be consumed in large quantities. They would—if truly frugal—reboil their coffee grounds and mix their stale bread with government-surplus molasses to make pudding.

There are probably as few such thrifty families among our present-day Welfare population as there are among Americans in general. Practically speaking, Welfare families are enticed by the same advertisements as the non-Welfare population. They do not know so much about home economics as the people who devise their budgets; and they often receive less than the stipulated budgetary entitlements. They generally have second-rate kitchen equipment

[2] In 1916 the City's Board of Child Welfare allotted such families an average of $25.09 a month. Given the enormous increases in the cost of living since 1916, when $16 a week was considered a good salary, it is anybody's guess whether the citizen of the Poorhouse State is much better off now as compared with then.

and tiny larders, so they prefer to eat canned meals, TV dinners, and lots of sweet things for taste. When they overspend on a meal, they have no resources to fall back on; they either run up a bill at the grocery store or do without.[3]

The 1963 Community Council budget included $14.70 a week for reading materials, recreation, tobacco, stationery supplies, gifts, insurance, and telephone service. On Welfare, every two weeks the thirteen-year-old boy and the eight-year-old girl members of the family would be given a total of $1.25 for their expenses "incidental to education" (paper, pencils, reading materials), but no members of such a family would be allowed money for tobacco, entertainment, telephone service, transportation (except, reluctantly, on Welfare business), gifts, toys, or even a daily newspaper. If the person wanted to have any of these items, they would have to be purchased out of the food budget or his sole clothing budget of $3.90 weekly, the allotments for personal care ($1.40)[4] or household expenses ($1.20), or the

[3] Welfare checks are paid out on the 1st and 16th of the month in the city of New York. In many Welfare neighborhoods the mails are tardy, and checks arrive routinely late to the budgeted family. This situation was further aggravated, until recently, by Welfare's practice of mailing the checks so they will arrive no earlier than the following Monday wherever either the 1st or 16th of the month falls after a weekend, so that the clients will not have the money to spend in bars over the weekend.

[4] Based on 1965 standards established by the homemakers of the New York City Department of Welfare, here is a list of items to be acquired with regular semimonthly grants for personal care and their proposed duration of use:

Women and Girls

1. Toilet soap   (12 bars per year)
2. Tooth brush   (2 per year)
3. Dentifrice   (2 four-oz. cans per year)
4. Cleansing tissue   (100 per year)
5. Nail file   (1 for 4 years)
6. Face powder   (2–3 oz. per year for employed woman)
                        (1–3 oz. per year for unemployed woman)

family would have to find ways of getting the extra income and face the risk of being penalized for the withholding of such income if they were caught.

The family living on the Community Council budget could expect to pay $82.00 a month for a four-room apartment, including kitchen and bath. It would have at its disposal the usual mechanical aids to facilitate housekeeping, i.e., access to a washing machine, a refrigerator, a vacuum cleaner, and an electric iron. When the Department of Welfare consents to pay $82.00 a month for rent, it is generally for the larger family. That family would have difficulty finding an apartment of value equal to the one described above, and the client would be required to pay his rent semimonthly. Although it is illegal to discriminate in renting to persons because of race, color, sex, or religious beliefs, there is no law in the State of New York prohibiting a landlord from discriminating against persons who are on Public Assistance.

The typical Welfare family is likely to reside in an old-law tenement or a tiny railroad flat with a bathtub in the kitchen in a neighborhood such as 80th Street. Once housed, it re-

---

Women and Girls (cont.)

7. Lipstick	(2 per year for employed woman)
	(1 per year for unemployed woman)
8. Deodorant	(2 per year for employed woman)
	(1 per year for unemployed woman)
9. Comb	(1 every 2 years)
10. Bobby pins	(48 pins per year)
11. Haircuts	(1 per year 16+; 2 per year 7+)
12. Permanent wave refill	(3 per year for employed woman)
	(1 per year for unemployed woman)
13. Sanitary belt	(1 for 2 years)
14. Sanitary pads	(144 per year)
15. Shoe polish	(1 can per year)

ceives money to purchase cooking equipment, beds, blankets, tables, chest of drawers, and chairs, if it can prove need, but it is assumed that the semimonthly allotment covers need, so each separate request has to be adjudicated individually. By special permission of departmental home economists the family can acquire a refrigerator if equipment on the premises is faulty, but a vacuum cleaner is considered a luxury. If convincing medical reasons are presented, the family may be allowed to purchase a semiautomatic washing machine with a "hand wringer." If hospitalization removes the mother from the household, the children, eligible for the services of a Welfare housekeeper, are usually sent to the shelters. A portion of the family's living space is sometimes rented to a relative—an "uncle" or a "friend"—without Welfare's knowledge and permission. Sleeping arrangements in such a home are deemed adequate if no more than two persons of the same sex share the same bed.

"We give people money for underclothing, and we find that they are using it to buy liquor," a Department employee complained to me one day. The same employee confessed on another occasion that he could understand "culturally" why it might be permissible for an old Italian couple to "take wine with their meals," but, though he thought most Welfare families should be teetotalers, he was particularly offended by the fact that his carefully-budgeted grants were being used by Negro and Puerto Rican women to purchase beer. Since there are no Welfare grants for beer, wine, or liquor, the only way a family can acquire such things is by dipping into the money for food, the new bed, or the new winter coat. A good deal of the petty cheating that goes on among Welfare recipients is merely an effort to obtain some of the comforts that have become more or less standard expectations—necessities?—in working-class America. Condemned to his meager half-world of preadded family budgets and special nonrecurring grants, the Welfare deadbeat learns to conspire against his wife's budget, his child's budget, or even his own budget. And when a family "makes it" on Welfare, it has learned to be as ruggedly individualistic, as resourceful, and as aggressive in its demands on the system as those earlier generations who crossed the wilderness or amassed large fortunes by hard work and thrift; but it is also learning to conceal, to lie if necessary, and to hide behind the protective coloring of the defective, which may be the only continuing grounds for eligibility. Such a family would make it its business to apply for every special grant, every tiny extra benefit, and it would probably be described by Welfare caseworkers in an unflattering way; but if the family did not lie, conceal, conspire, and manipulate, it might never even receive its entitlement, for not only do the economic penalties we impose on the dependent pervade every aspect of his daily life, defining his friends, his neighbors, his accommodations, and even his furnishings, but we also commonly do not take the trouble to instruct the recipient in the details of that entitlement.

Suppose, for example, that you or I decide that we need a new piece of linoleum for the kitchen floor. We can select the linoleum, buy it outright, charge it, buy it on time, or—if we are especially thrifty—save enough money each week to eventually purchase the linoleum. The Welfare deadbeat does not even know that he can have linoleum, so, lacking any of the above options, he applies to his investigator, bearing in mind, of course, that—as one New

York City Welfare manual points out—it is the investigator's "responsibility to establish that need exists" and that "mere statements to that effect are of little value." After listening to his client's "unsubstantiated assertion" of need, the investigator may decide that his client does not need the linoleum to cover his otherwise serviceable strip of concrete flooring, or he may feel that the old strip of linoleum can be cleaned another time, or, after inspecting the old linoleum to make certain another time that it has served out its "maximum durability," the investigator may consult with the home economist and decide to grant the recipient an amount sufficient to purchase a second-hand strip of linoleum or a very cheap new strip of linoleum. The recipient might be obliged to submit estimates from as many as three different storekeepers before he makes his purchase, and he might be charged a nonrefundable fee for these estimates. Whatever the estimated costs, the family may now have to use a portion of their linoleum grant to pay a bill at the grocery store, and the linoleum they may finally be able to buy with the difference, perhaps on another expensive credit arrangement, may be so shoddy that it will wear out before the payments are completed. Then the applicant will have to petition once more for linoleum, but it may take a while before his investigator will be willing to find the time to undertake another investigation of need (home visit), and when he does, the applicant's Welfare dossier may be used to show that he was improvident in the purchase of his initial strip of linoleum. The second grant for linoleum may, consequently, be smaller than was the first, and again it probably will have to be used to pay off creditors. Grateful for whatever linoleum he gets, never very troublesome about the linoleum he cannot have, the person who wants linoleum will probably not know enough to demand that his investigator pay him a visit. There may be reasons why he does not want him to visit. Probably he will never know (because he has never been told) what type of linoleum he is entitled to. At his local Welfare center he is exhorted with gaudy posters from the Department of Health, Education and Welfare about proper eating habits, but he will not be posterized to ask his investigator for enough money to buy a standard brand of linoleum.[5]

Nowhere that the recipient is likely to go during his dependency will there be signs advising him about his linoleum rights in such terms as those in which Social Security recipients are constantly advised that under such-and-such an Old Age and Survivors Insurance Program the claimant can now receive so many additional dollars in income. The War on Poverty has recently announced Operation Medicare Alert, an attempt to recruit all those over sixty-five to the Medicare Program, but no such effort has ever been made to recruit people to the public assistance lists. Persons on public assistance seemingly have no vested rights to their benefits. Whatever rights they do have are, as a matter of policy, kept deeply guarded secrets by the functionaries. Thus, whenever there is a raise in the level of public assistance grants from HEW, little effort is made to pass the news on to the potential consumers. When New York State, for example, made it possible for unemployed fathers to receive

[5] That nobody takes the trouble to tell the poor that they can collect public assistance can perhaps be gauged from this figure from the 1962 Annual Report of the Department of Welfare: An average of 59,000 persons in 12,600 family units in New York City received surplus foods but were not in receipt of public assistance.

AFDC funds under the provisions of a 1962 amendment to the Social Security Act, there was much self-congratulation among the professional social welfare fraternity, but nobody bothered to publicize the news among the unemployed fathers. One man thrown off Home Relief put the matter this way: "They don't want to know about us. We have to go looking for them."

And because it is this way, it is even more so in the administration of the individual semimonthly grants for income maintenance, which are to nurture and fulfill that dependency. When members of a four-person family received $24.15 weekly for food, they were not informed that they were strictly entitled to this $24.15. They knew with even less certainty that they could be allowed up to $150 a year in special grants for clothing before their case would be reviewed by a Case Consultation Unit. If they had a less knowledgeable or less charitable investigator, they might be given $23.67 a week for food and $50 per year for their clothing (or, more commonly, $5); and they wouldn't, typically, be in a position to argue with authority about what they were getting. There would be no published lists or schedules in public places notifying the father that as an unemployed man over twenty-one he could expect $6.25 weekly for his food and $7.35 for food for his thirteen-year-old son. In some Welfare Centers there are still rules against seeing such schedules. In others, if the client knows enough to ask, he may be given an explanation, but he will not be encouraged to ask, never advised, solicited, or otherwise stimulated to inquire. Even if his worker bears the client no malice, he may be such a newcomer to the system that he himself does not know that certain deserving sick people can receive money for special diets, or that young people are to receive so much for their cod liver oil, or that some slum families are to have their utilities allowances supplemented in order to keep their lights burning at night to discourage rats.

Despite the tiny increases, Welfare still has access to a body of information by which it makes decisions concerning its clients' standards of living, standardizing their needs even to the number of haircuts and razor blades they are to be allowed; but the needy petitioner cannot browse through such a "black book" at his local Welfare center during the many hours he must sit awaiting service. With every new action taken to minister to his need, his humiliation is made the more severe as his dependency is further stressed. If he objects to such a procedure, the benefit can be withheld. Presumably, that is why it took Antonio Ortiz nearly four months to receive winter clothing grants for his three children so that it was spring when the money finally arrived.

"It didn't astound me," this tall dark-skinned Negro with heart-shaped lips later told me, "until my wife said, 'What do we do now, Antonio?' So I decided to buy what we needed for the next few months and save the rest of the money for this winter because I am not what you would call a good manager unless I am being very careful. Even then my wife says, 'Anthony, maybe you ought to buy the coats now and I will put them in mothballs.' But I say there are other things we need, such as bathing suits for the CYO camp. By next winter, who knows, styles change. Let's at least be like other people for a little while . . ."

Ortiz frowned as if he had just at that moment realized

his mistake. He explained how little by little the money had been spent on a sick child, a loan to his brother, a confirmation dress for his eldest daughter. Now New York's streets were being dusted again with a thin rime of frost, but his children still lacked winter clothes. The longest strike of Welfare employees in New York City history had just ended. Although it had been announced to the poor during the course of the walk-out that they were being put on the "honor system" by the absence of their investigators, Antonio was still afraid, after the settlement, to ask for any more money from his worker. Probably he would have said nothing to anybody except that the children had been missing school on the very coldest days, and the authorities wanted to know why.

They told Antonio, "If you don't know your responsibilities toward these children, we will have to teach you." Then a neighbor told him that some social workers operating out of a storefront in the area had a supply of second-hand clothing that they gave away. Antonio arrived at the store in his only suit, a summer-weight black silk with long narrow lapels into which he had tucked a white silk opera scarf. Standing in the drafty entranceway, rubbing the chilblains along his arms, he was told he would have to wait until one of the workers was free. He sat next to me and started to chatter.

"That's a special coat you got there," he said. "That's a very nice coat." When he crossed his legs, I could see a hole in the heel of his black cotton lisle sock; and there was a white crust along the edges of his black dancing shoes where the salt, used to clean New York's streets on snowy days, had dried against a patina of shoe wax. Seeing me

stare at his foot, Antonio added, "I was 4-F in the Army . . .
arches . . . How much a coat like that cost?"

I told Antonio that my handsome alpaca-lined greatcoat of loden cloth had been a present from my mother-
in-law and that I could not remember the price.

"What you mean—you can't remember?" I told him
then I had overheard his conversation with the receptionist
and asked if I could be of any help.

"A coat like that must cost a fortune. Astounding!"
Antonio whistled faintly. He peeled away his silk scarf
so I could see that he was just wearing a T-shirt. Then he
explained that he wanted a warm flannel shirt for himself,
but he would need jackets and pants for the two boys, a
warm coat for his wife, and some big warm blankets for his
baby girl. "It won't astound me if they are not too pretty,"
Antonio smiled. "My wife fixes holes. Besides," he added,
"there is a new hotel opening uptown, and if I can keep
warm for just a little while longer, maybe I will have a job
through this friend."

"What do you think you will be able to do?"

"Don't you worry. When I'm ready I'll do something."
But, after staring at each other again, he seemed concerned
that I would misunderstand. "I'm just not ready right now,"
Antonio said.

Then he explained in his peculiar *patois* that at age nineteen he had emigrated from Puerto Rico to the Virgin
Islands, where he had worked as a bartender at one of the
resort hotels, but since he was a family man, he had never
liked tending bar. It was just too hard watching other people drink and not taking a few yourself, especially when
the management allowed for a certain amount of pilferage;

and he had never been an able drinker anyway. It made him
sick in the head, sick in the chest too; in fact, "it wasn't
so good for my whole system." By the time his wife started
having children, he had saved enough money to bring the
family to New York, hoping to find the same kind of work
temporarily, while he studied to be a television repairman
at night so that he would be ready when the right opening
came along. There just was not much demand, however,
for dark-skinned bartenders with fancy manners who knew
how to mix tropical fruit punches. When he did find work,
it was in a Dominican tavern in East Harlem. But there
was a health inspection, and they found that he was sick
in the chest and decided he "wasn't ready" again, so they
had put him on Home Relief and then on Aid to the Disabled, while the rest of the family received Aid for Dependent Children.

"I can't say I was surprised," he smiled, interrupting his
smile with a deep fierce hacking, as if to assure me that he
was, in fact, consumptive. "It comes and goes. Sometimes
I'm more ready than other times. Some days are just better
than others. The trick is to keep warm a little while longer
and then take the medicine and eat good . . . That is the
most important thing. Say, *if I had a coat like that.*" He
smiled again, rubbing a skeletal brown hand against my
alpaca collar.

The gesture sent shivers down my back. I asked, "How
long has it been since you last worked?"

"Nearly two years," Antonio said. He shrugged. "It could
be worse. I mean, I'm not so anxious to tend bar . . . All
that late work and broads and everything. It isn't the right
kind of job for a married man . . . although the money's

good. Anyway," he added, "I would need a coat to look for work . . ."

"You mean an overcoat," I said.

"Something like that," he smiled.

"Frankly," I said, "I doubt if there is anything like this here. Do you want to see what there is?"

"What do you think there is?"

I shrugged. "I don't know." But when I got up to go to the back room, Antonio followed me.

"Oh, no, mister . . . I'm not going to have my kids wear rags," was Antonio's only comment when he saw the cardboard cartons piled high with clean but rumpled flannels and corduroys. I picked up a child's sweatshirt and sniffed it to show him that it was clean, but he said, "Oh, no, mister, they have friends, too."

"They tell me everything has been boiled," I said.

Antonio merely said: "Uh uh . . ."

I pushed open the door in the giant wardrobe and pointed out the shabby woolen topcoats, the faded suit jackets without pants, a scuffed leather shortie, a pastel cubavera sport jacket without lapels, a field jacket, an Ike jacket, a plaid bathrobe, a plastic raincoat, an airman's fleece lining, and a pair of rubber hip boots.

After staring at each garment, Antonio said, "Some people are like awful pigs . . ."

"The stuff is warm," I said.

"Pigs," he muttered back at me.

"Look," I told him, "take a big bundle home and see what fits. That doesn't mean you can't get other things as soon as Welfare comes through . . ."

Antonio said, "I'm not ready for that!" He closed the wardrobe door and went over to one of the largest cartons again, plunging his hands among the various blouses and shirts so that they spilled over its sides onto the dirty floor. Holding up a woolen sweat sock, he said, "Uh uh."

"You know," he added, "I once earned a hundred and fifty dollars a week with tips."

"I know how you feel," I said, "but if you need to keep warm . . ."

". . . and you haven't got no rich mother-in-law," Antonio added, smiling superciliously.

He was now staring angrily at my greatcoat, which I had folded across my arm so that the alpaca fleece was showing. I tried to make a joke of our situation. "You don't want me to give you this coat? What would I wear then?"

Behind one of the nearby partitions a woman started to sob.

"Look," I said, "isn't there anything here that you can find for your wife and kids until Welfare comes through . . ."

Abruptly the woman's voice rose: "*No se puede dormir. No hay camas ni mantas ni almohadas!*"

As a social worker tried to quiet her with assurances that he would see that she got her sleeping things, Antonio said, "A woman like that could sleep in a coat like yours."

I started to pick up the apparel he had scattered across the floor. "It's no good. It's no use," he said. "These things are full of bugs." He turned and started for the door.

Less than five minutes later he was back again, coughing as if he had a saw working in his chest, his hands up in front of his face, which had turned gray and sweaty. When

I had found a cup of warm coffee and had led him over to a chair, Antonio Ortiz said, "Astounding. Fucking cold outside."

I made him take a sip of the coffee, which only started his coughing again. He demanded a cigarette. After a few long drags and more coughing, something seemed to click against his throat. He swallowed hard. "A guy like you . . . a coat like that . . . why don't you come with me over to the Welfare . . . I mean maybe they will believe me if they see a guy like you . . ."

I asked him whether he would take the old clothes if we were turned down. "I'll take anything," he said, in between another series of coughs, "because, shit, I can't go out like this."

I went to the wardrobe and found a poplin cap with fleecy earmuffs and a tweed overcoat with greasy stains on the sleeves. It was belted in the back like a Newport jacket, and it was probably two or three sizes too large. After I had helped him stick his skinny arms through the sleeves of the coat, Antonio wrapped the garment around his thin frame like a bathrobe, giggling, I clamped the poplin cap down on top of his head.

"There," I said.

Antonio went over to the wardrobe mirror to stare at himself. "Nice. Very nice, Mr. Ortiz," he said, with a shiver.

If he were behind barbed wire he would have looked like one of the American POW's during the Korean War. As Antonio toyed with the cap, tilting it back and forth on his head, I tried to find a warm scarf among the bins of clothing. "Don't bother," Antonio said.

"It's no bother."

"I once saw this movie from Italy," he said.

"What movie?"

Antonio shrugged his shoulders: "It really doesn't matter . . ."

"No," I said. "I'd really like to hear about it."

"Well," he smiled, "It was a movie about a circus, and there was this nutty woman who was dressed just like me. I mean even though she was white she was dressed like me . . . I used to go to a lot of movies when I first came to New York. Kept warm that way."

"What about the woman?"

"Astounding," he replied. "They had this big spic Anthony Quinn in the movie. I always like his movies. I don't know why. Anyway, Anthony and this girl in the overcoat lived in a wagon just like gypsies only they weren't gypsies . . ." He looked at me sadly. "I don't know why I'm telling you this story . . ."

"Because you were reminded of the woman in the overcoat."

"Oh, certainly," Antonio smiled. Then he walked over to the wardrobe to stare at himself again. "What a nice kettle of fish! I mean this is something. *Astounding.*" He smiled again. "Bet you didn't know I got a white wife."

"How should I know? Is she Spanish?"

Antonio said, "Uh uh—part Irish, part Jew."

He was making a fore-in-hand knot with his silk scarf, fluffing it under his collar, but when he saw me staring at him in the mirror, his glance immediately fell on my greatcoat again.

"I met her in the islands." He smiled. "What a funny thing. Where I come from you feel overdressed in just a bathing suit. You don't even need a fucking overcoat."

I asked, "Have you ever thought of going back?"

"Look," he spun about to face me angrily, "I'm not ready to do a thing like that. When I want your advice about going back I'll ask for it. I'm an American citizen. What do I want to go back there for? You go back there maybe later, but not now. Maybe to die. Besides, I got no family there. I've got young kids. You think I want them shaking tropical drinks?"

"I didn't mean what you think," I said.

Antonio said, "I don't know what you meant. All I want are some winter clothes."

To change the subject I said, "Maybe I remember that picture you were telling me about. Was it called . . ."

"Fucking Anthony Quinn pictures," Antonio said. "Everybody goes to see them . . ."

It is about a ten-minute walk from the bottom of Stanton Street to the Lower Manhattan Welfare Center. To get there you must go north across the wide, heavily traveled boulevard known as Houston Street, continue north to 5th Street, turn east past the grounds of a new middle-income housing project. At the other side of the project 5th Street resumes, a narrow street with the green light of a police station in the middle of the block and the Welfare Center diagonally across from it. During my previous visits to the Lower East Side I had taken this walk many times, always alone. Now, walking with Antonio, every step that brought us closer to the center made the trip seem more problematical.

As soon as we stepped outside the door, Antonio said, "What do you want to do this for?"

"Let's say I want to," taking his arm to lead him across Houston Street.

"What a stupid idea," Antonio said.

"Let's say I'm writing a book," I added. Antonio shrugged me off again and then stared at me and started walking; but when we got to Houston Street he could not seem to make up his mind to cross in the traffic. The wind was piercing cold, and it bent him over like a reed as we stood a few feet from the curb with our hands stuffed in our pockets. Once I started across and found myself alone in the traffic, so I hurried back to the curb just in time to see him make a break for it. He too got stranded among the racing autos and trucks and seemed so bewildered that I feared he would be hit by one of the rushing vehicles. Just as he started to lean toward the other curb, a car came at him and he drew himself back again, squaring his shoulders to his full height. "You can't stay there," I yelled, but another truck drove past just then, and I wondered if he had heard me. Running into the traffic, I grabbed his arm and pulled him across the remainder of Houston Street.

His breathing was so labored that he was coughing. I held him in my arms against a lamppost. "Are you all right?"

"Fucking traffic," he said, "it's inhuman . . . fucking wind."

A prolonged cold blast from the river was striking our backs as I pulled Antonio behind a building off the corner of Avenue B. After resting another few moments we started toward 5th Street, but at the parklike entrance to the project he hesitated.

"It's all right," I said, taking his arm as we walked quickly past the gray-uniformed guard to the other side of the common. Not far away were the windows of an Army-Navy store, and I started to guide Antonio across the street toward its displays. "That way you'll know what you want," I suggested.

"Later," he said, shivering. We started down 5th Street.

The Lower Manhattan Welfare Center is housed in what was once a decrepit red brick elementary school but is now a decrepit red brick emergency food distribution point, as well as a Welfare Center. More than five thousand Lower East Side families are served here. On the outside of the dingy old building there is a large white sign advising passers-by to come to this place to be "registered" if there is a bombing or other emergency. Beyond this there is a small sign in black:

CITY OF NEW YORK
DEPARTMENT OF WELFARE

When we came to the small black doorway, a few flakes of snow were falling, and Antonio told me that until recently he had always had to travel 60 blocks north to Yorkville to see his caseworker. In fact, he had been to 5th Street only once during his two previous years on Welfare. Then he had come to inquire about tuition money to continue his course in TV repairs.

"In those days I had this man for an investigator," he smiled bitterly, "and don't you think he didn't think so? You know what he asked me? He said, 'Can't your wife help out?' So I thought I knew what he meant by that. I said, 'You don't really mean that. You mean don't your wife peddle herself?' And this guy he just grinned at me . . .

". . . Now what kind of a question is that to ask? My wife don't peddle anything. She got the kids to take care of. What kind of a question is that anyway?

". . . So anyway I just got up and left the place, but they must have taken down my name because a few days later I got a letter to report to this office where they asked me if I had ever done janit—janitorial work."

Antonio coughed. It had stopped snowing, but it was becoming so blowy outside that, although I wanted to hear more, I did not think it would be a good idea to expose him to the weather any longer.

I said, "I take it you no longer have a man investigator . . ."

"Not here," he said, "it's a girl. Miss Oltarsch. You ever meet her, this Miss Oltarsch?"

When I shook my head no, Antonio said, "I only saw her a couple of times before the strike. Nice looking . . . but don't let that fool you."

"You mean she's tough?"

"Breaks balls," Antonio said.

We entered the center and the police guard stuck out his arm and directed us toward a small intake desk. Beyond the desk was the bullpen, with rows of glass-walled cubicles surrounding it. "Please do not bring children to this office," one hand-lettered sign declared to the hundred or so applicants, mostly dark-skinned, who were sitting in the bullpen, a few hugging their children close to them. A tall white man in a blue suit appeared. He walked between the files of chairs, pulling at his nose as he called out numbers. After a number was called there was a barking of voices, and the man shouted, "Quiet down there! One at a time!"

I started to lead Antonio toward one of the vacant chairs in the bullpen, but a young Negro at the intake desk stopped us. "What do you want?" he demanded.

He was making columns of vertical chicken scratches on a pad. Above his head was another sign: "Please do not bring children to this office." A red one proclaimed: "Smoking prohibited." He was a very tidy young man in a well-cut gray suit. As Antonio and I approached his desk, he made a fourth chicken scratch and then quickly inked it over with a horizontal stroke of his pen. He blotted the paper and picked up a large, shiny apple, biting deeply into its flesh with his big white teeth.

Chewing, he asked me, "Are you a social worker?"

I nudged Antonio.

"We want to see Miss Oltarsch," he said.

"You're his social worker, aren't you?" he asked, before taking another big bite of the apple.

I told the fellow I was not a social worker, just an acquaintance.

"What does he want to see Miss Oltarsch about?" he asked.

"Look," I said, "he speaks English. He just wants to see her. I am only along because he asked me to come."

"And I thought you were his social worker . . . Well," he added, as he thoughtfully chewed more apple, "you can wait here, I guess."

"I would like to go with my friend," I said as I heard the sound of a slap reverberating in the bullpen.

The young man also heard the sound. He said, "He won't need you inside . . ."

"I'd like to go anyway," I said.

"Suit yourself." He picked up his phone, asked for Nan Oltarsch, and waited a moment. Then: "There are two people waiting to see you." There was a pause, during which he took another cracking bite of apple. Then he turned to me, again with his mouth full: "What did you say his name was?"

"Ortiz, Antonio . . . I'm disabled," Antonio replied.

"He says it is Antonio Ortiz and he is on Home Relief . . . I think he means TADC . . . Oh, I see. Maybe he is a composite . . . and he has this friend with him . . . I don't think the friend is on anything . . . Yeah . . . I know. He makes it sound like it is his patriotic duty. Where did you say you lived, Anthony?"

Antonio said, "Twenty-nine Clinton Street."

"Twenty-nine Clinton Street," the fellow repeated . . . "You want me to get the friend's name? . . . You want me to have them wait?"

He put down the phone, took up his apple again, frowned upon seeing that it was already turning rusty, then dropped the core into a wastebasket.

Looking up, he said, "She had more than one Ortiz, but she found him all right. It just took a little while. He's got the prettiest investigator in the whole Center. She'll come and get you. You wait in there."

"Will she be long?" I asked.

"Why not wait and see?"

"Look," I said, "I am in a hurry. Maybe if we went upstairs . . ."

"It wouldn't be right. Him walking around upstairs . . ."

"You mean," I said, "he's not allowed upstairs?"

"None of them are," the man smiled. He pointed again toward the bullpen.

When we took our seats among the other applicants, Antonio smiled. "I bet we'll be here an hour."

He was mistaken. It was nearly an hour and a half before we heard a woman's voice. "*Mr. Ortiz? . . . Mr. Ortiz?*"

Nan Oltarsch wore her hair in a big, honey-colored bun at the back of her head. She had an ink splotch on the tip of her nose. She wasn't really pretty but she dressed as if she thought she might be. A tight mauve skirt of nubby wool showed off her hips; it was topped by a soft, light pink sweater. Her eyes were big, staring; she had a strong jaw. When she came into the bullpen, she stood on tiptoe staring out across the clients: "Mr. Ortiz?"

Our eyes met, and the lines around her heavily rouged lips softened into a smile. She motioned me to come forward. I took Antonio's arm and pushed him along with me.

"That really wasn't necessary," she said, when we were next to her.

Antonio was trying to smile. "Hello, Miss Oltarsch . . ."

"Hello, Mr. Ortiz," she said. Then she turned to me. "Are you a friend of Mr. Ortiz?"

"You could put it that way," I said.

"Can I speak with you alone?"

We walked a few steps toward one of the cubicles; because she was carrying papers, Nan Oltarsch stuck out her left hand. "My name is Nan Oltarsch." I shook that nice, warm hand, on which she wore a gold wedding band, and then introduced myself.

"Are you a social worker?" she asked.

"I'm afraid not," I said. I was going to leave it at that, but Mrs. Oltarsch stared at me until I realized that I would have to explain. "I just happened to meet Mr. Ortiz after not seeing him for a long time," I lied. "When he told me he was coming here to see you, I thought I would like to go along. Mr. Ortiz needs winter clothing for his family, you know."

"We'll see," she said. And she smiled and started back toward her client. "This way, Mr. Ortiz."

She led him toward a cubicle, and I followed. She turned and saw me still there. "That's all right, Mr. Elman."

Antonio was looking around, bewildered. I didn't move.

"I think we will be able to talk just fine now."

"You mind if I listen?"

Nan Oltarsch crimsoned. "If it is all right with Mr. Ortiz."

"I would like him to . . . you know," Antonio said.

"I see . . ."

She sat behind a desk and invited us to take the two chairs. Then she offered me a cigarette. Opening a manila folder marked *Confidential* in green, she scrambled through some forms and ran a finger down a column of figures. I struck a match and lit my cigarette. Mrs. Oltarsch kept hers unlit, using it as a pointer. At last she looked up.

"What happened to that money we gave you last year?"

I said, "How would you like your husband to ask you such a question?"

"I'm separated," she said.

I said, "I'm very sorry," and Antonio said, "Gee, I'm sorry."

Mrs. Oltarsch tried a smile; when it didn't work, she closed her folder and asked, "Did you spend all that other money?"

Antonio started to explain how the money had come in the spring and he had hoped to save it for the winter, but it had to be used for other things. Then he got disgusted with himself and said, "It wasn't enough anyway . . ."

Nan Oltarsch flicked a glance over toward me. "You see what it's like," she said. "I have a slip here that he missed an employment interview. We can't just keep giving out money all the time . . ."

I said, "You act as if it was your money . . ."

"I don't think that's very funny," she said.

"I didn't think it was funny. It's true . . ."

"Please, Mr. Elman. There is no reason for us to quarrel in front of Mr. Ortiz . . ."

"How else is he going to get money for his winter clothing?"

"I don't think that's very funny," she answered.

She looked at the papers and started to run her finger down another column of figures. "I don't see why he missed that appointment," she said, as she found another form among the papers and proceeded to scan it as well. Then she scribbled some figures on a scratch pad and said, "Mr. Ortiz and his family receive a regular clothing allowance of $6.00 [every two weeks], which may have to be adjusted a bit. I'll have to do some figuring later and speak to people around here. That isn't the point. The point is last winter we were able to find him a nonrecurring grant of $85.00 to purchase galoshes and quilted coats for his wife and children plus a separate $25.00 for galoshes and blankets for himself. Now he tells me he still hasn't got anything for the winter. Well, I think we have a right to ask how he's been managing."

"Who are *we?*"

Mrs. Oltarsch ignored my question. "There was also a grant of $50.00 for a new bed. Did he tell you about the bed and the blankets?"

"No, he didn't mention the bed."

"Why should I mention the bed?" Antonio asked.

Mrs. Oltarsch went on, "Anyway, I may have to pay him a visit soon because if he doesn't have that bed we will want to know why. Do you have the bed?"

Antonio nodded stubbornly.

"Well, that's something . . ." She glanced down at her figures again. "Anyway," she said, "I just can't give him another nonrecurring grant until I have it cleared with my case supervisor." Staring at Ortiz, she crumpled the cigarette between her fingers. "Don't you know how to save?"

"Save what?" I asked.

"I don't think that's so funny either . . . After all, a man has to learn how to be responsible sometime or other . . ."

Ortiz said, "Who isn't responsible?"

And I added, "I think he's got a point there."

"Well," she said, closing the Ortiz folder, "I guess there isn't much more I can say . . ."

"I'm sorry," Ortiz said.

And I said, "*What are you sorry for?* Look," I added, "can't you just put it down as a matter of administrative error? He got the money in the spring, he was in debt, he used it for other things. Strikes me that it was an administrative error if the money didn't come in time to buy winter clothing. I mean I know you are busy around here . . ."

"Are you being funny?"

"Look, I would just like to see Mr. Ortiz walk out of here with money for clothing. His kids can't go to school because they haven't got clothing. Now what's so complicated about that?"

Mrs. Oltarsch stood up. "I don't know whether you are being funny or not . . ."

"Can't you scrape up a little money?"

"I'll be right back," she said. "I'll see what I can do."

"Don't take an hour and a half this time . . ."

"Look," she started to say, but she stopped herself and left us alone in the cubicle. Less than ten minutes later, she was back, smiling broadly. "Very well, Mr. Ortiz, if you and your friend here will wait out there a minute or two, a check will be coming from the accounting office for the children."

"And Mr. Ortiz?"

"Look," she said, "I didn't tell him to lend that money to his brother. If his brother needs money so badly, tell him to apply to Welfare."

"And get turned down?"

"I don't think that's very funny," Mrs. Oltarsch said, and she added, "You know, I don't have to talk to you if I don't want to. Let's see how you like that. I don't have to deal with you at all, you know . . ."

"Don't," I said, "just give my friend here his money. After all that is what you are here for."

"Very funny," Mrs. Oltarsch tried again to smile. She asked if I would step out into the corridor once more. "You know," she said, "it is one thing to talk this way between ourselves, but I don't think it's such a good idea in front of Mr. Ortiz . . ."

"Are you going to give him his money?" I asked.

She said, "I just can't do that. It should go into case consultation. You want me to get into trouble?"

"Honestly," I said, "I don't want to get you into any trouble. I just want him to have an overcoat. You can say you made a mistake . . ."

"It isn't that easy," she smiled. "He missed his appointment . . . but," she added, "if you promise to make sure he buys the clothing . . ."

"I won't promise anything."

Mrs. Oltarsch walked a few steps further down along the corridor saying, "I don't understand you. Somebody has to take the responsibility. What's so special about Ortiz? If you want me to help, no questions asked, the least you can do is sort of look after him."

"I'm not a social worker. Besides, I never even met the guy until today."

"Really, that's . . ." She swallowed hard and continued, "I can't understand. Why didn't you just mind your own business?"

"I'm sorry," I said. "I suppose I deserve that . . . Only I wanted to know why it took so long for him to get a winter coat . . ."

"Oh," she said then. "He won't freeze. He already has a coat . . ."

"It's a rag," I said.

She said, "It's not supposed to be a Burberry . . ."

"It says in the book," I reminded her, "he's supposed to have a new coat once every three years . . ."

"Once every five if he isn't working," she corrected me. "What am I talking to you about this for? We already gave him the money. Is it my fault if he didn't buy what he was supposed to buy?"

I said, "Mr. Ortiz likes my coat. He has TB."

"Don't you think I know that?" She put up her hands, as if to stop me from saying any more. Then she added, "I'll be fair with you. Do you know if he has chairs?"

"Don't you?"

"I'm trying to be fair with you," she said. "I'll give him money for a new chair, and he can buy the coat with it . . ."

"Then if he ever needs a chair you'll say . . ."

"Cut it out. I may not even be here then," she said.

A head poked out from one of the adjacent cubicles. "Any problems, Nan?"

"Really . . . it's nothing," she said, trying to collect herself. Then she said, "Oh, what difference does it make anyway?" But she started back toward her office, and I followed her. Seeing us enter, Ortiz started to cough. "All right," she said, "you needn't do that." But Ortiz was coughing badly. Mrs. Oltarsch put her hands on her hips. "You can tell him he can shop around for himself, select a garment, and I will have a check written payable to the store."

Ortiz stopped coughing and looked up. I said, "Why don't you tell him?"

Mrs. Oltarsch was staring at me. "Besides," I asked, "How much should he spend?"

"He'll tell me," she said, "and then I'll tell him because I'll have to look it up."

"You mean you really don't trust me," Ortiz said flatly.

Mrs. Oltarsch stared at him as if he couldn't have put it

better, but she merely said, "May I suggest that Army and Navy store on the next corner . . ."

We nodded.

"I'm sorry. You'll have to go now. There are others waiting."

Two hours later we were standing in the cold in front of the Welfare Center with the snow beginning to stick fast. Antonio Ortiz had a check for $85.00 in his hand. "You want to go to that Army-Navy store?"

"What's the hurry?" He smiled. "You know," he said, "I would still like to buy that coat off you if you would sell it."

"It would be too big for you," I said.

"Besides," I added, "I don't want to sell it."

"Yeah," Antonio said. "You're not ready."

"You want to go to the Army-Navy store?" I asked again.

Antonio shrugged. "You know," he said a moment later, "if I don't get a coat it will be no great loss."

"You should have a coat," I said.

"It would be nice to spend the money," Antonio smiled. "I'd like to take this money and spend it. That's what I would really like to do. Fuck the kids. Fuck everybody. Welfare will take care of them sooner or later. I could have an astounding good time with this money. And then I would like to come back to the center with you and ask for more. I could get you to come with me. I know we could. Like right now, I would like to go out with you wherever you are going and have a good dinner and some drinks and then we would take in a movie, maybe . . . I would get one of the neighbors to look after the kids, and the three of us, my wife and me and you, we would really have a good time because I think you would like my wife, you know . . . and then tomorrow you would take me here, and I would come back and ask for more. What do you think they would say? We could go on demanding more from them until there wasn't anything left . . . and I wouldn't have one thing more to show for it . . . not even a coat . . .

"I'm kidding," he added. "You get that way sometimes." Shyly, he pocketed the check.

I asked, "Where are you going now?"

"I see you don't trust me either."

"It isn't that way," I started to say, but I realized that he was probably correct. Then I said, "What difference does it make if I trust you or not? You got the money."

"Big deal," Antonio said. He scooped up some snow between his ungloved hands and squeezed it into a hard little ball. Then, without even a word of thanks, he lobbed the ball in the air and started down the street alone.

4

SOME PORTRAITS FROM THE POORHOUSE STATE

• In the early summer of 1965, I stood outside the Welfare Center on 28th Street, stopping people when they left to ask whether they would submit to a brief interview about their life on public assistance in return for five dollars. I got good value for my money. Many people rambled on for as long as an hour; just a few were reluctant to answer my questions; and a few regarded me with suspicion. In the end, although I found I had many more interviews than I needed to illuminate the technical problems of maintaining eligibility, I decided to be generous in my selections so that these clients could be heard. Here then, is a selection of views about life in the Poorhouse State. Each of these interviews was later transcribed from my notes in the form of a monologue. Whenever possible, I have excised my questions.

• THENIA: "My mother gets $7.10 a month for gas and electricity. She pays about $30.00 [every two months]. You want to know why? I'll tell you why. We use the stove to heat the rooms. We burn the lights at night so the rats won't go near the baby. Also, it's dark where we live, even during the day. So if I am reading or sewing or studying from a book, I've got to burn lights. The Welfare knows all this, and they are supposed to do something about it, but they never do. Every month we get this bill, and my mother pays it with the food money. Then she has to prove to the Welfare that she has used the food money to pay for the lights. They say, 'You should bring us the bill and we will take care of these people,' because they don't mind paying the Con Edison half as much as they mind paying us. But we don't like to do that too often because we know what happens when you wait for the Welfare to pay the bill. You want to know what happens? They turn off the lights, and it is very cold.

"I can remember the last time they turned off the lights. It was the winter they killed Kennedy. My mother was so cold she started to cry. Then we all started to cry because it was so dark. We had to eat cold food out of tin cans until the Welfare called Con Edison and they turned the lights back on again. When he comes, my mother is angry with the man. 'Pray to God you have not hurt these children. Believe me.' He is just a man, and he has to do as he is told. It is different with the Welfare. They must help you. Afterwards, my little sister was sick for a week. And when spring came, we moved to a new apartment . . .

"Then my mother said, 'We are never going to have the lights turned off again,' because you don't know what it is like for Spanish people who are not used to this cold weather! So we are always paying Con Edison first with the food money and then we eat from the *bodega* on the book until the Welfare pays us, but we are never able to get the Welfare to give us more than the $7.10 for the utilities.

They say sure we spend more in the cold months, but we spend less in the hot months. They say they are only willing to make adjustments. It is like the special garments. You get them 'as needed.' You ever try to get anything that way?

"It is like my big sister's truss. Nina hurt herself real bad in the schoolyard on 4th Street, and the doctor at the clinic says she needs this thing. So the man writes a note to our investigator, and a month passes and there is no truss. Poor sister! She can hardly walk. So my mother tell me call the social worker [at Welfare], and this man he says she should go to the clinic and they will take care of her, not *Bienestar*. Nina has no money, so I ask can he come and give her the money for the taxi. He say she must take a bus, that she should borrow the money. 'Can't anyone there lend Nina fifteen cents?' So we find thirty cents for Nina and another thirty cents for me, and together we go to that clinic. This doctor is very surprised to see us. 'Has she got what she needed?' I tell him that the Welfare says we must come to him direct. 'Yes,' he says. 'They are always doing that. They don't do the right thing, so we must do it for them.' He is a nice man, this doctor. He gives Nina a paper, and she is able to get what she needs in another week from the clinic. Then this man from the Welfare comes to see my mother, and he is very angry. He say, 'Why do you tell such things about me to the doctor? Do you wish to cause trouble?' And when he leaves, he tells my mother to be careful because he can tell she has been drinking. He can smell it on her breath . . .

"If you think it is ever any different, you don't know what you are saying. When they are after you, they are very mean. When you want something from them, it is hard to find anybody. That is why we want to get off the Welfare as soon as we can. It's hard. When Nina's father, Mr. Alvaro, died, they took away his pension. I mean it goes toward the Welfare. We have nothing now except for Welfare. My mother says we must finish school, I don't know. It's hard. Sometimes I want to leave and get a job because I see that my friends have things, but we only have the Welfare. And when you want something from them you got to sit and wait all day, and if you complain they say, 'You got nothing better now to do.'

"It's hard. Everybody says we are supposed to have such things like Nina's truss and that the people want us to have them, but you know how it is. They don't act that way.

"I go to school with my pass on the subway. Every day I see the same notices. On the Delancy Street station there is one. It says, 'If you got worries, call a certain telephone number and they will help you.' Could they have such notices for the Welfare? My mother says yes because the people only want what they should have . . .

"What will I do with your five dollars? I don't think I will save it. Maybe I will buy things for myself . . . and some things for Nina. My mother has all the money now, so I don't have to buy anything for her, but I would like to do something for myself and Nina, and maybe I will buy them. Like what? I don't know. Do I have to decide this minute? It is sometimes nice to have the money to think about . . ."

• ZENOBIA: "With the $5.00—if you really give it to me —I will get my coat cleaned for the winter. They don't give you the money for dry cleaning, and this coat smells very strong. It should be cleaned. Maybe I will use some of the money for that if I don't lose it . . .

"There are now three of us at home. My husband visits. What I don't like about the Welfare is the insecurity. When my husband was working, we had to worry all the time if he would lose his job, but those jobs . . . there were always others. On the Welfare it is different. You never know if you will lose it, and if you lose it, you lose everything. I don't like that. If my husband and I patch things up again, it will be better because now the men can get the Welfare too. Why didn't I ever get a divorce? The judge [in Family Court] said it was not the right thing to do, and I am not like Sophia Loren, I just can't fly to Mexico . . .

"One thing I will never do on the Welfare is take the money from my children. Some of the women I know do do that. That is a terrible thing to do because, you know, they give us that money for the children. That is why I am glad to have your $5.00. What would I do if I had more? I would buy things for myself and maybe a present for my husband so he would feel better, and if my investigator said anything, I would say I have the money from other people. He would have to say that was all right, okay. Or else he would say you must not, and he would take away the *cheque*. It is hard without a husband who earns money, but it is harder still without *cheques* . . .

"Two things I would like from the Welfare are the telephone and movies. I don't care for the TV, but I love movies —in Spanish or in English—it doesn't matter. Now I know I am not supposed to spend the money [for the children] on such things, so I don't go very often and when I do go, I worry. They ought to let us go to movies. If I had the right clothes, I would go sometime to see the Mayor and tell him. It doesn't seem right not to let us. But if they say no, I won't go. It is too much of a risk. Maybe they ought to have a movie here for all the people who are on Welfare. That way they would know it was all right, that we were doing the right thing. It would be like the clinics, but I think they just don't want us to go. Maybe, if I have something left over from the coat, I will take my young one to the movies . . .

"I would like the telephone to speak with my brother, who lives in Queens. Also, sometimes, when the children are sick, it would be nice to have a telephone because now I have to take them with me to a neighbor's house . . . If it is late, I must send somebody to use the booth on the corner. Once my brother said he would give me for the telephone if it was all right with the Welfare, but they said if he can give me for the telephone, he should help to support me. I don't want to do that to my brother. He is just starting out in life. He has a store in Queens, and although they are not yet on the Welfare, they are very poor. How do I know? I sent my oldest to live with them once, and there was nothing but rice and beans.

"If they don't want to give me a telephone, they should put one in our building. All the people there are on Welfare, and none of them have telephones. If only they would put a [pay] telephone in our building, it would be better, but the Welfare[1] is the landlord, and they don't want to do it.

---

[1] Evidently this is one of many tenements taken over by the city in receivership.

It is a shame. It is very cold when you have to go out at night because of the children.

"When we first got on the Welfare, it was because of the unemployment. My husband lost this job, and they told him to go to the unemployment because they would give him money until he found another job. But the man [at the unemployment office] didn't speak Spanish. He said my husband had been fired [with a warning] because he was a bad worker. My husband is a good worker, but we couldn't collect the unemployment, and then my husband got angry and went away and I had to go to the Welfare. I think a lot of Spanish people get trapped that way. I don't know. Sometimes it seems that they don't even like us to have the unemployment, so how can we expect them to like us to have the Welfare?"

• CONCEPCIÓN: "When the Welfare doesn't come, you hear it all the way from Rivington Street. *El Cheque . . . el cheque . . . el cheque.* It is everybody thinking alike on that day. Then the men must watch the children while the women go *Calle Cinco,* or 28th Street, and some have to go all the way up to Yorkville. Sometimes they all go together, because many times my mother has asked another woman to bring back her check and there is nothing doing. They don't trust these other women with our checks.

"The trouble with such a life for the children is the bad moods. When the check is late the [older] women are vile. When my mother is vile, she goes to the social worker at Henry Street [a local voluntary settlement house]. They talk together, and then she comes back and must go to the

93

Welfare. My uncle says this vileness has to do with the cycles of a woman. I think it has to do with the Welfare.

"I hate New York. All the boys make trouble and the men are no good for anything. I like to get dressed up with my friends and walk along Clinton Street on Sundays, but the [middle-class] people don't seem glad to see us. I never go to the Welfare for my mother except this once. Why am I here now? It is because I must have this new uniform for school, and my mother is feeling vile. If my mother finds me with your five dollars, I shall have to give it to her, so what I will do is hide it until I know how to spend it. I don't want to spend it for this uniform. What fun is that?"

• PETO: "At the Welfare they got this man they call him the Resources' Man, and sometimes he is also a woman. Whenever you apply for the Welfare, you must be sent to him because he must ask you a lot of questions. All kinds of questions. Like he may ask if you belong to a union or are in the Army. Then he will try to do something about that to keep you off the Welfare. I don't understand what.

"When I applied for the Welfare I was here two months from PR and I couldn't find any work. In PR I was a field hand with my father's sister, but when the speculators took away most of the good land, my father's brother said I should come to work with him in the store. It took two years to save that much money, and by then things weren't so good with my uncle, and he was on the Supplementation from the Welfare for his children. So the investigator said I must move out because how did he know I was not eating the children's food. He said apply if I think I have a case, and they will consider me as a special case.

"So I came here to 28th Street, but they said they couldn't help because I was from PR. They sent me to another place on West 31st Street near the Sears Roebuck. It was just a place. A lot of people there. You know. Finally, this man says to me, 'You come here for a reason?' So I tell him about my uncle, but he don't believe me, I guess. 'If you are telling me the truth, your uncle is now on Welfare. How can he do anything for you?'

"Then he said, 'You think I won't know if you aren't telling me the truth. If I find out you will get in a lot of trouble. I think you came here,' he says, 'because your uncle told you that you could collect the Welfare. Is that true?'

" '*Pocas-vergüenzas*,' [not so true] I tell this man in Spanish because it wasn't even that true, but he is not such a nice man. He sends me to the Resources. Now this Resources was a woman from Ponce [the second largest city in Puerto Rico], and she wants to know all about the way we lived in PR. When I tell her about the farm, she says, 'If you go back you could have a job there?'

" 'I don't want to work on no farm,' I said.

"This woman is a lot nicer. She can speak Spanish. She tells me she understands that it would not be so nice as New York. Then she asks if there is anything that I would like to do.

"I say I would like to work in a store or a factory until maybe I can open up a business for myself. 'You know,' I say, 'I would like to go to school at night and learn a little about business so when I have the money I could open up my own place.'

"Then she says to me that I can't expect the Welfare to put me through such a school. 'If you want the Welfare,' she says, 'why not go back to PR, where you still have family?'

" 'I don't want to go back there. You know,' I tell her, 'I only want the Welfare until I can find work here. I will look hard. Believe me,' I say, 'it wasn't my idea to collect the Welfare, but the man told me if I don't move out he is going to be very angry at my uncle and his family.'

" 'People here are very cruel,' this woman at the Resources says, 'and you must get used to it.' But she doesn't mention that I go back to PR again.

"Now I must go to another man, who asks me the same questions. And when he hears that I am only nineteen years and still no wife, he wants to know if I have ever thought of joining the Army.

" 'What I want to do a thing like that?' I say, because it is already Vietnam, and there are lots of Spanish kids getting killed.

"But he says jobs are real tough, but if I were to do the Army they would teach me certain things, and when I came out I could have money, so I wouldn't need to go to the Welfare. Well, I don't want to do a thing like that because it may be that they will never get me, but when I tell this to the man he says, 'If you are willing to collect the Welfare, you should be willing to serve your country.'

"It becomes a little crazy now because I tell this man *muchas gracias*, but I will wait until they call me, and then he wants to know if I have a record.

" 'You know,' he asks, 'have you ever been in jail or in trouble?' Now I am getting very angry, because it is clear that this man does not want to give me the Welfare, so I go back and see the first man and we talk again, and he says he can't help me anyway unless I can prove that I have been looking for work.

"So I go away from that Welfare center as rich as when I came there, and when my uncle sees me he sends me to his friend in Hunts Point. It seems this man knew my father, and he is very nice to me. He tells me of a job in his place in Queens. After another month I am given the job. It doesn't pay much, but it is a living. Then I go back to my uncle, and he finds a room near him and since he is still on the Supplementation, I give him money but I won't eat with him for fear of what the Welfare will say. This new job—it isn't much of a life. We are making decorations for lamps, which we dip into silver. It is hard to learn very much. Just too many Cubans in that factory. A few months, the union comes, and we go out on strike. I have no savings yet, so I must go again to the Welfare. But this man wants to know when I got my last check. Then he says he can't help me because it is not so long ago that I shouldn't have some money. And he tells me then to come back in another week if the strike isn't settled, but today when I went to see him he said, 'Look for work and come back again in another week.' I just don't think he wants to give me the Welfare.

"So that's the way it is again. I have moved out of my room and I am staying with my uncle. He and his wife are very worried, but there is nothing they can do. I just hope that there is no trouble. If the strike ends soon, maybe I will save my money and go to another city. I have friends in Philadelphia. They say it is not so cruel about the Welfare."

• PETO'S AUNT: "You want to know how they close a case? I'll tell you. They know the mail is always late for people like us. If the investigator writes a letter to come for an appointment the day after tomorrow and he mails it tomorrow, you will not get the letter on time to come for the appointment. Then he closes your case just like that. It's punishment—you know. Sometimes it takes three months before they write all the papers again to put you back.

"Another way to close a case is when you have grown children. They can make the children work. If the children don't cooperate, there are reprisals. When my daughter was eighteen, she got married. The Welfare couldn't touch her then, and they still had to give us the Supplementation.

"Getting by on the Welfare is a matter of *suerte* and *dinero* [luck and money]. I don't say that all of the investigators are bad. Some are very *familiar*. When all the children took special diets, it was good times. My husband was working. He was given money for the lunches and carfare. It made a difference because they didn't know that he walked to work and that his firm gave him lunch anyway. When we had the store it was because of the money he saved [from that job], and it was not so good having the store, but there was always enough food. Now times are hard. Two of my children are married, and there is Peto to feed, because the Welfare told him to stay with us, but I still have to eat with one eye cocked at the door. Sure they give us the surplus food, but we Spanish don't like their rice. It is not tasty like ours. And the beans you have to soak forever. Sometimes I get my husband to trade what I have with the Negroes on the fourth floor. They don't like the canned meat.

"There are many things you can get from the Welfare, but you have to know about them. There are also many things you can get other places. Sometimes there are church fairs where you can buy clothing cheap. I know Orchard Street and the Essex Market. They even sell good things sometimes. If you buy at the *bodegas* you just can't make it. I used to take my boys to Hunt's Point for haircuts.

"If a family gets sick on the Welfare, it is bad luck for you. Somebody has to visit the sick ones. Maybe they don't like the food, so you have to bring them to eat. While you are sick, you don't have them on the budget. It can be hardship. When somebody in my family is sick, I tell them to go to Gouverneur Clinic or the Jewish Hospital on Stuyvesant Square because the nuns—and even the Negroes from the City—they don't care if you die if you die a Catholic. It is different with those Jews. They know a little better . . .

"Peto is my husband's nephew. He is a good boy. He wants to work hard. When he had money, he gave us some, but we could never tell the Welfare. Now we must feed him again, and we still don't want the Welfare to know about him. Where I grew up in Caguas the priests said it was a black sin to lie. I never did so much lying since I came here [to New York] and got on the Welfare."

• PETO'S UNCLE: "If you want to find a good apartment, you got to have the money in your hand for the security, but the Welfare won't give you this money until they approve the apartment. And because they won't give you the key money for the super, you don't ever get the apartment. When I moved in here, which is not so good, I lent the super twenty-five dollars the Welfare gave me for a dresser. Then the man wanted to know why I didn't buy a dresser.

What could I do? I told him it went for other things. It is the same way with jobs. All the men will tell you. You can buy a good job that will last maybe a year on 42nd Street for a hundred dollars, or you can go upstate to the hotels[2] if you pay fifty dollars. The Welfare don't like to pay for its jobs. They send you to State Employment. But the jobs on 42nd Street, they pay better. If I had the money I would buy myself a summer job in the mountains. It would be better than staying at home all summer, but I would have to pay my debts on the store—and then what would I have?

"I got my money from the Welfare because I was in Berlin. My friends tell me this is the best of all the Welfares.[3] Well, I don't know. I don't get so much as some other people. My friends say with me they only have to come once a year. Believe me, sometimes they are here once a month. It is to see the children. And when you ask them for something, they just pretend to be writing in their books.

"If I were a woman, I would sell myself rather than go on the Welfare because, before we patched things up, she and I, I had this other woman for a while, and she was getting money all the time for her children. They used to come into her house and open up all her drawers. All right, a whore gets arrested once in a while, but don't you think she's got more privacy than that? She gets more money too and nobody is always trying to catch her in the shower . . .

"The truth is, it isn't good with the Welfare and it isn't good without it. My kid, she is now married. Her husband bought himself a good job in a dress factory. I hope they

---

[2] The Catskill mountain resorts around Ellenville, New York, where many Puerto Ricans are employed as kitchen helpers.

[3] He is on Veteran's Assistance.

never have to collect, because it can make you hate each other. You are always at home, and there is never anything good to eat, and you have to stretch yourself a million ways, and if you are the least selfish, like I was, you hurt everybody. Some people say it was better in PR because there you didn't see all these people living off the Welfare like dogs, and you could always go to your family in the country when you wanted food. In PR we had chickens and pigs. That was nice. But you know what they give people in PR who want the Welfare? $4.00 a month . . ."

• MRS. CABALLERO: "God help all of us if they take away the Welfare. God help us! It was the Welfare that put these clothes on my back. It was the Welfare that put my daughter in that home. And when my husband died, it was the Welfare, I think, that buried him.

"My husband died because he could not live any longer. We were staying in Williamsburg [Brooklyn]. My husband had no job. My daughter was sick. The apartment was small. Just too hot. One day my husband took my daughter up to the roof. He was going to throw her off because he said it was all useless, but a policeman told him you must not kill your daughter. So he jumped . . .

"Then the Welfare came, and they took away my daughter because she was so sick, and they helped me to find work. It was useless. I cried too much wherever I worked, and the other girls resented me so much the bosses got rid of me . . . and ever since then I have had to collect the Welfare. It's not a good life, but it's the only life I have. I go to see my daughter when I can, but nobody ever comes to see me . . . not even the Welfare. They know I'm harmless. What I would like is that they send me back to Puerto Rico, but they won't do that unless you got people there, and when I got the Welfare I told them I didn't. Don't ask me why. A friend said I should. Maybe, with your five dollars, I will send a present to my sister so she will write and ask me to come back. It's hard. If I go back I won't see my child. People there will say, 'Look. She has nothing!' I'd like to go to work again, but who wants me?"

• ANDREAS: "Some people here really work at what they got, but I don't. I figure if I'm disabled, it's not my fault. Why work at it? They're not giving me anything I don't deserve. I think some people feel differently. They just pretend. If you ride up here on the bus with them, they will look all right, but when you see them later in the Center they look as if they are about to die. It's very impressive to see such people. Me? I wouldn't carry on that way because I have no reason. Everybody knows what I got. In fact, I don't even think they like to see me at a place like this, but I come sometimes when I need things. I'm not going to feel ashamed just because I'm sick. I'm not so anxious to get off the plate yet. Today I think I came to the wrong place, but I'm not sure. I'll have to go back and see . . . if I don't have to wait too long.

"Of course, if you're really sick, they can put you in a home, or, if it's mental, in a place like Pilgrim State. That's why it never pays to exaggerate. The State people will get you then if the City doesn't. In my case, exaggeration wouldn't be necessary. I've lived here a long long time, and I think everybody knows about my heart. I could die just like that . . . if somebody did the wrong thing. The only problem is because I'm still a young man they probably worry about how long will they have to put up with me. I don't say they do. I say they probably do. I would if I were in their shoes.

"I tell you it gets pretty boring with no money and nothing to do. If I weren't so scared, I'd ask to do something. But it's like everything else. In my condition it doesn't pay to ask. How do I know what could happen to me? When I was living uptown once—it was a long time ago—I did a few things on the Q.T. Nothing much. It's just that I'm very good at building model airplanes, and some of the people in the park would buy them for their kids. I charged whatever I could get. Well, I had this friend, and he said you better be careful they don't find you out. So I lost interest after a while. Now I make things for my nephews, but how many can you make for them?

"Another thing I'm good at is cooking. I learned it in the mountains. I make the best onion soup because I brown the onions first and I know how to make hot apple pie with a crust in cold water, but I guess nobody wants to take the chance, that I would . . . you know . . . get sick on the premises. If I ever get well, I'd like to get a job in a real restaurant —not one of those *comidas criollas*—but, to tell the truth, I worry about all that steam and my heart. One thing is certain—I don't get a chance to do any cooking on what I earn. In fact, if they say it's all right, I'm going to ask for a restaurant allowance because it isn't too nice eating all your meals alone.

"The best thing about being on Welfare is that it got me to stop smoking. With my heart that was a necessity, but . . . you know . . . I found it very hard. Well, when you're on

Welfare, things are so tight you realize if you want to eat good, you better stop smoking. At least I did. Why? Because I guess I do like to eat a lot. The doctor even says I should lose weight. I don't know. Eating is such a pleasure. It's hard to cut down.

"When this first happened to me they said, 'What you need is a warm climate,' and they wanted to send me back to PR. Not me. I hadn't been there since I was three. To tell you the truth, I speak much better English now than Spanish. Why go back? Well nobody ever mentioned it again, but that doesn't mean it won't happen. That's why I want to ask if I can live with my brother. It would be nice for his wife to have the extra money, and I would also be a little less lonely. If they say no, then I'll ask for the restaurant allowance. But I just don't want to stay as I am. I got no friends this way.

"If I ever get well, I'm not going to be like some of those alcoholics who go right back to the same old life all over again. I'm going to become a real chef because they earn good money, and then I will see a bit of the world, too, before I die. You don't see the world sitting at home watching TV. Yeah, I could have a set if I wanted it, but it seems like such a boring idea. So sometimes I read books and sometimes I go to see my brother. I like all kinds of books . . . especially cookbooks and novels. Now I'm reading *Catch 22* because my investigator told me it was funny. It's funny, I guess, but I was never in the Army."

• MARINA: "From the social workers uptown we got ice skates last winter. There is no good place to use the ice skates

here, and the money from the Welfare is for more important things than for going to Rockefeller Center. So today is
my little one's birthday, and since I know that we are never
going to use these skates, I took them to a shop to sell them,
but the man says it is the summer and what is he going to
do with ice skates. He offered me only $2.00, which is not
enough for a present even for such a little one. So I am coming to the Welfare because they still owe me for the utilities,
and I thought I would just use that money and pay it back
when I got my next check. Now I have your $5.00 maybe I
won't even sell these skates after all, because it is not so nice
to sell a present to buy something else. What do I think
about the Welfare? I wouldn't be without it. Anybody down
here tell you differently, he is a big liar . . . The only trouble
is they are so stingy. Last winter some people I know got
warm coats, but I got only the mittens. It's crazy. When I
asked the man what about a coat, he doesn't even seem to
hear me. I don't understand it. I know a woman from San-
turce lives on Stone Avenue in Brooklyn who got a sectional[4] at her Welfare . . . and I don't even have a carpet on
the floor."

• ARTY: "I don't think they ought to give Welfare to
the people. They ought to get them jobs. If I had a job, I
wouldn't need Welfare. I collect Relief. Why? Because I
got sick and my family needs the money. It isn't very much.
Nothing is even less. When a man takes he feels ashamed of
himself. They make you feel that way—even when you are

---

4 Sectional: a couch that comes apart in sections to follow the contours
of a room.

sick. I don't know why. I'm not lazy. I'm sick. I'm not so sick that I can't work at anything. I'm just too sick to do the things that I have to do. What do I do? I've done a lot of things off and on, and they don't add up to much. The last job I had was in Dry Cleaning. I delivered things . . ."

• LARGO: "I have never collected Welfare in my life. Yes, my wife gets a little. I have done a lot of things to stay off the Welfare because it is important to me to stay off. Right now I am working for the *Centro Medico* in Harlem.[5] They pay me $1.30 an hour, and I get overtime once in a while because somebody has to clean up. It is not bad. I don't get too much, but it is more than the minimum. I also get a little Welfare—through my wife because we have six children. I like work. I don't like to collect the Welfare. You want to know why? Because when you collect the Welfare, they think they know who you are, and they treat you like you collect the Welfare."

• HECTOR: "Agostino here will tell you. I am a good guy, a good father, everybody where we live knows that. So if I am coming now to the Welfare, it is because it was fated that way. It was not my fault. I've worked all the time. Worked hard. I can't remember when I didn't work. And what do I have to show for it? Now I come here to Welfare with Agostino, and I feel sick and we still don't know if I am to get it. What did they tell me to do? They said I must come back again with a paper . . . a proof . . . so it is a good thing that I met you and your five dollars because I think

[5] A group of store-front doctors.

106

that without you I would have to go to see the social workers. Believe me, this is the first time on the Welfare and I also don't like the idea, but I don't like to fool people either. I have nothing, so I must come here. Tomorrow I will come back again, and then they will say go to this other place. I know what it's like because Agostino has told me. He says they must give it to me sooner or later if we really have nothing. I just hope he is right."

• AGOSTINO: "My real name is Secundino Agostino. People here call me Agostino or Dino, which is an Italian name, but I am Spanish. I speak many languages. I can speak to a Haitian or a Dominican, a Cuban, a Brazilian or a *Borinqueño*.[6] Now I do not collect the Welfare because they say they will not give it to me, but I help others who do. When they don't speak good enough, I go with them to the Center. The investigator asks questions and I translate. Some investigators won't let me work with their clients. They say these are matters between the Welfare and the person, and I've got no business to know about them. Many times I have to say that I am a relative. If the man or woman is nice, she would usually give me a little something . . . for friendship' sake . . .

"It is much better in that respect at the Unemployment because there—on 13th Street—nobody speaks good Spanish and they are glad to see me. If they know I am getting a little something, they don't seem to mind. It seems they are not so strict as the Welfare.

"How did I learn so many languages? I am very intelli-

---

[6] Puerto Rican slang for a former resident of the island.

gent, and I like to talk to people. If you know Spanish and you talk slowly you may learn French. Brazilians speak Portuguese. I know a few. Dominicans speak different from us. So do the Cubans. But it is no great problem for an intelligent man. Once I had a woman from Mexico. She was a problem. She spoke like a stranger. They wouldn't give her the Welfare. She was not a citizen.

"I have a family in Puerto Rico to whom I still send money when I have any. Here I just live with friends. A big problem is looking good when you go to the Welfare. I spend a lot of money on my clothes, and I like to shave every day and I always like to have a good haircut. I work all over the city through friends, and it is important that I look good. I have two suits, which I bought on Orchard Street, and I buy my shoes in Spanish Harlem. What will I do with your $5.00? Maybe I will go on Saturday night to *Caborojeño.*[7] What are my plans? I have my profession. There will always be the Welfare."

[The interview below took place a few days after my first meeting with Secundino Agostino, when we happened to run into each other a second time. A worker from Welfare, who noticed us talking together, approached me afterwards and agreed to talk with me.]

• A WORKER: "Last year when we went out on strike I worried a whole lot about the clients. You're wrong if you think we don't worry. I thought about those who were being dished out of special grants, and I thought about some of the mothers with young children and about some of the older

[7] A Puerto Rican dance hall in Spanish Harlem.

people. Then the strike dragged on, and I had to start worrying about myself because I have a family. Was anybody worrying about them? It took six weeks to settle that strike. I came out of it a poor man. My wife said, 'You should apply for Welfare.' Very funny.

"The thing that bothers me about people like you is that you all seem to know it all. I'm not saying that you mean any harm, but you certainly think that money can buy anything. Well, it won't buy honesty and it won't buy decency. It won't buy me. If you've got $5.00 you want to throw around, make a contribution to the *Hundred Neediest Cases* next Christmas.

"Why do I seem angry? Listen, if I told you some things about these people, you wouldn't even believe me, so what is the use of telling you? You really think they are just poor. Well, I have to go into their houses. I see the way these people live. I have to sit with them, and I know about their habits. Probably they don't mean anybody any harm, but you just can't let people live that way. They need all the help they can get, and my only complaint is that this department is so fouled up we don't give them near enough of it. They ought to be made to learn better things. They ought to be helped. No, not money . . . money never helped anybody. What they need is help . . . I came over to you because I saw you were talking to that little wise guy from Harlem. If you listen to him, you'll get in a lot of trouble. You know, some people give him money to come down to see us. I don't think that's right—taking money from poor people. If I could prove it, I would report him. *Don't tell me that.* He should get a real job. He doesn't need that much . . . I know you think I'm being queer when I talk to you like this, but

I'm just trying to let you in on the facts. That little guy isn't honest. He'll get his people to say anything to us. Listen, it is one thing if they come down here with a social worker . . . we can talk it over like humans . . . but when we have to start hollering at people like him . . . it is just not fair.

"If I had my way, I wouldn't allow anybody except people on official business inside our center because we have enough problems taking care of all those people as it is. I am sure you must know about all the forms. And those damned people are always screaming at us. Sure some are better than others, but that doesn't mean it isn't trying. They ought to have maybe ten cases for each worker, and then we could really visit them in their homes and help them and decide who needs what. This way it's like murder. Somebody has to wind up getting hurt. You just can't expect people to work hard under such circumstances.

"You hear a lot of people talking about how bad the Welfare is, but did you ever stop to think what these people would do without it? It is their life blood. Some of them don't have families . . . what you and I would call a family . . . and the rest of them have habits like you never saw before in your life. I was brought up in poverty. I know what I am talking about. Believe me, Mister, it isn't pretty and I'm not saying it is their fault. You won't get me to say that. I think a lot of these people are just the product of their environment . . . and, of course, a lot of them are psychotic. A lot of psychotics never get to the hospital, you know. They keep them on pills, tranquilizers, things like that. I have this woman who likes to wear rags. I give her money for clothes, and she never seems to have anything on her back but those same dirty rags. Well, I'm going to keep watching her, and then I will recommend that she see somebody. If she puts up a fuss, we have ways of forcing her . . .

"Before I came to Welfare I worked in an office—it was a showroom, I guess you could call it—and I have also been a car salesman. Actually, I studied accounting in college. You know, you have to have a B.A. to do this kind of work, and I still take courses at night at Adelphi. I know I am not an expert about things, but I read a lot, and I think I know the facts of life. What did I read recently? I read the Midtown Mental Health Survey [L. Srole *et al.*, *Mental Health in the Metropolis*] and I read a book about Lesbians . . . a serious book. I also read a lot just for entertainment. What kinds of things? I'm finishing *Ring of Bright Water*, and I want to read this book about a schoolteacher in New Zealand because my wife read it and she told me it makes you feel good . . . I mean some of the things that woman was able to do in New Zealand . . .

"Just one final thing: because they told you those things about the Welfare workers, I wouldn't give it a grain of salt. I'm not saying that you shouldn't believe them. Things like that could happen any place. But these are mostly, honest, hard-working people. I'd hate to see any of them get a black eye just because of what some people are saying. If you don't believe me, ask some of the others. It's a thankless job. Occasionally you have a satisfying relationship with a client, but most of the time it's just give me, give me, give me . . ."

• MRS. SHAPIRSKY: "When they had a different type of person, it used to be a lot better. Now it's not so good . . . you know what I mean by a different type of person? I mean a different type of person. These people—they have no standards. It isn't Welfare's fault. They should have better standards, and there would be better Welfare. I know what I mean because I've had it for many years. What would I be without it? My husband is dead. I buried two sons before my time. I won't take your five dollars. I don't take charity. Look around here someday, and you will see the type of people I mean. They will take anything from anybody. They've got no pride. Sure, they should be helped when they need it, but they should also have a little more pride."

• BILL BRIGHT: "How would I change Welfare? Who cares what I think? If they bought everybody on Welfare an annuity, like some people have, you know, that would make a difference. I mean, suppose the government invested $100,000 in everybody. At six percent they would get six thousand dollars a year. Then, if they wanted more they would have to work for it. When you invest money it's not like spending it, and then there would be enough for everybody. No! I never told anybody about my idea. I don't know what I'm talking about . . ."

• COADY: "I don't hate anybody. I'm poor. I've always been that way. If you are poor like me, you know what you have to do, so why should I hate anybody?

"Some people are willing to take it out on everybody except themselves. I know that. They collect Welfare because it is for poor people, and then they never stop feeling sorry for themselves. Down here you don't see anybody but poor people.

"I never knew anybody who made a living on Welfare. Some people say we cheat a lot. Maybe some people like to think they do, but they are poor just the same. Welfare is for poor people. It's not right to say those things about people because only the poor can collect it. You know what I mean? If it is for the poor people, how can people say they are cheating?

"I don't want to make excuses for myself. It's my own fault that I am the way I am. I had a lot of chances to be somebody. Well, I didn't. So what? Maybe I was just too sluggish! You talk to some people, and they will tell you it's because people who took care of you didn't know any better. They didn't give you the right things . . . or tell you what to do. People who took care of me were poor. So what? Just because I'm poor now people don't always have to be such bastards because of what I am. I will not make any excuses to anybody. People say it is because you didn't get the right education or the right food or because of the juvenile delinquency. That's not the point. I never was in that much trouble or else they wouldn't be giving me the Welfare that they are giving me now. I figure I get what I deserve because it is my right because I am poor . . . and I don't like to go any further than that. You know what I mean? They wouldn't give me anything if that wasn't so. How much do I get? I get for the room, and I get meal tickets . . . Only, the other day a man came to my room and stole all I had, which is why I am here now."

• MRS. PETERSON: "I pity the young ones. They still want things. With me it's different. I'd go to a home if I didn't have all my furniture. Why should I get rid of these things? They are all I have got.

"When I was younger I used to like to see my investigator.

I would give him instant coffee and we would talk. Sometimes I think I talked his ear off. It was like that. Now I have another man, and he is always cranky with me. *Why don't I think of going here? What about doing that?* I've seen that place in Neponset.[8] It isn't as nice as I've got here.

"I suppose I've had the best of them all these years. They fed me, clothed me, and took care of me. I haven't had many troubles with them. But you know, it never seemed as if I had the right to expect anything. I remember when I wanted to visit my niece in Lake George. I had to ask them for the money, and they made it seem like they were doing me such a favor. Ever since then, I have always felt that they have been doing me these favors, and I don't like to ask for anything more than I need. That's what makes my investigator so cranky. He is always saying I can get you this, that, or the other thing but you must do such-and-such. At my age there isn't much you need, so I always say, 'No, thanks' as nicely as I can. It's better that way because if they can say yes, they can also say no. Why start trouble?

"I am partial to lamb chops, though, and if I had the money I would eat them every day. Why don't I ask for more money? I wouldn't want to start anything. You see, I think if they wanted us to eat lamb chops, real lamb chops, they would give us enough money. I can't use your money for that. In fact, I won't take it at all. It wouldn't seem right. I haven't done anything for it.

"The nicest investigator that I ever had was this young colored girl, Lorette. She was very pretty, and she used to let me call her by her first name. She got married, had children,

8 A home for the aged run by the Department of Welfare.

114

and left; and you can't blame a person for doing that. When Lorette came, she would see that I had all my winter clothing, and she would say, 'Well, I don't see why we can't give you the money anyway. You can have a TV.' She would say, 'You'd like to have TV, wouldn't you?' She probably meant well, too, but I would never let her do it because what would happen when she left? I was just too afraid I might get in trouble with the next one.

"Then, after Lorette, there was Mr. Provenzano. He kept wanting me to go to Neponset, but he wasn't too bad. After him came Gottschalk. He was on my case when I wanted to go to Lake George that summer. People I know say that Gottschalk had trouble at home. I don't know. I just think that he was trying to do his job.

"The one who used to talk to me a lot was named Philipson. He was from somewhere out West. I don't think he had a family. He was one of those funny type of men. They're almost like women. But I never let it bother me because he was so nice, a very sweet young man. I think he had a tough time of it at the office. One day he came to see me and he had this patch of tape over his left eye. He said, 'I'm very sorry about the way I look.' Well, I didn't want to ask any questions. It doesn't seem right to ask a man like that questions. It was the last time I saw him. He was a nice boy, whatever he was . . .

"You ask me what I would do to make Welfare better? For myself, aside from the lamb chops, I would like people to know that we aren't doing anybody any harm. I only come here when it is absolutely necessary. Today I came about my electric bill. But whenever I come I always feel as if people are staring at me. I try to dress the best I can, so I know it's not because of my clothing. They just seem to know that if I'm going in that door it's because I'm something. That's why I pity the young people. They may have to live with this all their lives. I know. When I was young, people were talking then of eliminating poverty. It didn't do me any good. I've seen three big depressions in my life and three or four wars, and I've known a lot of people on Welfare. They are just like everybody else except they are different. You know what I mean? They don't have anything . . . anything at all except Welfare."

5

BARBARA DUGAN'S STORY

• "I wish I could remember when I got this sickle-cell anemia. A lot of us here have got it. They say we got it down South, but when you got it you just don't feel like doing too much. It makes your blood slow. Hard not to do too much when you are on the Welfare. They give you the pills and the special diets, and they send you to homemaking classes if they think it will help you, but they don't help you otherwise, so you still have a lot to do. They is picking up the kids after school because you don't want them walking home alone in a neighborhood like this . . . and they's cooking and shopping and laundry and housecleaning, and then well-baby clinic and sick-baby clinic and the clinic for yourself and that sickle-cell anemia. It's a full day.

"What I mean by a neighborhood like this is they's a lot of junkies and queers around here. Well, you just don't want to take a chance on them. So you carry your kids to school in the morning, and you carry them home after school. My kids live ten blocks away from the school. Ain't no buses down here . . .

"Ain't no lazy people on Welfare. Oh, maybe they is a few, but they ain't many. Seems like you got to pull your lazy butt from one place to the next, and you got to pull your kids with you wherever you go because they ain't no place you can leave them where they be safe . . . And sometimes you just don't feel like doing too much, but you still got to do it if you don't want them to take your kids away from you. *They find you lying in bed with nothing to do that's just what they going to do—sickle-cell anemia and all.* I got two sick kids like me and another in the Kennedy Home in the Bronx . . . I don't know about him . . . and sometimes you get pretty tired, but you just got to do certain things. After all, they say, if you don't take care of these kids, who will? They got a point. Ain't nobody else around here . . . and, after all, they's givin' you a special diet . . .

"But every time you want something extra from them, it's a whole nuisance. Like carfare. Sometimes I got to spend ninety cents for carfare for me and the kids to go off to Bellevue, because, as I told you, you can't leave them alone if you got to go there for some reason. And when I come back from Bellevue clinic, I got to rush over here to 28th Street for that carfare money or else I'm going to run short on food. Well, even so, they don't just give you your money like that. Sometimes they want proof. Sometimes they say they will owe it to you. You got to be careful about the ones who say that. I learned you got to insist right then and there you want that carfare or else you don't get it. So you just got to sit there and wait for the man until he gives it to you. You think they care? Sometimes I think I spend half my life waiting somewhere for ninety cents.

"And what I mean is, if I send my boy to get the money for me, how do I know if the man is going to listen to him? They don't like kids there. You know what they tell my boy when he goes? 'You make sure that gets to your mother. Don't you go spending on yourself.' Shit!

"And if they think they can get away with it, they liable to ask your boy all kinds of questions which they just know they got no business asking. They ask. Nothing private with them . . . Except when you want some money. Then you got a case against them.

"Shit! I could put up with anything if it weren't for the going this place and that. It's just about enough to make me give up everything sometimes, especially when I wake up feeling like I just can't do too much. But you know as well as I do that if you stay that way you are going to end up in a lot of trouble. So it's off to well-baby clinic and sick-baby clinic and now they even got my big girl seeing this psychiatrist. You think I let her go there alone? She goes there with me. Otherwise they say, 'Look at Barbara Dugan. She don't give a good goddamn,' and they try to take my kids away from me.

"Barbara Ann goes to the psychiatrist because they said so at school but if you ask me, it's because we've been pushed down for so long even the kids know it. She cries a lot. I used to be that way. You mustn't believe them when they say we get something for nothing. You may not have to work when you are on the Welfare, but you don't get anything for nothing. They make it hard as dirt. If you want something, you got to go and get it. And you can't ask the man to help because how should he know. He don't even know you're alive half the time, and the other half it's always so much this and that. Takes a genius to know what anybody is talking about.

"Worse thing of all is when they decide you haven't done

119

right. Then they get awful mean. They'll threaten you. Some of these women get sulky after one of those visits. They get sunk down real low. Every time they's a visit they get that way . . . real low . . . I don't get that way anymore. Any time they get after my tail, I take my kids and march right over here and I just start scuffling. They see me barging in like that, hollering for the man, and they just know I know my rights. You think they would treat me like those others?

"Well, you can't do that every day of the week when you got sickle-cell anemia. Sometimes you just wake up too tired. Sometimes you just don't want to go out looking for bargains. So, when night comes, you send your kids out for some of the *cuchifritos* or maybe delicatessen or a pizza pie and cokes and you just sitting around having an early supper when he comes by.

"He says, 'I just wanted to see how things are coming along.' Or he says, 'I thought I would like to find out how you are getting on.'

And then he looks at all that food and he gets real mean. Gives you a big lecture about how you got sickle-cell anemia and should eat the proper food or what is the use of the special diet anyway. And sure enough, next time you get a check they have taken away that special diet and you got to start all over again at Bellevue with a letter from the doctor.

"Seems like you're always doing the same things over and over again. You get an apartment. You start furnishing it. Then you got to move because of the relocation and it starts all over again. The man won't give you security. The man don't want you to live in that building. You go to look for an apartment and the man say, 'Who's looking after the children?' Seems like they always got to make remarks.

"That's why I don't want my boy to come home from that school. I know Welfare would give me more money. You think I want them snooping around? Kids grow up too fast here. That little Puerto Rican girl next door—she's fifteen and Welfare just give her money for the layette.

"Well, you just can't expect any different from people like us. It is the way people live, I guess. I think they ought to take all the kids away from some of these women. The way they bring up kids. You wouldn't want it to happen to your kid. They just don't know any better, and they afraid to ask without getting into trouble. It's a hard life. Every time you want something they's somebody there to make it hard for you. You say, 'I don't want to cause any trouble. I'll do just as they say.' Then you get a new investigator, and he's changed his mind about everything . . .

"I guess the Seventh Day Adventists do best on Welfare. They just like Jews. Strict about everything, even food. If I was going to stay on Welfare, I would become a Seventh Day Adventist. But it is hard. You got to keep kosher. I think the Welfare likes these people better than us because you never see one of them getting into any trouble. They know how to live on the Welfare better than anybody else. Don't kid yourself. It must be hard, living like one of them. You can get money for the special diets, but they make you live just like a Jew . . .

"Some of the Puerto Ricans also do good because rice and beans and bananas are cheap, but they don't speak good English many of them, and some of them can't read or write. They can get all fouled up sometimes. I've seen it happen. Seems they will never understand why you don't ever get the same check twice. Well, I don't understand it either. I once asked the man and he said if you got a complaint to make . . . I ain't complaining, I told him. I was just wondering why. You think he ever told me? Probably he don't know himself. Like that time I caught that girl making a mistake in my arithmetic. I told her, 'You know you cheating me for fifty cents?' Well, she give me the money, but she turned red in the face and screamed, 'Keep a civil tongue in your mouth, Barbara!'

"Worst of all, though, are the special men who come at night. Like this one man asked me, 'If you got no man in the house what you got those pills?'[1] Well, I told him they give me them over at the Planned Parenthood two years ago and I ain't used any of them, as he can plainly see. Then he says, 'You make sure you stay that way,' as if there was a law against going to bed with a man—I mean if he is not your husband . . .

"Speaking of husbands, they used to come around to some of these women. Early in the morning you could hear them running down the stairs. You think they'd ask these women when they suspected something? No. They come around asking you. Well, I ain't going to tell on any of these girls when I know I'm likely to get my head split in.

"And what's so wrong if the men do drop by? Most of them got no place else to go. You know it's hard on women

[1] Welfare agencies commonly attempt to ascertain the presence of a man in the house, capable of providing support, as a way of avoiding or terminating their obligations to women with dependent children.

too not having their enjoyment once in a while. I don't do any of that stuff any more and I'm used to it. I don't even miss it. Maybe it's this damned anemia. But if I had a man I would want to have a separate room. It's not so nice when you sleep in the same room with your kids. Once I lived in a place. They was plaster falling on us every time. You go tell that to the Welfare. I have three rooms here, but one of them got no heat so we all sleep here in the living room as a practical matter. When I asked the Welfare for a bigger apartment, they said you got enough for just the three of you, and the man told me not to apply.

"And that's the way it goes. You're always asking and being told and going from this place to that place. You're always waiting on lines. And all you ever think about is your Welfare. You're right. The way they got it fixed, it's just like being a junkie. You get your checks twice a month, but you got to keep going over there every few days for that extra little fix, and sometimes when you need it worst of all the man ain't nowhere to be seen.

"Worst of all, though, is when you got kids. They need gym shoes. You got to go to Welfare. They need a doctor's examination for camp, and again you got to arrange it for the Welfare. If you spend the money for food to buy your girl shoes (because she needs them for school and you figure you can save yourself a trip), the next thing you know the man wants to know why you ain't got no money. Kids just don't understand budgets, and when they want something, they really want it. I'd like to see the mother who thinks differently. But it don't work that way on Welfare. I get maybe $4.00 a week for their clothes and for me, but I am always using it to do other things. So then, when I need something, I got to go down and get the money from the Welfare, and they likely to want to know why. When you got kids, it's not a good thing to be on the Welfare.

"Well, nobody wants to get rid of their kids. Least I don't see how they could. So you are always buying now and asking questions later, and then they get angry with you and you catch hell. It's the goddamnedest life. If you buy at the store, they overcharge. If you go to the supermarket, you got to carry all that stuff back—and who's taking care of your kids meanwhile? I tell you it isn't easy when you got sickle-cell anemia . . . And some of these women got worse things than that. My neighbor's daughter is an epileptic . . . so when I asked the doctor for a housekeeper because they give her one, this man say, 'You got anybody with brain damage?' Seems it's different if you got brain damage because this man said if he gives me a housekeeper what am I going to do?

"Yes, seems like they always going to make remarks. I don't care if they white or colored. They make remarks. The colored's the worst sometimes. The young ones are a little better, but the way some of them come sniffing around, you think maybe they looking for the wrong thing. Worst of all is that you got to put up with this every day of the week. Except Sunday. They can't do much to you on Sunday. Last Sunday I took my kids in the subway up to the Bronx because this social worker said I should go to visit that other boy. I made a picnic lunch because it was supposed to be a nice day. Then it rained, and then we had to eat in the classrooms. Anyway, when we got back I only had 50¢, so I made my kids hot cereal with raisins for supper, and early next morning I sent my boy with a note to the Welfare center to get us back some of that money.

"Well, my boy say the man had this white stuff all over his face. He had a bad sunburn. It was the week before school was supposed to close, but he say, 'What are you doing out of school?' So he called the guidance counselor and told him he had my boy in his office, and then I had to come to school the next morning with my boy and explain or else they said they would suspend him. Well, I told that man at the school that we just didn't have any money so I had to send my boy over to the Welfare to get reimbursed because I had all this laundry to do else there wouldn't be clean clothes for anybody. You know what that man say then? He say, 'Next time that happens you just telephone.' Can you imagine? He wants me to telephone. Don't he know they don't give us any money to do that?

"It's like when I first started on the Welfare, and they said I was 'mismanaging.' This nice girl—she was a social worker—heard about me and she said she would take my case. So every time I would get a check from the Welfare, I cashed it and brought the money to her and she would put it in this little metal box in her desk. Then I could come over there every day, and she would give me a few dollars for the shopping because she said it was better to shop every day on what I was earning. She was a good sweet girl and she liked me, I think. It was better leaving the money with her than leaving it at home where I could get robbed. So every day I would come to her and get some of that money. Then one day toward the end of the month I come to her and she says,

'I'm sorry, Barbara, I just haven't got any more money for you,' and she opens up that box and shows me that it is empty. Sure enough, we sit down then and do some figuring, and I've taken out more than there was, but she says it isn't my fault. There just wasn't enough to begin with. And she says, 'Let me give you something from my pocketbook until the end of the month.' But when she opens her purse, she's only got about three or four dollars and some change.

" 'I don't know what we are going to do now,' I say. I look over at this girl. She's crying.

" 'Barbara,' she says, 'I'm sorry. I'm really sorry. If I give you this I just won't have anything.'

"So I had to go out then and buy at the Spanish grocer, and I've been paying him back ever since. You know, because I was short. Well, after that I figured I'll hold onto my money myself because if they ain't enough, they ain't much sense to budgeting. You know what I mean? I mean it's a little silly. Course, things can change. I get this special diet now, and I get a little more money. I don't wish to sound ungrateful. I just wish it wasn't always so hard. You know what I mean. And those remarks all the time. You know what I mean, don't you?"

6

BROWNLEAF'S STORY

• Brownleaf is a tall thin Negro in his early forties. If you ask him his name, he will tell you it is Brownie, or Brownleaf, but he will never mention his first name. Although Brownleaf lacks one finger on his left hand and has a cloudy yellowish cast in his right eye, he appears to be otherwise physically fit. One day, in a bar near 5th Street, Brownleaf told the following story.

"About six month ago I come back north from my mother's funeral and started living with my family near Chinatown. My mother had ulcers. I worried I might have them too. One day the man comes to see us.

" 'Brownleaf,' he asks, 'how long your family been on ADC?'

"Well, I started telling him how I had been going out pretty near every day to look for employment when I didn't have to go to the clinic, but he says, 'You don't have to put me on, Brownleaf. I ain't going to do anything to you. Just tell me if you ever had a real job.'

" 'It's been a while,' I say, 'even before the last baby and she is now two.'

" 'Well,' he says, 'I guess I knew that. You can consider yourself lucky. You're going to be retrained.'

" 'I never been trained,' I say, 'so how am I going to be retrained?'

" 'It's just a word,' he says.

"I ask him then if I have to go to any school. 'Don't you worry. It'll be easy,' he says, 'you'll get $17.00 a week and your family can still collect the Welfare.'

" 'Just what I got to do?'

" 'Oh,' he says, 'it isn't anything you got to worry about. All you got to do is make sure you show me attendance slips. It isn't bad, you know. $17.00 a week, and you will be re-trained.'

" 'And I don't do nothing?'

" 'You just do as you are told,' he says, 'and I'll play ball with you. You might even learn something.'

"Well, I don't like the way he puts it, so I ask, 'Suppose I don't want to.'

" 'Don't be foolish, Brownleaf,' he says, 'you have to start learning how to take care of your family.'

"So this man—his name is Santos and he has a twitch in his face—tells me he has made an appointment with me the very next day at three o'clock over at that big building over on 9th Street. He tells me you go see Miss D'Angelo, and then he reminds me about the attendance slips and he be-comes real twitchy because he says, 'Goodbye and good luck. If you hold up your end we'll hold up ours.'

"Well, since there wasn't any way I could argue with a white man like that, the next afternoon at three o'clock I drag it over to see this Miss D'Angelo. Now, she was just like him. Big smile. You know. Couldn't be nicer. And she told me first thing how I was going to get $17.00 a week and all I had to do was make sure about the attendance slips.

" 'What you going to train me to be?' I ask her, and she smiles and asks what did I ever do.

"Well, I've been a laborer and a farmer. I also worked in a factory years ago when I lost this finger, and I've been in jail a few times. Nothing much, but I don't lie to her. I told all of these things, and she said then maybe I ought just to take it easy and get a little orientation first. Then she asked me could I read and write, and when I said yes, she said that was good because all I would need now was a new attitude, a little orientation. She was sending me to that big building over on Church Street.

" 'Don't you forget about those attendance slips,' she says to me, and we shake hands with her telling me to report Monday morning at nine o'clock.

"Well, when I go home and tell my friends what they going to do to me, they say you're crazy Brownie. Use your wit because they can't make you do that if you missing a finger, but I say you got to trust people or they won't trust you. So Monday morning I go down to this place to see this man and he reads my little note and then takes me into this room where there are a lot of other spades just like me. And he tells us to write our names on this piece of paper, which he takes away from us. Then he tells us how the government realizes you just can't give men like us money because you also got to give us opportunities. Then he tells us how lucky we are to be taking this retraining because it will mean so long as we remember our attendance slips we'll get $17.00 a week and our families will still collect the Welfare. Then he asks if there are any questions, but nobody raises their hands.

" 'Come on,' he says, 'let's hear them if you have them.'

"So I raised my hand just like in school. 'What we going to do?'

" 'You see this fellow here. He seems very anxious, don't he?' and he looks and finds my name on that slip of paper and he says, 'It's Mr. Brownleaf, isn't it? Well,' he says to me, 'if you're so anxious to begin, Mr. Brownleaf, you go down to that cellar and ask for Mr. Romeo.' Everybody is laughing. Then he says, 'Go on, now. You go on down there quick and don't disrupt this class anymore.'

"So I took my coat and things and go down in the elevator to the cellar, and it's easy enough to find Mr. Romeo because he is in charge of the trash. A little spic with frizzy hair, speaks with an accent. You know. So when I tell him how I got here, he says, 'You're one of the boys from the Welfare, aren't you?'

" 'That's right,' I said.

" 'Well,' he says then, 'you come here to work for the City, you get busy because this is the taxpayers' money. You see that big barrel full of garbage? You carry it over to the incinerator.'

"I look at this barrel and it is one of those great big cardboard things just full up to the brim with nasty things. So I say, 'You going to help me?'

" 'I work here,' he says. 'You here to learn. You do it. Get busy.' And he leans back against the wall and lights himself a Tiparillo.

"Now maybe I'm just stupid old Brownie, but nobody is that stupid, so I say, 'I ain't here to do your work. I'm here to be retrained.'

" 'First you got to learn things,' he says.

" 'What things?'

" 'You got to learn things,' he says. 'You got to learn the value of a job. You got to learn work habits.'

"I say, 'Who you to teach me these things?' But it's awful hot down there in that cellar, so there ain't no use getting worked up.

"I say, 'You just never mind what you think. You and me ain't got no business being like this. You got something for me to do it's one thing, but I ain't here to do your work, you understand?'

"Seems being nice just didn't help. That Romeo says, 'You get busy or I call the supervisor.'

"Well, I didn't want to cause trouble on my first day, but I didn't see why this spic should be bossing me around. So I say, 'If it's that way I'll help you but you got to understand. I ain't going to do it all alone . . .'

" 'Son of a bitch,' he screams at me, 'You pick up that barrel.'

"So I remembered some stuff from when I lived over near the Broadway Casino, and I say, *'Haga la ponienta chica!'*[1]

"Then this guy who was half nigger himself was fit to be tied, and he tells me to get the hell out of there and see Mr. Auerbach on the fourth floor or there will be trouble. I say, 'I don't want no trouble. Who's going to cause trouble?'

" 'Man,' he says to me, 'you don't know what you are doing. You want to be thrown off the Welfare?'

"Now how the hell should I know they would stoop to that? I say, 'Look here, I got a wife and kids.'

[1] Literally, "abuse yourself."

131

" 'We all got,' he says. 'Don't you think I got? You should have thought of them before this . . .'

" 'Give me another chance,' I say, but this guy Romeo won't even let me come near his barrel. He says, 'You go see Auerbach. I don't want you here, you troublemaker . . .'

"So I go upstairs and wait for maybe half an hour outside this office, and then they bring me in to see this little Jewish man and he seems to know all about me, how many kids I got, where I live, what happened downstairs with Romeo, just about everything except my ulcer; and he says he is very angry and disappointed with me.

"He says, 'You think you can walk right in here and be the boss. First you got to learn something. Then maybe we can make you a clerk or something.'

" 'What they put me down there with the garbage for?'

" 'Well,' he smiled, 'you know you got to start somewhere.'

"Then he tells me to go home and cool off and think it over. He says I don't have to retrain if I don't want to, just like I don't also have to collect the Welfare.

" 'What about my family?'

" 'You go on home,' the man says. 'You think it over real good. We'll come to that bridge when we cross it.'

"Well, I went home and talked to my wife and these friends, and we did some figuring together and hell, that $17.00 was just a few cents more than I could get from the Welfare.

"My wife says, 'If you going to work, why don't they pay you a real salary?'

"And my friends all say, 'Use your wits, son. You're a fool if you work for that. They can't make you.' So the next day

I don't show up at that place, and along about four in the afternoon I'm having a beer with a friend when Mr. Santos drops by to see me.

" 'Brownleaf,' he says, 'what the hell you trying to do to me?'

" 'You didn't say I was going to be a garbage man. You said I was going to get retraining.'

" 'You know what I got to do here now,' he says, 'I come here. I see you drinking beer when you supposed to be in your class. I got to throw you off the Welfare.'

" 'You can't do that. I know my rights. I don't have to go to work in the cellar for some spic at $17.00 a week.'

" 'Brownleaf, you're too choosy when you got nothing to be choosy about,' the man says. 'So I'm going to teach you a little responsibility.'

"He goes away, and about a week later I get a letter from the Welfare that my case is being closed. That motherfucker really meant what he said. So I'm fit to be tied, and I borrow a dollar from my wife and call Santos down at the Welfare Center and I say, 'You son of a bitch. You doing this to me or the whole family?'

" 'If I had my way,' he says, 'your wife would leave you because you aren't doing her and the kids any good . . .'

" 'How do you know that? You ain't been around all the time. You're only here when you want to see something.'

"Santos is very angry at me now, but he says if I'm still willing to be retrained, he'll give me another chance. He'll get me put back on the Welfare, only I'll have to wait for the next cycle to begin. In other words, for the next two weeks I don't get no Welfare."

Brownleaf lifted his lean body off the bar stool. "Time

I got going home," he said. "Kids ought to be back from school in a little while. The wife is out doing work." He winked at me.

"Suppose the Welfare finds out?" I asked.

Brownleaf dropped thirty cents on the bar. "You know what I think?" he said. "I don't believe this shit about cycles. I just think old twitchy is trying to get me. Whichever way you look at it, he's got me. You know," he said, "over there on 4th Street they're training all the young kids. Teaching them how to be carpenters. Teaching them spelling and reading. They don't got that kind of training for people like me. You know, I went down there one time because I got a nephew down there being trained, and I said, 'What can you do for me?'

"'Well,' this nice man say, 'I think you a little too senior for our programs . . .'

"Well," Brownleaf said, looking at me steadily through that cloudy yellow eye, "if I'm too old what they playing around with me at the Welfare? You know why they play around with me like that?"

"No," I shrugged. "You tell me."

Brownleaf laughed. "They think we niggers going to riot. They think we going to kill Whitey. Let me tell you something," he said. "When you get to be my age, that's the farthest thing from your mind. You're toothless and old, and all you want is that sugar tit. Violence . . . that may be all right for the young kids because they don't know any better, but I know better. Who I going to kill? That bunch down there? Don't you kid yourself," Brownleaf said, "You got this sugar tit, you don't want to kill nobody. You just want that sugar tit. Don't seem much of a chance of that so you get angry, but even then you don't want to kill. You just want more of that sugar tit . . ."

"What does your wife say about all this?" I asked.

"She knows what's good for her."

"And your kids?"

"They got nothing against the kids," Brownleaf said. "It's just the fathers."

7

DOROTHY MUDD

• "You know what I did the first day I got off?" Smiling, Dorothy Mudd daintily pulled a gobbet of cream cheese off her green Chock Full o' Nuts uniform and wiped it on a tissue-sized piece of wax paper, which she then crumpled up and threw into a bin. Spatula in hand, she began to spread cream cheese on one piece of toast after another as they came sliding out of the toaster.

"Actually," Dorothy said, "they didn't make me get off. I wanted to get off. I was sick of that life for good. People always poking around in my business. You know. And I never had a penny to my name. Not that I got that much now. You don't ordinarily, working in a place like this . . . paying for carfare and clothes, you know . . . but at least it's mine and nobody can tell me what to do with it. You know what I mean? I mean, actually I ain't any better off than I was before because they were supposed to help me with the kid, but you know, I just don't want to have anything more to do with them. You understand?"

"I understand."

"So anyway," Dorothy continued, "I was telling you about what happened when I got off. Actually," she smiled, "it was the first day I got paid. That's the truth. I had all this money in cash in my pocketbook and I went right from work to 5th Street and asked to see my investigator. You know what I did then?"

Dorothy's chatter was causing the toast to pile up as it slipped off the rack, so she began spreading the cream cheese faster.

"So anyway, it wasn't much money but it sure looked like a lot because I had it all changed into ones. And when he came down those stairs I took it all out of my purse and waved it at him. 'I'm Dorothy Mudd,' I say. 'You remember me? Case No. 1348635? That's right. ADC—I got this boy Jimmy. That's right again,' I say, when he begins to nod, 'and I also got this friend Leslie. Now you remember? Well,' I say, 'you see this? I earn all this at Chock Full o' Nuts. I don't need you anymore. And don't you worry. You're never going to see me inside this place again.'

"Anyway," Dorothy continued, "this man was so flabbergasted that he just says to me, 'Good luck, Mrs. Mudd.'

"Well, then I really fixed him. I say, 'It's Miss Dorothy Mudd and you just mind your manners. You understand, because I'm a taxpayer just like everybody else and I don't need you anymore. As a matter of fact,' I said, 'I'm going to go up and get a bag on my head as big as this whole room, and you can't do a damn thing about it!'

"And I did," Dorothy added, laughing heartily, "only it was all a mistake. He wasn't my investigator after all."

She wiped the sweat off her brow with the short sleeve of her uniform, on which was pinned a Chock Full o' Nuts badge complete with her name: Dotty. Then she said, "Excuse me a minute, I got some catching up to do."

She was a lean, light-skinned woman, whose age was hard to determine at first glance; but when she started to work again, I saw how lined and worn her hands were, and I saw the heavy knot of muscle on each of her forearms. She worked effortlessly, wielding her spatula with well-contained fury. Next to her a darker girl in the same green uniform was grabbing up the freshly daubed slices of toast on a sheet of waxed paper and closing them against pieces of toast that popped from another machine; then a third girl wrapped each sandwich in wax paper and deposited them in the stainless steel bins under the counters. The three girls worked well together, with sober faces and an unjoking demeanor, until one of the men behind the counter walked past Dorothy and pinched her on the buttock. I expected her to express outrage, but she merely winced and said, "Don't do that!"

When the man came back a second time and patted Dorothy, she giggled. For a moment she was like a flirty little girl. "What you up to . . . you watch yourself, you . . ." She was squirming, so she missed the toast with her spatula of cream cheese and spread it all over her palm. The man laughed, and Dorothy turned back to the counter to catch up with the other girls. After a moment she said, "Pig!" The other girls solemnly nodded.

Because it was still early, and there were very few customers to distract them, this trio made up for the delay very quickly and soon had their bin stuffed with sandwiches. Then Dorothy said, "That ought to hold the buggers." Again she wiped the sweat off her brow, and she dropped the spatula into a tin of murky hot water before rejoining me at the counter.

"You still here?"

"I'd like another cup of coffee," I told her.

Dorothy went to refill my mug with the same casual toughness with which she had greeted me when she saw I was reading *Policies Governing the Administration of Public Assistance* at her counter.

Then she had said, "You ain't going to learn nothing out of that book," as she shoved the mug of coffee at me. Now she shoved a fresh new mug at me and said, "When I was on the Welfare, I could never even get out of the house. You think they give you money for a baby sitter? Now I'm in church choir . . . I'm in the PTA . . . It's a different life . . ."

"And your boy doesn't miss having you at home?"

Dorothy's face became a little stern. "My boy and I never got along that well . . . I just wish Welfare would do as they say and help take care of him as they say they should, but I ain't going over there begging. I don't want to have anything more to do with them people." Dorothy added. She poked her fork at some frankfurters on the grill and said, "If you ask me, they ought to get more of the women away from home. Then they would be doing some good."

"I guess so," I said. "But are you able to manage without the Welfare?"

"It's hard," she said. "My boy is now fifteen, and he can run through clothes quicker than anything you've ever seen . . . they don't pay that well here." she added, "and there isn't any tipping. But when the man from Welfare said I ought to go down and apply, just so long as I was bugging him so much to get off, I did it in a minute. Anything to get off that Welfare. And I don't intend to get back on either, even if I get laid off here. I'll collect the unemployment insurance. I'll do housework. Don't you worry—I'll find something. You think not?"

"I hope so. Still," I added, "it does seem a shame that you can't get Supplementation if you need it."

"I don't need it and I don't want it," she said. "I mean, I could get it if I wanted it badly enough, but I don't need it that bad. I would rather work forty hours more a week than get it. You don't believe me, do you?"

"I believe you. Still," I added, "you could probably use it, couldn't you?"

"I could use it," Dorothy said. Then she became sober for a moment, reflective. "One thing is," she said abruptly, "I got rid of old Leslie fast enough. I said to him, 'When Welfare supported me it was different, but you don't expect me to support you, do you?' You should have seen the look on Leslie's face. Serves him right. I still see him occasionally, but I wouldn't have him living with me . . . not on what I earn."

"Just how much would that be?"

Dorothy said, "None of your business!

"When I was on Welfare," she quickly added, "everybody knew my business. Now it's different. It's a lot different."

I asked, "Don't you get lonesome?"

"Sure I do, but I got PTA and church. I got things to keep me busy. I make my own dresses. What do you think of that?"

"That's very impressive," I said. "I mean it," I added. "And Leslie, he's all right?" . . .

"He got to take care of himself, that Leslie . . . We all got to take care of ourselves."

Then Dorothy said, "You wait and see how good it will be when that boy stops eating me out of house and home . . ."

"Is he a good boy?"

"He's good," she said. "He's bright enough, all right. That's how come I'm in the PTA . . . Only he just favors his father. Son-of-a-bitch never gave him anything or me anything, but he favors him, all right . . . Son-of-a-bitch got me on Welfare to begin with . . . Well, anytime he wants to go looking for him, I'll tell him just where he is and he will have the surprise of his life. He'll come running back with his tail between his legs to Momma."

"You mean he never sees his father?"

"Oh, he sees him, all right," Dorothy smiled. "He comes by every now and then for a little food, maybe some money. I can't be that much of a son-of-a-bitch . . . You know what, down South I taught school, but I don't have the credits to teach up here so I always used to say to the man, 'Why don't you send me back to school again so I can get more credits and maybe teach.'

"But he says, 'Who's going to take care of your child?'

"Well, I didn't know what to say to that, so I stayed home taking care of this kid, who never even liked me, until I couldn't stand it any longer, and then I said I'll take any kind of job you got—anything.

"But he said, 'Don't you think you ought to think of your child?'

"Well, I said, 'Why don't you think of him for a change, Mister, because I'm going to get a job and get out of here whether you like it or not.'

141

"So I took this—it was the first thing that came along—and I've been here eight months now, and I can't say that I like it, but I like it a lot better than the Welfare. And as for my kid, the less we see of each other, the better. He knows he can always come to Momma for a good meal or a new suit of clothes. What more you ask of me? I'm in the PTA and church choir, and I just don't have any more time for this shit. If Welfare wants to help out, they know what to do. They know where to find me. Only they will have to beg me, because I ain't going begging to them."

"And you're getting by?"

"Man, who said I'm getting by? I just say it's better than the Welfare."

Dorothy had to interrupt herself then to serve a cream cheese sandwich and a glass of orange drink to a bald squinting customer who kept tapping his quarter against the counter. When she came back later, she said, "Well, I bet you won't find any of that in your book."

"No," I said. "I guess not."

"Sure you won't," Dorothy said. "And what's more you won't go looking for it either. You people start out all right, but after a couple of weeks you're just like all the rest of them . . ."

"Look," I said, "you got me wrong. I'm not an investigator."

"Then what're you reading that for?"

"I'm writing something," I said. "I'm interested."

"Come off it. You got people on the Welfare."

"I'm afraid not," I said. "I'm just interested."

"That's a funny one," she said, and she went away again.

A moment later she was back. "How about some more coffee?"

But when I said no and got up to go, she said, "You're interested in the Welfare. That's a hell of a thing."

She removed my dirty mug and made a quick swipe with her rag across the counter. Then she said, "I don't know what you're interested in. Do you? There ain't nothing to be interested in. They treat you all alike. They're just a bunch of bastards, that's all. They treat you like dogs. When I was on Welfare I got maybe $25.00 a week. You think I'm doing a hell of a lot better now? Not with carfare, I ain't. And you know what they can do with those fringe benefits? Bunch of bastards is all they are. Well, I decided long ago that the thing to do is to be just as big a bastard as them. Then they'll never touch you. Just as long as I don't need them for anything, they can't do a thing to me. Look at me, I'm in the PTA! You think I could have done that if I was still on the Welfare?"

"What about your kid and Leslie?"

Dorothy smiled. "Sooner or later they're just going to have to take care of themselves."

"And you?" I asked, "You think you'll always be able to do that?"

"I can do housework," she said. "I can always do something. Maybe sooner or later I'll get a husband. Only," she winked, "you gotta be careful about these men. They're just looking for somebody to support them."

I said, "I don't suppose you'd want to do that . . ."

"Who, me? I can't afford it." Dorothy smiled. "Things keep up, it may be different. We ain't supposed to get tips, but I'm pretty good and people throw me a little something now and then. Well, I haven't got anything saved, you understand, but I will someday. You wait and see. I'll have something . . . and then we'll see which fish we want to fry."

I wanted to ask Dorothy how old she was, but her supervisor walked by just then, and she winked at me and said, "Looks like I better get back to business. I don't want to lose this job if I don't have to."

She started to turn to her frankfurters, and then she added, "You come back some time, and I'll tell you just what it's like. I used to have a lot of friends on Welfare, only I don't see them any more. They're all a bunch of money-grubbing whores and bums. You better believe it. I can tell you all about them."

As I went out through the revolving doors, I could see that business was picking up at the Chock Full o' Nuts. Dorothy was standing at her counter, spearing frankfurters with one hand while jerking rolls out of a dispenser onto a piece of wax paper with the other; she served and then made change. I stood watching her for perhaps five minutes, because she was really fast and good at what she did. Then I saw her suddenly stop. Frozen in mid-motion, she wiped the sweat off her brow, and there was a tight, hard, anxious look between her eyes.

When a customer demanded his change, Dorothy shouted so that I could hear her even out on the street. "I got you, Mister. Don't you think I got you, Mister?"

PART TWO

The investigator is responsible for seeing that no needy person eligible for assistance is denied assistance and that no ineligible person receives assistance. He is not fulfilling his function until he recognizes that denial or withdrawal of assistance is as constructive a factor as the granting of assistance, both to the client and the community.

Chapter V, page 65, *Policies Governing the Administration of Public Assistance,* City of New York, Department of Welfare.

1

HOMELESS MEN

• For every New Yorker on Welfare, 1⅔ eligibles are not. Of these, in Manhattan alone, as many as 37,000 may be homeless. Not only do they lack regular domiciles or employment, but they are not even considered members of the labor force; and few are collecting public assistance. In general, they have never been given the opportunity to obtain public assistance. They are eligible for relief (variously called Home Relief or General Assistance), but this is perhaps the most strictly administered and discretionary of all our public assistance categories in regard to eligibility.

As one unsuccessful applicant told me, "Nobody trusts you when you apply for relief. It costs the city only about $2.00 a day to keep you on relief, and it costs maybe $9.00 a day to put you in the poke . . . I don't care whether it's Hart's Island or Riker's . . . but they would just as soon put you in that poke as give you that $2.00 . . . and even when they're giving it to you, they're saying try to use as little as you can because it's better for you that way."

Getting on relief can present a major difficulty to the person without a family. To be eligible for Home Relief in New York you must establish that you are sickly and needy;

but if you are too sickly or needy, you will be institutional-
ized or offered Aid to the Disabled. The policies of the
Department are very clear in this respect:

> Any person who is unable to provide for himself or to secure
> support from any other source and is not receiving needed
> assistance or care under Veteran Assistance nor receiving,
> eligible to receive, or presumptuously eligible to receive, Old
> Age Assistance, Assistance to the Blind, Aid to the Depend-
> ent Children, Aid to the Disabled, or assistance and care
> under Child Welfare provisions, is eligible for Home Relief.[1]

The need of the Home Relief applicant is consequently
more difficult to establish than simply proving that you have
dependent children who are needy, or that you have a lame
leg that makes you needy, or that you are needy by the
virtue of your advanced age, all of which are federally supported categories of assistance. And you must also be able
to avert the suspicion of being a mere vagrant.

In effect, then, the relief applicant has to play a game
with the City. He wants it to give him something for nothing. He wants $2.50 a day. But there is nothing terribly
wrong with him except that he lacks money. To be eligible
for such a catch-all program, he will not only have to establish his pauperization, but he will also have to prove that he
lacks prospects, legally responsible relatives,[2] and, neverthe-

---

[1] *Policies Governing the Administration of Public Assistance*, City of
New York, Department of Welfare.

[2] Advised in their policy manuals about the legal limits on the laws regarding the responsibilities of relatives, Welfare workers were also urged
until recently, as a matter of policy, to seek out any other close relatives (or
even friends) who may be cajoled or embarrassed into supporting the indigent applicant. I made inquiries on behalf of a friend who had a married
daughter who was not legally responsible for his upkeep. Since her husband

less, has a domicile. Of course, people in such straits rarely
have domiciles, so they are offered the shelters, at worst, or,
at best, a "flop," for an indeterminate period of time while
their case is being investigated. These, I suspect, are the
fortunate ones. Welfare also reserves the right to question
such applicants about how they have supported themselves
thus far; if any inkling of possible solvency is detected, it
will be used to justify the denial of relief. If, for example,
a person has engaged in casual labor, the Department will
assume that he is capable of becoming self-supporting. If he
is penniless but living with a friend, the Department might
encourage him to remain there and defer its support. It is
through such reasoning that many thousands of potential
"reliefers" in Harlem, Bedford Stuyvesant, East Harlem, and
the Lower East Side move in with AFDC mothers and are
pursued and punished when such illicit unions put more
children on the Welfare roles.

Another equally unfortunate outcome of such a policy
is that it causes a further economic drain on those who are
poor. Many Welfare families in a city like New York are
underbudgeted because their investigators may not know or
may be too lazy to give them their full entitlements; but a
substantial number are underbudgeted because they are supporting family members and friends who are not yet eligible
for benefits. Not only is this true among the Puerto Rican
community, in which distant relatives and friends from one's

---

was having a hard time supporting her and the children, my friend wanted
to make sure, before he applied, that no "unpleasantness" would come their
way. The Welfare worker told me, "We can't make his daughter do anything, but don't you worry [winking at me], we have our ways to get people
to volunteer."

former village may be taken into the home and supported for indefinite periods of time, but it seems equally true among other Welfare recipients. Many AFDC women continue to support the men who have abandoned them—on an occasional basis. Just as often, these men alternate between the homes of their sexual partners and those of their mothers or other close relatives, always disappearing, of course, when there are official visitors. It is a fairly widespread assumption that the Negro matriarchy has been consistently bilked by its itinerant males, but one reason for this is that the men have an extremely difficult time getting relief unless they are married. And, contrary to the prevailing mythology, there are very few men who are willing to get married to collect Welfare.

Welfare is stingy in giving relief because the city and the state must pay the entire bill without federal reimbursement. Some form of emergency assistance is supposed to be given to anybody presumed eligible, pending the formal investigation. To make certain that this arrangement is not used to defraud the city, the caseworker can satisfy the above requirement by handing the applicant carfare and a slip of paper to report to a shelter. Operating the shelters is costly, and it might appear that it would be cheaper to give people cash assistance; but if the threat of the shelter can be used as a deterrent to those who apply for assistance, it becomes a long-range economy. The unattached male, living as described above, does not want to make use of the shelters. At the shelters the deserving are sent to cheap hotel rooms and given assistance, and the undeserving are classified as vagrants and alcoholics. They receive assistance according to their deserts. Often this means referral to a job.

One Negro from South Carolina who had been trying to make himself eligible for relief for nearly three years told me his story.

"Seems like all I ever got was that slip of paper. You go to 5th Street, they tell you 'case closed.' They send you uptown to 28th Street. They tell you go to 5th Street. It's a real runaround. Pretty soon you ain't careful, you run right up your own asshole . . . Downtown they say go uptown, and uptown they say 'case closed' again. That's the hardest two dollars you'll ever earn . . ."

When I asked him why he thought this was so, he explained, "Seems like they always trying to say you can work, and then they send you to that office on St. Mark's Place for work . . . because they know you ain't gonna keep a job, and once they got you down at that shelter they got you for good. Next stop Hart's Island . . . or else they send you upstate to one of the hotels—Goshen, Ellenville, Sullivan County—I've worked in just about all of them. They don't even pay the minimum wage. If you're lucky it's $90 a month, and they deduct room and board. So they got you back on the Bowery again, and then you got to spend all your money until you got to go to the shelter. Then it's uptown, downtown and downtown, uptown and your case is closed. When they think you got nothing better to do, it's off to St. Mark's Place. You think you ever get relief like some of those nice little old ladies get? Bullshit."[3]

Welfare's intake statistics on Home Relief seem to bear out some of these intemperate assertions. In a typical month, June, 1964, the Department reported that it had

[3] In some localities the itinerant applicant for relief is still escorted out of the jurisdiction by the police.

received approximately 500 more applications for Home Relief than for AFDC, but there were almost the same number of acceptances for each category. Although the AFDC caseload was nearly three times as large as that for tiny Home Relief, approximately the same number of applicants were disqualified from each. Of these, more than one thousand cases of Home Relief were dropped for reasons the Department's monthly report left unspecified.

These apparent injustices were partially the result of the City's curious system of double bookkeeping, whereby it tries, whenever possible, to qualify a person for federal assistance. That procedure has been responsible for a great deal of public misinformation about the Welfare problem. Early in 1966, for example, the Social Security Administration announced that the number of those on relief had dropped to a nationwide low of less than 300,000 for the first time since 1957. Ever anxious to find some reason for optimism about the national effort to eliminate poverty, the *New York Times*[4] Washington economic analyst promptly reported that this shrinkage among reliefers had been caused by the creation of new jobs, a consequence of the tax cut of 1964 and the War on Poverty. The article also mentioned that the economic growth rate had not significantly affected the number of those on AFDC, who were said to be increasing, but this was attributed to the breakdown of the urban Negro family. The following day the *Times* reported from New York that within the city there had not been a decrease but an increase—as much as 59 percent—in the number of

[4] *New York Times*, "Relief Load Cut to an 8-Year Low by Nation's Boom," January 17 and 18, 1966.

those on relief. City officials laid the blame on population influx and the dwindling of low-skilled jobs. Neither story pointed out, however, that since 1962 it has been possible for states to grant federally reimbursed AFDC funds to male applicants for relief who have families. In other words, the drop in the relief roles was basically a realignment from relief to AFDC because men who had previously been considered employable were now being classified as unemployable. While this arrangement probably benefitted some heads of families, it did little to redress the condition of those without dependents. Now the majority of states and localities have even more justification for not wishing to give unattached persons relief. If New York has seemed somewhat more liberal in this respect (so that its rising relief rolls reflect the intensity of the problem), it is probably because New York uses relief as a limbo category in which the applicant is placed pending efforts to make him eligible for one of the federally assisted programs. That many states now refuse to give even this much assistance out of their own funds may account for the much-heralded drop in the number of those on relief, which, in turn, is used by those who wish to convince the public that the status should not be legitimized by greater federal participation.

In New York, then, the unattached relief applicant still has a difficult time establishing his credentials as a bona fide pauper. He can be denied relief if he misrepresents, if his behavior is considered obnoxious at the intake interview, or if the Department believes he is not making a suitable effort to find work. The New York State Constitution recognizes that the aid, care, and support of the needy are public concerns, but the extent of the *right* to benefits has never been adequately tested in the courts. In general, relief is still administered *de haut en bas,* as charity. It is left to the discretion of the functionary to decide whether or not a man is employable or whether he can be rehabilitated through job referral "therapy."

If there is a strong fiscal reluctance to grant cash assistance to the single man or woman who walks into the center to apply for relief, there is an even greater reluctance to set up housekeeping for persons who are presumed to be rehabilitable, because the Department does not like to invest unnecessarily in the cost of their furniture, living arrangements, and clothing. In 1960 the city spent approximately $18 per capita on furniture and $32 on clothing for its caseload. Proportionally, AFDC and Home Relief received the smallest share of these grants. The Department could be so stingy because it did not have to abide by the "inalienable" right to cash assistance that is written into all federal programs for income maintenance; nor does it have very many firm ideological guidelines about its objectives (i.e., AFDC is given to encourage family stability).

Obliged to register for work, vulnerable to accusations of malingering, the potential reliefer becomes a victim of such automatic distrust when he applies that he can be easily denied, and if he tries to assert his formal rights to appeal, he may find them so vague and ambiguous that for all practical purposes they would seem to have evaporated. In denying relief a functionary is not required to keep elaborate records as he would with an AFDC family. Many applicants never even reach the formal intake, and the clerk or functionary they encounter can, should the question ever arise, justify his decision to deny by producing a carbon of the shelter voucher or perhaps by declaring that the man was offered a job that he refused.

But rarely do such questions arise, because applicants are kept in ignorance about the rights they have. Just how far states and localities are willing to go in making the rights of relief applicants obscure is revealed by two question-and-answer pamphlets prepared by the New York State Department of Social Welfare.[5] One is for Home Relief Applicants, the other for AFDC applicants. Both of these booklets are written abstractly, in dull, rather too intricate language, without setting forth specific examples of procedures and with no attempt to outline benefits. But although their formats are identical (questions and answers chosen by the Welfare authorities), it is interesting to compare the relative degrees of obscurantism of these questions and answers concerning the applicant's right to an appeal.

Neither booklet advises applicants of the efficacy of legal assistance; they do not offer to provide such assistance; nor do they point out that there may be legal avenues for redress beyond administrative review (i.e., the courts).

The applicant for AFDC is made to understand clearly that she must receive a written notification about the status of her entitlement. If her application is denied or assistance is discontinued unfairly, if she thinks her benefits are too small, or if the local agency fails to respond within thirty

[5] *Aid to Dependent Children* and *Home Relief and Veteran Assistance,* 1962, New York State Department of Social Welfare. Many state offices I've visited don't even have these on hand.

days, she can appeal by letter to the State and must be granted a formal hearing within sixty days of the receipt of that communication.

But the relief applicant may apparently be notified verbally about all decisions affecting his entitlement. If he remains unsatisfied, he is to ask the official who has just denied him for a reconsideration or further explanation. If after this he still remains unsatisfied, "he may report the matter to the State Department of Social Welfare" but *only* when a decision has been delayed beyond thirty days if "an applicant has been denied or a grant discontinued after a public Welfare official has determined that an applicant . . . came to this state for the purpose of receiving assistance . . . can the applicant appeal such decision . . . and may also ask for a hearing thereon."

I have read this passage about three dozen times, and about all that seems clear is that the State of New York is not anxious to sit in judgment on relief decisions. If I understand the policies set down here (and presumably I stand a better chance than some), New York feels an obligation to reconsider decisions affecting nonresidents but no obligation to review the cases of those who are residents. But when rights have been made so obscure, all residents find it arduous to apply for benefits. In New York needy persons are defined as those who are not receiving or who are unable to "secure sufficient support from relatives, friends, or other sources" to meet their requirements, but they are not told when they apply what constitutes sufficient support. Instead they are interrogated. One middle-aged middle-class man of my acquaintance applied for relief when his drinking became such a problem that he could no longer procure work. He was asked a lengthy series of questions about his relatives, friends, business connections, and former employers. He was asked for the name of his landlord and his former wife. When it became obvious to this man that the Department was planning to call on these people, thus making it even more difficult for him to rehabilitate himself if he ever again was in a position to pursue his profession, he demanded that his application be withdrawn and never again went to Welfare. Perhaps this is the intention behind the intention of the Department's insistence that the worker check out every conceivable "resource" on the odd chance that assistance may not be necessary at all.

But even if a man is willing to put up with the humiliations of this initial application, even if he is willing to sleep in tawdry and overcrowded dormitories and to feed on poorhouse fare, he may not be willing—for a variety of illicit and semi-illicit reasons—to become involved with the policing mechanism that is considered a major correlary function of such institutions. If he is a vagrant, for example, he may not be willing to involve his legally responsible relatives. If he is an alcoholic, he may be afraid of some of our presently crude methods of rehabilitation or unwilling to swear off drink. If he has been engaged in illicit transactions, he may not be willing to risk the penalties implicit in the Means Test, or his behavior may be such that he may not be willing to submit to the mandatory home visits. I even met one frightened man who had been disabled in an industrial accident a few months earlier; he was afraid to apply for Welfare while his case was being decided because he expected a windfall from the lawsuit, and he was not going to "let *them* get any of it."

This man had been led to believe that his compensation would be considered a resource that Welfare would attempt to apply against his benefits, and the decision would be made without his participation. If there are policies against such procedures, applicants are rarely informed of them. In fact, it may seem entirely up to the discretion of the worker and his supervisor to decide what shall be considered a resource and how to apply that resource. Usually these decisions are made with reference to the man's character as well as to his circumstances, and inferences are drawn from his "living conditions" as well as from the documents he must supply to establish need.

Thus, Welfare policies often seem so lawless that even those who are themselves lawless may come to resent and fear such behavior. If, moreover, an application can lead to Hart's Island or to the observation ward at Bellevue, it is prudent to find independent ways of maintaining yourself. Thus we promote a kind of pauper rugged individualism— men who drift from bed to bed; and the shelters and work camps remain the habitual drying-out places for Bowery-based alcoholics, many of whom are given their pittance by Welfare. Such men rarely argue about what they are given. Not only are they not told in advance what they are entitled to, but they are often willing to take whatever they can get. They use shelters as our middle classes use spas, retreats, resort hotels—to restore their shaky equilibriums.

"I'm an alcoholic . . . they don't like to give us too much," one filthy old woman on the Lower East Side explained when I came upon her eating out of a garbage can. If you ask the average worker about such a person, they will admit they exist, but they will also tell you that some people are poor and some people merely "feel poor." Perhaps so! But even if he also happens to be a drinker, it is doubtful that an unemployed male such as Benny Mosca would ever feel that poor unless he *was* poor. On November 9, 1965, Benny, formerly of Mayaguez, P.R., walked all the way from the Coney Island section of Brooklyn to the Lower East Side in order to find his older brother Ephemio, who had owed him one hundred dollars for more than two years.

Benny Mosca is such a thoroughgoing liar that it is some-times difficult to understand why he has not been more successful in his various self-help projects. Then one realizes that Benny lies to other people so that he can more success-fully con himself. He needs to plant the false evidence else-where so that in stumbling on it he can find verification for his own fantasies. Perhaps this is a rather creative adaptation for a man in his predicament. At first Benny told me that he needed the $100 because his Unemployment compensation had been falsely terminated for nearly two months; when I asked why, he admitted to me that he had never been covered by unemployment because in the last year he had only worked two and a half months for a hospital and about three months at the Aqueduct Racetrack. Nobody likes to think that he may be incapable of performing more work than that, so Benny probably lied because he did not want to seem "like such an oddball."

"I mean," he explained, "what kind of a guy can't even make Unemployment?"

Benny Mosca was so extremely candid with me from the beginning that I had to assume that his lack of circumspec-

tion was, in part, the result of his talents as a liar. Even now
I have no way of sorting truth from fiction in what Benny
told me, but I am reasonably sure that there are large
elements of both. Benny explained that when he had been
laid off at Aqueduct, over three months ago, he had gone to
live in Brooklyn with a friend, Rosalee Vasco, and her three-
year-old daughter in a two-and-a-half-room furnished bunga-
low near Coney Island. Benny claimed that he had not been
able to save anything at either the hospital or Aqueduct.
Now that Rosalee was having a difficult time taking care of
him on her tiny AFDC allotment, she was afraid that one of
her neighbors might say something to Welfare or that Benny's presence might be construed as a bad influence on little
Iraida.

Benny said he had even offered to marry Rosalee, but she
said, "Not until you get a real job."

He said he was just as glad anyway because he was not
anxious "to get so tied down."

Finally Rosalee had said to him, "I know you don't mean
any harm. You just aren't doing any good. Don't come back
unless you can take care of yourself."

So Benny Mosca decided that he would search for his
brother Ephemio. He was pretty sure that Ephemio could
not afford to give him the $100, but he hoped that his older
brother might allow him to stay with his family until he
found work. Benny had an old postcard with an address for
Ephemio on Hester Street near the Williamsburg Bridge.
When he finally arrived there at four-thirty in the afternoon,
two men named Peto and Charley, whom he had known in
Mayaguez, told him that Ephemio had moved away some
three weeks earlier to live in Hempstead, Long Island. It was

growing dark outside. Benny had only fifteen cents in his pocket, which he had borrowed from Rosalee earlier that morning. Fortunately, his friends from Mayaguez invited him to a bar to have a beer. Benny told me what happened then.

"We were taking our second beer when the lights began to blink. Then everything turned black. Some of the people were old-timers, and they said it was just a fuse. Others said they were testing something. So the bartender's brother comes in, and he says it is the Consolidation Edison and that it is happening all over the city.

"Another man says, 'It is even happening in Canada.'

"So the brother says, 'Don't anybody panic,' and he will go away and come back with more news . . .

"So it is just blah blah blah between all of us for maybe fifteen minutes because we are naturally all very frightened because you can never tell where a thing like this in a city like this can lead. Some people are even saying it is the Negroes. Then the brother comes back and he tells us everything will be okay by eight o'clock. Peto and Charley, these two friends of mine, they have to go home to see their families, but they say if nobody is hurt they will come right back to get me. So there I am, alone in this bar, listening to all that blah blah blah, and after an hour this bartender sees that we have no more money, so he is giving all the people beer on the book because he knows they just can't leave and walk around on the dark streets on a night like this . . . in a neighborhood like this.

" 'You I never saw before, but I can't send you away if you don't want to go,' he says. He gives me a glass of beer and a hard-boiled egg . . .

"Well, it wasn't so bad after that. They had lots of candles and there were no fights. I had two glasses of beer and two hard-boiled eggs, which always gives me a lump in the chest, and it was very gay and blah blah blah, you know. So I had maybe four beers altogether, and I was beginning to feel very sleepy because I had taken such a long walk. When this girl with the bad teeth says she is going to take me home with her because now she has lots of room with her brother in the Army, I say all right blah blah blah because maybe she isn't too beautiful, with her color and all, but I needed a bed. The bartender's brother gives us a piece of candle and we start walking to her place . . . it was a place called Henry Street . . . and now it was so dark outside you couldn't even see the sidewalks. This girl is asking me all kinds of questions about where I live and what I am doing down here [on the Lower East Side], so I take her hand and I start to tell her about my job at the Big A, about the horses, you know, blah blah blah, about Rosalee and Iraida, and how I have come to find my brother Ephemio . . .

"Holy Christ! As soon as I say that name she is very angry. 'This Ephemio—is he a tall skinny one with a gold tooth in the front of his mouth?'

"When I say yes, she says son of a bitch she has been look-ing all over for that son of a bitch because that little faggot gave her an infection and now the Welfare says what is she doing getting that kind of infection, for which they have to send her to a special doctor, if she don't have a boy friend. She says they are going to punish her so that her oldest kid won't come home for Christmas . . .

" 'Oh,' she says then, 'I hope you are not like that dumb son of a bitch . . .'

"What can I say against my own brother? We are facing each other by candle flame, and I am feeling cold but I am also worried that I will get such an infection myself, so I say, 'Ephemio and I had different fathers, but I am very sorry about what he did to you ...'

" 'Son of a bitch little faggot, he's sorry,' she says. 'Well, you can go fuck yourself because I may be a nigger but I am not getting into any more trouble.'

"She ran away then. I didn't mind, only she took the candle.

"So now it is even darker and there is nobody but myself on the street, although I can see all these other candles in the windows. It's like Christmas maybe, only dark, you know. So I don't hardly even know where I am, but I think I will trace my steps back to the door of that bar to wait for these friends. I felt very silly ... walking slowly along that pitch dark street ... I was afraid even to run because you never can tell in a city like this ... someone will think you have done something wrong. I mean, you don't like to get caught running at a time like that. People may get the wrong idea ...

"So when I came to this deep dark place in the sidewalk, I am not running but sort of walking fast with my hands in my pockets ... real innocent-like, you know. Hell, I probably should have known that maybe somebody yesterday or the day before yesterday left his coal chute open, but to tell you the truth I'm saying to myself it is just another of these wet spots which you can get from all the rains. I'm telling myself that and a lot of other things ... you know, blah blah blah ...

"Holy Christ! I take one step more then and the next

thing I know there is no sidewalk underneath me, and I'm falling down through all that darkness. I'm scared—so scared I don't even know what has hit me. So thank goodness and all that shit I landed on this big pile of what they call soft coal because who knows otherwise if I would be alive now to tell my story. I mean, the coal was soft all right, but I got these bruises on me just the same . . .

"So when I am able to get up after that I am feeling very groggy and my joints just ache all over. I figure then maybe I am hurt bad. Then I realize that I can't be hurt that bad or I would not be able to think so clearly. Anyway I go blah blah blah and, sure enough, I am thinking just fine, so I decide then that I will sack out down there in that cellar until the lights are turned on again.

"Come to think of it, I must have been hurt worse than I thought I was because I fell right to sleep, and the next thing I remembered it was like daylight with all the lights turned on in that cellar. Here I am, lying next to this big old boiler with this bad taste in my mouth and a knotty feeling in my stomach . . . and there is this old Jewish man standing over me. He has this very funny look in his eyes. I figure maybe he thinks I am some kind of troublemaker because he is what you would call a real old Jew, you know, dressed like the undertaker . . . well, I knew a little Jewish from Coney Island so I say to him, 'Wus willst du, momser?'

"Jesus! Holy Christ! The next thing I know he is screaming at me in Jewish so fast I can't understand a word he is saying—gurgle gurgle gurgle—blah blah blah—and then I feel this knot beginning to loosen on me only how do I know how far it will go? So when I get up, then I have this awful

headache between my eyes and I am trembling all over like
the Fourth of July ... Suddenly this old man yells '*Bum!*' and
I put my hand up to my head ... and look at me, here I am
shitting into my pants like I haven't done in maybe twenty
years. ...

"'*Animal!*' this old Jew screams, but I tell you I just
couldn't help myself. A lot of good my blah blah blahs are
doing anyway because this old Jew starts to chase me out of
his cellar with a coal shovel. I look at him as if he must be
crazy, but I start to run just the same—all the way up the
steps ... and as I am running my cuffs are just dripping shit
... like I tell myself, if only I had a hose, then I could hose
myself off like we used to do with those horses, but there is
really no time to think. Sure it was just an accident. Try and
make that old Jew understand ... Because you think I go
around shitting into my pants every day in the week?

"Which is exactly what I told that man over at the Welfare when this bum told me to go over and see them because
he figured maybe a guy like me—I don't sound like no spic,
do I?—anyway, he figured that maybe the Welfare, seeing
what kind of a guy I am, would want to give me some money
to find Ephemio and get myself cleaned off. You see, I
thought maybe I ought to get to Hempstead before the lights
went out again because this bum he swore to me that if they
went out again another time, it would prove it was sabotage
and then the cops would be out looking for all the guys like
us ... I don't know where he got that idea ...

"To make a long story short, I started walking through the
door of that Welfare and there is this man sitting at the
desk. When he sees me, he doesn't even ask any questions.

" 'You go to Great Jones Street. They'll take care of you.'

"And he starts to write on a little slip of paper.

"Well, I don't want to do a thing like that without know-ing what I am doing because this bum told me to watch my-self they should never give me any slips of paper.

"I ask, 'What's this Great Jones Street? What is this anyway?'

" 'It's on Third Street,' the man smiles. 'It's a place for fellas like you . . .'

" 'Oh,' I say, 'I don't believe that I want such a place as that, after all, because I got a little something here in my pants and all I need is a little money for a room and food and the train so I can find my brother who lives in Hempstead . . . Isn't this the place where they give out the money?'

" 'Wait here.'

The man goes away and comes back five minutes later with a lady she has purple hair. She must be maybe sixty, and she looks mean.

" 'Why do you smell like that?' she asks.

" 'That? That's just shit,' I tell her, 'because you see I fell down this coal bin last night during the eclipse, and you must understand I was frightened because I guess I just shit into my pants when this old Jew found me lying there . . .'

" 'I don't want to hear that kind of talk,' the man says then. And he looks like he is about to call the cop.

" 'Mister,' I say, real quick, 'I don't like it any better than you do, but I got shit in my pants just the same' . . . and blah blah blah . . . you know. I say, 'I came all the way over here from Brooklyn to find my brother Ephemio, who owes me this hundred dollars. People I knew in Williamsburg says he lives near the Williamsburg Bridge by a postcard he once sent them, but they are mistaken, as I found out when I met these two friends from Mayaguez, where we used to live, who tell me that Ephemio is now in Hempstead. So all I want is a little money to take the Long Island Rail Road train to Hempstead because Ephemio owes me $100. Look,' I say, 'I'll even take a bus.'

"She says, 'There is no bus goes to Hempstead . . .'

" 'If you're from Brooklyn,' the man says then, 'you should go to Welfare in Brooklyn.'

" 'Well,' I say, 'it isn't that simple. I'm not from anywhere at the moment. But if you were to lend me ten dollars, I would go to see Ephemio, and I will then pay you back with interest when Ephemio pays me that hundred dollars . . . You think I want relief?' I ask them.

" 'The best I can do for you,' the man says, 'is to send you over to Third Street, and they will put you under the showers.'

" 'It itches like hell,' I said. 'You think I like shitting into my pants? Say, listen,' I added, 'I bet you even got a revolving fund of some kind . . .'

" 'No,' the man says, 'you are thinking of the Traveler's Aid . . .'

"Then the woman says, 'Why are you telling him that? If his brother owes him a hundred dollars, he don't need the Traveler's Aid. You go to your brother.'

"Blah blah blah! She gives me that slip of paper and fifteen cents carfare, and the man says, 'Sorry!' "

Benny Mosca wanted to believe that it was all just a case of mistaken identity. Nobody could seriously take him for a bum. When he had spat out that final "sorry," a deep black rictus gaped between his thin parted lips; I half expected him to cluck at me like a hen. Benny shut his mouth tight, and then he opened it half way, shrugging.

"I guess I got a very bad break . . ."

"I would guess you did," I said.

"It happens." He smiled wanly, as if he had to believe that or else lose his self-esteem. Then he produced his shelter voucher from a pocket. "You don't think I would want to go to a place like that? They got all kinds of bums and queers . . . a place like that . . ."

I asked why he had not yet gone any place to get himself cleaned off.

"You know how it is," Benny smiled. "You get this way, you figure you ought to stay this way or people won't give you anything."

"Right now, I guess," he added, as if he were carrying about the family jewels, "you could say right now it was my selling point." Again he tried to smile.

"It must be uncomfortable," I said, pointing.

"Not only that," Benny replied, "it's humiliating . . ." Then he added, "I know . . . you probably find it hard to believe . . ."

"Not a bit," I lied.

"It's all right," Benny said. "I know it's a little out of the ordinary . . ."

For a man who smelled as if he had a dead animal trapped inside his trousers, Mosca still had some curious notions about decorum.

He said, "I wouldn't lie about a thing like this. You think I'm lying? I'll show you if you don't believe me. Because it just wouldn't be right . . ."

"What wouldn't?"

"I know," Benny said. "You think I'm lying. Making up some story . . . It just wouldn't be right . . . I would be too self-conscious . . . "

Benny was a thin man, of less than medium height, with a tiny black mustache and woolly brown hair. He looked thirty, but I was sure he was older. How dare anybody say he was not self-conscious, that he lacked self-respect! How dare anybody accuse him of being a derelict? Derelicts did not wear fancy black rodeo boots and specially tapered jeans. Neither did they own Levi jackets with leather piping around the cuffs and the pockets. Even if they did, they certainly would not have patches consisting of two Louisville sluggers crossed against a catcher's mitt, in front of which was emblazoned MARINE PARK LUCKY TIGERS, sewn across their hearts.

Seeing me stare at his insignia, Benny smiled. "I never could hit worth a shit, but I was a very good fielder . . . You understand," he added, "I'm not making any excuses for myself. You understand that . . ."

But what was there to understand? Why should he not make a few excuses? Benny could have told me that his mother had never loved him, that he was "culturally deprived," or that he had never been able to earn more than $1.25 an hour, and I would not have held it against him; but I was a little angry that he thought I believed he had connived to defecate in his pants before approaching me for a hand-out. Even if he had, what harm would a few good alibis do Benny now?

Again, anticipating me, he said, "I don't think it's right . . . people wanting something for nothing. If this hadn't

169

happened to me," he said, patting his hindquarters, "I would never even think of going to the Welfare."

Then I realized why I had bothered to talk to him at all. I am not usually such a humanitarian that I let myself be panhandled indiscriminately; but a man who leaps up from the sidewalk on Avenue C and Houston Street as you are walking to the Public Library and, with a blathering aplomb worthy of a candidate for public office, borrows two dollars from you in quick succession is sometimes disarming. Benny said he wanted to give me a receipt. He also promised that I would be repaid with interest. As he spoke in his queer monotone, my initial fear and astonishment gave way to an amused, stammering self-righteousness that he could have anticipated through this wild bit of self-caricature all my objections to such an arrangement.

"Say you were to give me a dollar and a half." Benny was smiling at me crookedly. "Just say it because you understand it's only a loan and I'm not saying that you should . . . or even that you will . . . So why not just say it? Well, I will take down your name and address on this little piece of paper and by registered letter with a money order for three dollars I will send you just as soon as I find my brother Ephemio. What do you say to that?"

"I never saw you before in my life," I said.

"Aw, come on," Benny said, as if I was the one who had the seatful, "have a heart!"

All that was lacking from his performance was the by-now-standard "seriously" or "honestly" with which we all preface our most corrupt acts of deceit. I decided that either Benny was sincere or his behavior was such a perfect imitation of artistic sincerity that it did not really matter whether he was sincere or not because he believed he was. If the latter was the case, what right did I have to be offended that he had dreamed up such a line about being ethical? How would I have liked a man with shit in his pants to behave? Did I really need his humility?

So it was with a sense of the abused innocence with which Benny might have panhandled others before me that I consented to give him his first dollar. As soon as we had negotiated the initial touch, he was asking for a second. Benny explained that the first would get him to Hempstead, but with the second he could also buy a meal and get himself cleaned up.

"And if I gave you a hundred," I said, "you could buy waxed calf shoes and a bowler hat . . ."

"Don't be silly," he said. "I don't even know what you're talking about."

I suppose he really didn't, but I still felt put out that he had picked on me twice rather than choosing to go to the shelter. One dollar, you see, is rather a large touch, but two dollars is more like an investment in a person. I needed certain assurances that my money would be well spent.

"What are you?" I found myself asking. "Some kind of junkie?"

"Honestly," he said, as if savoring all the word's implicit hypocrisy, "do I look like such a guy?"

"Then," I demanded, "why not go to the shelter?"

"That isn't exactly what I would call a picnic," Benny replied.

How could you argue with such good sense? It occurred to

me that despite my criticism of the people at Welfare, when the bite was put on me, I still had to know the man's case history. Just who the hell did I think I was? I had been panhandled, not "reached out to," and if I didn't like the smell of his shit at the moment it was just too bad. The people at Welfare were probably just as appalled. Either I was going to give Mosca his money or I should walk on and let some other sucker get the bite. As I started to go, Benny said, "Hold it a minute! . . . I just wanted you to know, it itches like hell. Holy Christ. When you got something in your pants like this, it's awful hard to keep up appearances."

The more I came to know Mosca, the more I was impressed by his talent at understatement. What could I do then but give him the second dollar? But I found that I had only a ten-dollar bill.

"Look," I said, "can't you get some of this money from your friends?"

When Benny winced and started to frown, I added, "Never mind . . . only I'll have to get change . . ."

"You do that. I'll wait right here . . ."

"Why don't you come with me?"

"You know," Benny shrugged, "it's just a little hard to walk."

Upon my return, no more than five minutes later, Benny had revised his plans. He would look for his friends from Mayaguez after all; he hoped they would let him take a bath in one of their apartments. Benny said he would offer them money, if necessary—my money! He said he also thought he could borrow a clean pair of trousers from his friend Peto Basuto, who was about his size. Then he would take the

BMT back to Brooklyn to see Rosalee because "by now she is probably very lonely." Puzzled, I asked Benny what he thought he would do about his brother.

"What do you think I'm going to do in Hempstead," he said, "with just a dollar in my pocket? . . . A guy like me in Hempstead," Benny continued, "a fish out of water . . . Say, listen, you mustn't get me wrong. I could give you a lot of blah blah blah, only I am trying to be straight with you. I got a little something in my pants. I don't want to go all the way out to Hempstead for a thing like that. Besides, Hempstead is in the suburbs. It's a great big place. I don't even know where Ephemio lives. I'd have to be crazy to go looking . . . No," Benny concluded, "I didn't make you any promises to go to Hempstead . . ." He was pushing a worm of dirt out from underneath the cuticle of his thumb with the edge of a match book. "It is much better that I go back to Brooklyn because Rosalee is really a nice girl, and if I tell her how they treated me at the Welfare, she will say, 'All right, you can stay here, Benny, just so long as you don't bother me and the kid . . .' "

I asked, "Will there be enough to eat?"

"She's really a nice kid," Benny replied, his eyes blinking with moisture, perhaps of reverie, "only sometimes it takes a girl like her a while to loosen up . . ."

"What do you mean——loosen up?" I asked.

"Women," Benny Mosca replied, "got a funny thing down there!"

I wasn't very sorry to have to leave him then, although I went away two dollars lighter. An hour later, at closing time, I walked out through the front door of the library and started up Houston Street, and there was Mosca. He had not moved from that street corner. He saw me and waved.

"Don't you worry," he said, when I had come as close as I dared, "I don't want any more money. I just didn't think you would like me to come inside because I know what these places can be like . . ."

"Tell me," I said, "what are they like?"

"It's a hell of a thing. Jesus Christ," he said. "Before, when I didn't have any money, I walked all the way here from Brooklyn. Now I got your two dollars in my pocket, and I feel like I should spend it wisely. I mean, I can't afford to make any mistakes because how do I know if I'm going to find another guy as nice as you. It makes me worry. Suppose Rosalee doesn't want to see me again . . ."

"What about your friends?" I asked.

"You think I like to go calling on people from Mayaguez with shit in my pants?"

"Well," I said, aware that my voice was growing unnecessarily loud with anger, "I'm not your social worker. If you want to stand here all night that's your business!"

Benny Mosca put a finger up to his lips as if to hush me. Then he smiled crookedly, "I could tell by the way you gave me that money you are a man of ethics . . ."

"Cut it out!"

"I mean," he said, disappointed that I had not been hooked by such bait, "I just thought you wouldn't mind striking up old acquaintances again . . ."

Mosca was so loathsome to my nostrils that I had to face the wind to keep from gagging. I was anxious to hurry home to my family. "Look," I told him, "I've done about all I can for you. You'll just have to make up your own mind where you're going."

"Isn't there," Benny asked, "anything I can do for you?"

"Honestly, what do you think you could do for me?"

Benny winked. "I don't know. I just thought there was something I could do." As he spoke, he deliberately passed his little pink tongue across the narrow gap between his lips, like a Third Avenue hairdresser.

The gesture was too inept not to be deliberate. "Sorry," I said, "I'm not interested ..."

"Don't get me wrong," he added, obviously taken aback by his own miscalculation. "I like girls too ... and I would clean myself up first ..."

"Just forget it, Benny," I said. I started walking west on Houston Street toward the Independent Subway.

"Remember," Benny yelled at me. "I didn't make you any promises about Hempstead or anything."

At the corner of Avenue B I felt a twinge of remorse and stopped to glance back again. Benny apparently had not made himself any promises either because he still had not moved. In the gloom of early evening he stood with his hands in his pockets, bow-legged with his own squalor. A patrolman on a scooter was cruising slowly along Houston Street. From an open window nearby somebody was playing a recording of *The First Nowell* in Spanish.

It was nearly two weeks later before I ran into Mosca a second time. I was walking through the grounds of the Lillian Wald Housing Project when I happened to notice a well-dressed Puerto Rican man hurrying by. He was wearing a fine brown topcoat I had admired only the week before in a shop window, which is why I noticed him in the first place; he wore a moss-green tyrolean hat tilted jauntily down over his forehead so that only the whites of his eyes showed through the shadows. The fellow walked with a lively step, keeping his gloved hands stuffed inside his pockets. After we had passed each other by perhaps fifteen yards, I realized that it was Benny. He had simply shaved off his mustache. While I was trying to decide whether or not to let him know I had recognized him, I heard his hoarse voice.

"Nice to see you again!"

Mosca had stopped twenty paces down along the walk. I started back toward him. "*Qué tal*, Benny . . ."

"Speak English," he said, shaking my hand.

Benny did not seem at all embarrassed for having been caught in such a display of affluence. After we shook hands, he said, "Nice . . . Yeah," he said, agreeing with himself even before I could nod my assent, "pretty faggy . . ."

He must have realized that he had chosen precisely the wrong adjective, for he said, "Not that it's like that, you understand . . . As a matter of fact, these aren't even my things. They belong to one of our young men in Vietnam."

"What do you mean?" I asked, "*Our* young men?"

"In the patriotic sense," Benny said. "Honestly. I'm not kidding." He unbuttoned his topcoat so that I could see his fancy tweed sport jacket, the candy-striped shirt underneath, the rep tie, the freshly pressed chocolate trousers. "You don't like?"

"It's very nice," I admitted. "I just hope you and your friend there will be very happy together..."

"Look," Benny said. "Cut it out! Do I seem like such a jerk I would do such a thing? Besides," he added, "as I told you, I like girls..."

Mosca was staring at me with cold gray eyes. Feeling that he had probably been convincing on that point, he said, "Anyway, it's a woman friend..."

When he saw that I was unimpressed, he added, "Now I am staying with this Irma Boldín," as if that were precisely the same thing as saying, "You are looking at Liz Taylor's new lover."

"I guess you wouldn't know this Mrs. Boldín," he added. "Maybe... you'd like to meet her. I'll introduce you if you like..."

"Well," he said, when I was still too speechless to leap at his invitation, "I don't see why not, because she is a very respectable lady..."

"Come off it," I said. "What kind of respectable lady would want a guy with shit in his pants?"

"I tell you it wasn't like that," Benny said, blushing deeply. "It wasn't anything like that . . . Look," he said, "I may have had a little something once but I got rid of it. Look at me. Do I look like that type of guy? You come along with me now. You'll see for yourself. I'll even make you a cup of coffee. Honestly," he said, "it would help out a real lot if Irma knew what kind of friends I had..."

Friends? First I was his old acquaintance, now I was his friend. I wanted to remind Benny that the sole extent of our relationship was that he still owed me two dollars. But I was beginning to sense something about him that would have made that an impossible thing to say. If I had told Benny I wasn't his friend, he would have said, "That's funny . . . because, you know, I consider you *my* friend."

On the way to Mrs. Boldín's Rivington Street flat, I tried to find the opportunity to remind Benny about my two dollars, but he was much too busy "confiding" in me.

"Confidentially," he said to me, "in Ponce Irma's family is very well known . . . big money there."

He also told me that her son Jaime—"we call him Jimmy" —had been in the trainee program at Abraham & Straus, a Brooklyn department store, until he was drafted and had to close his apartment, leaving "all the good things with his mother."

"You think Jimmy is going to miss these things where he is now?" Benny asked, stopping short.

I ignored his question, pressing him once again about how he had gotten to know Mrs. Boldín. Was she another of his *old friends* like me?

"You know how it is," Benny frowned, "one thing always leads to another . . ."

"So what led to this?"

"Blah blah blah," he said. "You ask an awful lot of questions for two dollars . . ."

"And the last time I saw you," I said, "you had shit in your pants . . ."

"Okay," Benny said, "take it easy."

Without breaking stride he immediately started to explain how he had cleaned up in the men's room of the Delancey Street subway station before departing for Orchard

Street to purchase a new pair of cotton trousers. "They cost
me ninety-five cents marked down," he boasted, "and this
man let me change in the back room for another quarter.
So then I was just walking around on Orchard Street in my
new pants, wondering what to do with only $1.25 in my
pockets, you know, stuff like that, blah blah blah, when I
see this Mrs. Boldín. She has two big shopping bags full of
groceries, and one of them has split open so that it is leak-
ing all over the sidewalks. I figured maybe she would offer
me a tip if I helped her. Holy Christ. I started putting all
her things together. We are talking. She tells me her name
is Boldín.

" 'That's a good old family,' I say, because—you know—
Spanish people like that kind of thing..."

Benny paused with his hand up to the brim of his hat, as
if he were just about to salute himself for his recent display
of acuity.

Then he said, "Honestly, I was just as surprised as you
when we got to her place and she invites me for a cup of
powdered coffee. So pretty soon," he added, smiling wist-
fully, "one thing leads to another . . . She's a little bit old,"
he concluded. "You know how it is . . . you get lonely when
you get old . . ."

"So," I said, "you really hooked something good this
time."

Benny said, "I don't want you to get the wrong idea. She's
a widow . . . she's on Welfare."

We were now standing in front of the *cuchifrito* parlor
which Mrs. Boldín lived above. "Come on up, and I'll show
you around," Benny said. "You don't have to be scared."

Climbing up the stairs Benny told me that his new mistress kept a supply of more groceries than he had ever seen in any one place.

"She could run the A&P. I bet she has two hundred cans of Campbell's Chicken Gumbo soup . . . Listen," Benny added, fumbling for a new key as he became quite animated by his own trembling response to Irma's greed, "I bet she has fifty cans of tuna. The big cans from Chicken of the Sea. Every time there is a sale Irma is out there buying. That's probably where she is now. You mustn't be too tough on her," Benny explained.

"Been on the Welfare ever since her boy turned eighteen . . . I mean," he added, "she was always on the Welfare, I suppose, but when her boy started working it turned out the little son of a bitch could show that he didn't have more than ten dollars a week to spare for his mother because he said he needed all the rest to live decent . . . over there in Brooklyn . . .

"Irma's a good-hearted woman, only that son of a bitch kid she has got is just like too many other Spanish kids from what she tells me. If he gets hurt over there it will teach him a lesson."

When the door opened, a chain lock still held it fast from the inside. "Shit," Benny exclaimed, "she must be at it again!" He gave the links a short quick karate chop, and the chain dropped. Then the door opened wide.

The flat itself was small and clean and crowded. It was little more than a cage with a bright red linoleum floor; it consisted of a tiny square kitchen with a bathroom to one side and a little alcove to the other, into which a big double bed had been jammed.

180

When the door to the flat opened, the orange light was dimmed momentarily by our shadows, and I saw a fat black cat leap off Irma Boldín's kitchen table and scamper under the bed. Benny flicked a switch on the wall, and another small light went on over the sink. The apartment brightened. Benny had not been exaggerating about the hoarding: there were stacks of canned goods in neat rows on the shelves above the sink, the stove, the tiny yellow icebox, along the opposite wall, above the bed, alongside the sink, and even along the window sill beyond the bed. Benny was clearly delighted that I was also astonished by such an array. He opened the icebox door. It was crammed with large, heavy blocks of government surplus cheese and margarine, wrapped in khaki papers—enough margarine, perhaps, to grease the wheels of the Twentieth Century Limited on a transcontinental journey.

"Come on in." He slammed the icebox door and walked back over to me. "I'll make you some soup . . ."

"I don't want any soup."

"That's right." Benny snapped his fingers together. "So I'll make you coffee . . ."

He shoved me through the open doorway.

Being in Mrs. Boldín's apartment while Benny puttered about at her stove was like sitting in some well-stocked air raid shelter deep underground during an imaginary blitz. Benny banged pots and pans, dropped things, spilled other things, yet the apartment remained a vacuum of silences. In fact, in between these barrages of clangings and bangings the room remained so quiet that one could be hypnotized just listening to the steady ticking of the large black-faced

Ingersoll clock above the icebox. At the far side of the great double bed Mrs. Boldín's one window was separated from us by a bunchy plastic shower curtain, which hung from the archway on tiny hooks. Under the front door there was a metal ratcatcher, so the darkness from the stairway was completely locked out. Sealed off inside those two small rooms, one might have been fifty fathoms beneath the sea, or perhaps inside an enormous food chest with a faulty cooling system; and all around were those stacks of canned goods.

I counted forty-six green Heinz bean labels before the kettle started to whistle, at which point Benny reached for a jar of coffee, and I started counting columns of bright yellow Niblet corn. There were cans of black and cans of green olives. There were jars of olives with pimentos and a gallon jar of maraschino cherries against one wall. Above this, myriads of Green Giants were pouring tiny *petits pois* through a sieve against a glitter of silver. Behind these lay a brickwork foundation of four-pound khaki-colored cans of surplus beef and dried milk. There were stacks of sardines in cellophane, blocks of Carnation milk, and little cornices of fruit cocktail and corned beef hash, making a crazy quilt. Almost lost against that wall was a framed photograph of Jimmy Boldín, in cap and gown, with something scribbled across the white space in Spanish. Jimmy was smirking into the vacuum as if to say, "We wouldn't display things this way at Abraham & Straus." On a little shelf above the stove an upper and a lower bridgework soaked in a glass of cloudy water; next to it a glass of chickpeas was also soaking; and on the wall itself was hung a large poster declaring: THESE

ARE THE SEVEN BASIC FOODS. Once, glancing from the face of the Quaker Oats man back to Jimmy's portrait, I mistook him for still another type of cereal. Then the room trembled as somebody overhead stamped his feet. Inside the walls, pipes groaned. A toilet was flushing like some distant Niagara. I felt certain that this one-dimensional mural (for surely, it could only be that) was about to become three-dimensional and would converge on me. Closing my eyes, I heard Benny say, "Hot java coming up." He shoved the muddy coffee across to me in a green cup and saucer from Woolworth's and then pushed across an open can of condensed milk, a spoon, the sugar bowl.

"Doesn't Irma eat anything except out of cans?" I asked.

"She likes onions . . ." Benny took the chair facing the doorway. "And candy," he added. "Only we don't keep any sweets around the house."

Benny sounded like a keeper at a zoo. I asked why not. "Irma says it brings rats," he told me, "but I figure maybe she doesn't want me to have too much . . ."

Embarrassed by his own greed, Benny added, "So here I am, all dressed up, and I don't even have a cigarette." He patted the pockets of his shirt. "You got a cigarette?"

When I gave Benny the pack, he extracted two cigarettes, stuck one in his vest pocket, and took a swallow of the sweet coffee before lighting up the other and inhaling deeply.

"Irma doesn't like me to smoke around her house. She says it's because she is afraid of fire."

"And why do you think it is?"

"What the hell?" Benny said. "I figure a woman like her gets pretty cranky sometimes. Change of life. You know.

What the hell kind of life does she have to begin with? It hasn't been any picnic. Irma's maybe forty-six or forty-seven, because you know Spanish women like to say they are younger than they really are, but I figure she must be at least that old because Jimmy was six when her husband left and he got killed in Korea . . ."

"Try and figure it," Benny said with a shrug, as the icebox started chattering. "All I know is, it wasn't any real marriage. I mean, I don't think they ever saw the priest. So first Irma collected for the kid, and now she collects for herself. If Jimmy someday doesn't strike it rich, they'll be giving her for the old age too . . . Poor Irma. I feel very sorry for that type of person. She may even be fifty because I notice she don't even menstruate any longer."

He shoved my diminished pack of cigarettes at me.

I asked, "What exactly is the point, Benny?"

"There isn't any point," he protested. "I just thought you would like to know how it is for people like Irma. She gets cranky, you see, because every time Welfare thinks Jimmy is making a little more money they are after him to do better by his mother . . . and he gets nasty and she gets cranky . . . You know what they told her a couple of years ago? She said they sent her to this school to learn how to cook and make her own clothes, and she did so good they wanted to give her a job helping other people, but she wouldn't take it. She pretended she was disturbed because she said it would mean she would have trouble getting back on again when she was older, but I think she was afraid to be away from all her goddamn cans . . .

"I mean," Benny swallowed, "I don't wish to sound cruel,

184

but Irma should have her head examined. At least I think
so . . . Like, now they are telling her they will support her
while Jimmy is away, but when he comes out of the service
she should figure on living with him. Well, I understand. I
guess she doesn't want to take any chances. You can't blame
her. Suppose Jimmy gets married? You know what I think,"
Benny's voice suddenly became a whisper, "I wouldn't be at
all surprised if she had something socked away under her
mattress, just in case . . ."

"You really think so?"

"I would bet on it," he said. Benny was standing by the
bedroom curtain.

"Cut it out," I said.

Benny stared at me in angry bewilderment for a moment
and then went back to the table and sat down. He asked for
another cigarette. "Maybe I ought to get out of here," I said.

"Sit!" Benny said.

Five minutes later we heard footsteps. *"Benny? Are you
there? What are you doing in there, Benny?"*

"Come on in, sweetie," he piped back, even as the door
was already being opened.

Irma Boldín was a tiny, thin, ugly woman, about two
shades darker than her son. She looked her age, if not older,
and she had clearly seen plenty of hard wear; she had a
sinewy face, sunken cheeks, a hairy mole on her chin, and
straight black hair that looked as if it had been hacked at
with a pair of shears. She came into the flat in an old gray
coat with big pouch pockets. A shopping bag hung from
each of her wrists. As she walked, I could hear the clanking

of canned goods. Irma's nose had the shape and texture of a Jerusalem artichoke. When she unbuttoned her coat, I saw that she was wearing what thirty-five years ago might have passed for a "frock" but was now just a clean gray rag with little pink roses scattered across it.

Seeing Benny first, Irma said, "What you been doing? . . . As if I didn't know." She wheeled about, noticing me half-hidden by her open door. Kicking the door shut, she blinked her eyes. "So? Who is this?"

"He's a friend," Benny explained. "A guy I know . . . I happen to know him. He's a guy. That's all, Irma . . ."

She dropped her packages with a heavy thud. "What right you got to do this, Benny?"

"Do what?"

"What right you got . . ." Mrs. Boldín seemed surprised by her own anger. Walking past me, she peered over my shoulder into my half-filled cup. "I'm sorry, Mister," she said. "I don't like to be a pill. If I'm not careful, this bum will get me in a lot of trouble."

"What kind of trouble?"

Mrs. Boldín ignored me, turning on Benny again, "You been job hunting?"

He nodded.

"You had lunch?"

"Tuna."

"You know how many tuna you had since you been with me?"

"I got to eat something."

"He's like a cat . . . *he gotta eat something* . . ."

Irma started to empty her coat pockets of cans of sardines and plastic packets of condensed soup. "Here," she said, "they had these for special on 14th Street. Next time you get hungry, you eat these . . ."

"Thanks, Irma." He reached for the provisions. Then Irma got a better look at his outfit, and she drew back all her goods.

"What you doing wearing Jimmy's things?" she shouted.

"Cut it out," Benny said.

"What you doing in those things?"

"Irma, you are just trying to humiliate me," Benny said. I decided that it was definitely time that I leave. Seeing me get up to go, Benny pleaded, "Stay a while!" Then he added, "Honestly, Irma, take it easy. He's just a friend . . ."

"Never mind about him. You get out of those things. They are Jimmy's . . ."

He fumbled for another cigarette. Then Benny remembered smoking was also against the house rules, and he said, "I don't think you're being very fair . . ."

"I guess I'll be going now," I said.

Mrs. Boldín said, "Why not? Just take your fancy friend with you."

"You invited him," I replied. "Besides, he hasn't got any place else to go . . ."

"Yeah," Irma Boldín said, "take it from me, he's nothing but a bum."

She hung her coat on a hook against the wall and then hoisted one of her shopping bags onto the table. It contained a case of white asparagus, but some of the cans already lacked labels and others appeared dented, flattened on their sides. When Irma located her other bag, she spilled out about a case of Puss N' Boots. Then she started to sort through her cans until she came up with a number of red and yellow cellophane-wrapped sour balls, which she would have stuffed into the pocket of her dress if Benny had not been staring at her.

"I got a canker sore anyway," she said. *"Here,"* as she threw one at Benny and another at me, popping the third into her mouth even as she was twisting it out of the cellophane. Then she said, "So long as you're here, why don't you put those things on my top shelf . . ."

"Go ahead," Benny said, "give her a hand . . ."

"Now look who is giving the orders," Irma Boldín declared.

Benny had already thrown his sourball against the roof of his mouth so that in order to answer Irma he had to bite down hard; a look of extreme pain transfigured his features. "Take it easy . . . Irma . . ."

"I'll take it easy, you bum!"

She pushed the stacks of canned goods away from my hands and shoved them at Benny. "Here," she said, "you put these on my shelves and don't touch anything, Benny, unless I say so, and when you get all finished you take off my Jimmy's things. I got your stuff clean now. Just who do you think you are, Benny? What's the idea . . . dressing like my Jimmy?"

Benny said, "You are a bitch, Irma!"

"Sponger, don't you call me such a name. Don't you think I am wise to you, you bum?"

"Come on," he said, "calm it down, Irma. I got a friend with me . . ."

She said to me, "If you're a friend of this sponge I feel sorry for you . . . whoever you are . . ."

Benny said, "When she gets angry, she don't even sound like a Spanish woman. She sounds just like a nigger . . ."

"Sponging prick," Irma replied.

What domesticities they shared! Every new curse was obviously for my benefit because they were spoken in English. I wondered what they did when I wasn't there. Did they argue in front of the cat? Was Jimmy used as their sounding board? Benny kept calling Irma "bitch," and she answered back "sponge," but they seemed so accustomed to their own malice toward each other that either probably would have been shocked if the other had suddenly said "Sweetiepie."

Benny said, "You think I give a shit about her kid's things? I was just waiting she should do my things . . ."

"Don't you worry," Irma assured me then, "he cares. Benny thinks he has got it pretty soft here. Look at the bum. Now he even invites his friends. Well, let me tell you something, Mosca. You came around, you hadn't eaten in two days and you smelled awful. I been good to you, but I don't like you taking advantage. You want something, ask. If I got I'll give you . . . and don't you go walking around in my Jimmy's things," she added, *"because who the hell is he?"*

Irma had turned herself full face toward me to make her final accusation.

Swallowing audibly, Benny said, "Don't she remind you of an angry nigger?" But he immediately flinched and ducked behind the curtain, presumably to change his clothes.

Mrs. Boldín laughed harshly: "Finish your coffee, Mister. It's a shame to waste things . . ."

"I didn't want any coffee to begin with," I said.

"If you don't eat your sour ball," she warned, "I'll have to give it to Benny..."

"So give it to him," I said, having had enough unpleasantness. Finding my coat, I started toward the door.

"You understand," Irma said, "I wouldn't want you to be angry at me for your friend..."

"I'm not angry," I said.

"You know," I added, "I'm not even sure how I got mixed up in this. I only met Benny a few days ago. He was looking for his brother..."

Mrs. Boldín asked, "Do you believe that story about Hempstead?"

From behind the curtain Benny shouted, "IT'S TRUE ABOUT HEMPSTEAD. MY BROTHER OWES ME A HUNDRED DOLLARS..."

"Crap," Mrs. Boldín said, "he never had a hundred dollars. I've known him a long time..."

"IF YOU TELL THAT TO THE WELFARE," she shouted, "YOU'LL NEVER BE ABLE TO COLLECT..."

Then she turned toward me again.

"What do you mean," I asked, "you've known him a long time?"

"A long, long time," she said. "This isn't the first time he stayed here..."

"ALL RIGHT," Benny yelled, "SO I WAS PUTTING YOU ON. THAT DON'T MEAN THAT I WAS PUTTING YOU ON ABOUT HEMPSTEAD..."

"He wanted me to pay for this Hempstead business," Irma said, "only I am not such a sucker. You want this little greaseball to go to Hempstead, Mister, you pay for him . . ."

"WHAT'S THE POINT OF GOING TO HEMP-
STEAD NOW?" Benny demanded, still behind the curtain.

She said, "Shut up, Benny!"

"*You see what I mean,*" she added, for my benefit. "And
you believed him about Hempstead. Sure he's got a brother
Ephemio, but that don't mean there's a hundred dollars
anywhere. There never was. How could you believe a little
greaseball like that?"

She turned again toward the curtain. "IF IT AIN'T
TRUE WHAT YOU SAID ABOUT HEMPSTEAD,
MR. BENNY GREASEBALL, YOU HAD BETTER
GET THE HELL OUT OF HERE!"

"*You know what he wants to do?*" she said to me. "Benny
claims he is getting these awful headaches between the eyes,
so he figures he's got a case against somebody because of
what happened that other evening when he fell into that
hole. He says he read it in the newspaper that a lot of people
are suing Con Edison so he asks me would I please give him
the money for a lawyer. WELL, I AM NOT SO STUPID
AS THAT!" She was again facing the curtain. "YOU
THINK I WANT TROUBLE WITH THE CON EDI-
SON? YOU WANT TO CAUSE TROUBLE, BENNY
MOSCA, YOU CAUSE IT SOMEPLACE ELSE BE-
CAUSE I'M IN GOOD WITH THE WELFARE NOW
AND I WANT IT SHOULD STAY THAT WAY!

"He thinks I don't know why he got all dressed up," Irma
continued in a lower voice. "It's because he went to see the
social workers. He thinks they'll give him the money. Well,

191

maybe they will and maybe they won't, but I sure won't. If I weren't on the Welfare, he wouldn't even have anything to do with me. Don't you think I know that?" Irma slapped both hands down on the table. "IF ONLY PEOPLE LIKE HIM WOULD LEAVE ME IN PEACE! . . ."

"Talk talk talk," Benny Mosca said then. "Blah blah blah." Parting the curtain, he stood before us in his own skimpy cotton trousers, barefoot and naked above the waist. "For your information, I didn't go to the social workers . . . What's the use? You would think it was a crime to try and get ahead." He was staring at Irma. "Jesus, honey, I'm hungry again. Don't be such a bitch . . ." Then he glanced at me. "Before you go . . . give me another cigarette . . ."

"You want to smoke," Irma reminded him, "go out into the hall . . ."

"Shut up!" Benny's arms and chest were covered with gooseflesh. "I'm cold," he said. "Come on. Will you give me a cigarette?"

When I threw him the remains of my pack, Benny said, "You shouldn't talk that way, Irma. The neighbors . . ." He didn't seem to want to look at me any more. In fact, he seemed quite anxious that I leave. "Before you go," he said again, still staring at Irma, "I'll take a light too . . ." I threw him the matches. "Thanks . . ." Benny gave me a quick salute of goodbye. Slamming the door, I started down the stairs. Then I heard, "Make us some soup, will you, Irma?"

Three days later Benny and I ran into each other for the last time. Again I was going to the library when I happened to see him, standing on the corner of Houston and Avenue D.

"What did I tell you?" Benny said as I came closer. "I knew if I stood here long enough, you would have to come along..."

"How long have you been here?"

"Maybe a couple of hours..."

"What's the matter?" I asked, "Did Irma throw you out?"

"I wouldn't put it that way," Benny said. "Irma's such a funny woman. She just gets very funny sometimes."

He immediately bummed a cigarette but left it dangling at one side of his mouth, not even asking for a light. When I asked Benny what he thought he would do now, he said, "There is always Rosalee..." At the thought of his former girl friend, Mosca was reminded to shake a fresh crease into his clean duck trousers. "Yes," he said, "it's got to be Rosalee ... or maybe," looking up, "I will try Ephemio after all..."

"Cut it out!"

"Holy Christ. I'm not kidding you..."

"You're clean now," I said. "Why don't you go over and try to collect Welfare?"

"What kind of life is that?" Benny replied.

Then I asked how the headaches were.

Benny winced. "Now I am sure of it. I am definitely going to Hempstead. Ephemio will take care of me because he has just got to. He is my brother. He may not have too much, but he is my brother and he will give me what he has ...

"Funny thing," Benny added. "If I went to the Welfare

and told them about these headaches, they would send me to Bellevue. Irma told me that. She says it is one of the best ways of collecting. Who wants to go to a place like Bellevue? I once ran away from Kings County, which is in Brooklyn, but it's just like Bellevue..."

"What happened?"

"It's a long story," Benny said.

"No," he said, "it's better that a guy like me goes to my own flesh and blood, Ephemio, because blood isn't like water, and he is my brother and even if he can't give me he may know of a job. Brothers are brothers. Christ," he added, "I haven't seen the little bastard in over three years . . ."

"I thought you said it was two years ago that you lent him that hundred dollars."

"Maybe it was closer to three..."

"And were you very close?"

"We didn't even have the same father . . ." Benny laughed. "We didn't even have the same father, but we slept in the same bed..."

Then he frowned. "Look, whatever your name is, I don't want to be such a son of a bitch, but maybe you can lend me a dollar for going to Hempstead?"

I did not have an extra dollar, but I told Benny I would escort him to Welfare—if that would do any good.

"What the hell," he said. "Thanks anyway."

"What about it?" I insisted.

"I had enough humiliation with Irma," Benny said.

Then he put his hand up to his head and I said quickly, "You ought to get somebody to take care of you . . ."

"I'll take fifty cents," Benny said. "What I got to do for you for fifty cents?"

I ignored the inference, asking if he would use the money to go to Hempstead. "I'll go to Hempstead," he said, "when I can get a nice job and look decent. You think I want my own brother should see me looking like such a mess?"

I asked, "Why do you want my fifty cents?"

"Don't worry," he said, "I won't waste it."

"I didn't say you were going to waste anything," I told him. "I just wanted to know if you had a plan . . ."

"I got a plan . . . If you want to know my plan, I figured on buying Rosalee and the kid some flowers . . ."

"What about Irma?"

"Are you going to give me that fifty cents?"

I gave in again. As Benny stood there clutching my last two quarters, he brought his hand up sharply to his head a third time. "I don't know . . . maybe I'll go looking for Ephemio after all . . ."

"You got a hell of a lot of nerve," I said then. "You know you're only leaving me with two dimes and a nickel for myself. There's nothing I can do for you. You know that, Benny. Why tease me?"

"You start to get all types of ideas when you have a little money in your pocket," Mosca said. He touched my wrist. "Look, I am very confused. I'm sorry. I'm just a confused type of person. I don't mean to string you along like this. Holy Christ, I even forget your name but I'm sorry . . ."

"I'm sorry too." We shook hands.

"And it really was an accident," Benny said. "I mean what happened . . . with my pants, I mean . . ."

195

"I know it was."

As I started away from him, he did a little dance step with his hands thrust into his pants pocket. "It's cold, man. You think I wouldn't like some of old Irma's soup?"

"Poor Irma," I said. "She won't have you back?"

"Why does she need me?" Benny said. "I wish she did. It would almost be worth it if I could get some of that nice hot soup."

I reminded him of the address of the shelter and then handed over the remainder of my packet of cigarettes. Benny insisted that we shake hands a second time.

"You know, I got this feeling," he said, when I had started going, "I wouldn't be at all surprised if Rosalee would be glad to see me..."

There was nothing more to say. I didn't want to turn around, and I did not care to argue with Benny. What difference would it make? If not Rosalee, there would be Irma, or Ephemio, or perhaps somebody else. Whoever took Benny in would be impoverished by him and would punish him in return. What could be done? If he went to Welfare, they would tell him to look for work. If he found a job, it might not last long enough for him to collect unemployment insurance, and afterwards he might have to go looking for a new Rosalee or Irma. Poor Benny! He wasn't overage. He had no dependent children. There was just his dependent self. Wasn't it tough luck that he was trying to make that greedy little self dependent, when everybody else was convinced it would do him "irreparable harm"?

As I turned the corner onto Avenue A, the dialogue of an early afternoon movie blared out of an apartment building, and I recalled a public service announcement I had seen the previous evening on one of the late shows. It was for a city-run antipoverty agency called JOIN. The film showed a young Negro boy walking away from one of the tenements of Harlem. Immediately there was a quick cut-away shot to that same boy in the classroom. Then it dissolved to the same boy working over a lathe somewhere. With each new edit in the montage, the boy's ragged appearance was miraculously improving, and he seemed to be acquiring a nobility and presence; the final shot was of the boy walking home, shoulders squared, garbed in an elegant top coat and a felt hat. The narrator declared with a congratulatory air that because this young man had enrolled in JOIN, his mother was no longer collecting Welfare . . .

2

ON DEPENDENCY

• Dependency is the bogeyman of the Poorhouse State. It is to be discouraged whenever possible. The dependency we find so problematical and wish to deter is that state of moral and psychological debilitation alleged to arise from the individual's reliance upon government for his sustenance; but a major characteristic of dependency in this country is that far too many potentially dependent people are forced to rely on others who are dependent because they are not permitted to poach on the state. In America the poor are still obliged to feed the poor, and the weak must bleed the weak. We say we believe in self-help, and then we encourage this peculiarly symbiotic, mutually debilitating form of parasitism through the Poorhouse State.

Perhaps when all our poor have been made dependent upon government and assured of stability and decency, liberty and justice, we will be able to worry about how they work out their psychic destinies without seeming like hypocrites. In the meantime, data that the American poor are not yet dependent accumulates.

Every one of our states administers federally funded programs of public assistance. And in every state grants for four-

person families are below the $250-a-month minimum the
federal government has defined as "poverty." This makes it
very difficult for such families to abide by the rules of their
dependencies. On January 1, 1966, the nation's public assistance population was given more money; aged, blind, and
disabled persons were granted an extra $2.50 a month each,
and needy children were boosted $1.25 a month. But in-
creasing inflation, attributable in part to the Vietnamese
war, left the recipients no better off than before in those
states which elected to take advantage of such increases.

And then there are all the Americans who have never
quite made public assistance to begin with. Some states still
refuse to make unemployed male heads of families eligible
for federal assistance programs, which means that they are
left with three options: they can desert so that their wives
can benefit, they can accept substantially lower payments
under General Assistance (Home Relief), or they can accept programs of work relief, often verging on peonage.
These men are not yet likely to see their long-term dependencies as much of a problem. Some states and localities
offer no programs of cash assistance to such men or to unattached persons. If they are now dependent on anybody at all,
it is on their friends or on the Salvation Army. How apt we
are at encouraging initiative and self-reliance among the
poor even as we subsidize the stock-market speculator with
guaranteed cost-plus government contracts.

One of the most curious dependencies created by our
Poorhouse State is that which exists among the various
bureaucracies that attempt to govern it. This is a dependency to which the caseload *en masse* has never been ad-

mitted. If one were to graph the arrangement of power within such a hierarchy of public agencies and private contracting institutions, there would be the eight million clients at the bottom and the amorphous Department of Health, Education and Welfare at the pinnacle; but altitude within such a hierarchy does not always mean power. Power resides in those who deal with the client. The behavior of the Welfare caseworker in the isolation of Watts or Chicago's South Side is likely to have far more effect on the life of the client than the beliefs of the highly placed Washington official. HEW may propose and even devise new programs, but states will have to adopt them, localities must implement them, and sorely pressed human beings must administer them. Just so long as they are not being discriminatory *per se*, these coalitions of interests will encourage administrators to be as generous or as niggardly as together they see fit. These bureaucracies will find the means to exclude applicants as long as they are not being systematically exclusionary in violation of constitutional guarantees (which might provoke litigation).

From Washington the representatives of HEW's Bureau of Family Services will continue to publish their brochures describing how families on public assistance should be treated, even as they are driven by their own dependency on state and local officials to try—behind closed doors—to cozen these officials into being a little less harsh on "their" poor.

Thus, we maintain a Welfare system in which the federal government provides incentives for the states to play out their idiosyncratic bigotries against the poor; and then we attempt to rectify the matter by offering further incentives so that these states will substitute "rehabilitative" for punitive programs. Occasionally, though, HEW may actually try to police the behavior of local agencies, which must attempt to be somewhat responsible to federal policies because they are dependent upon federal matching funds. But such scrutiny will have to rely on information supplied by the agencies of the state in question. What is likely to happen? The agency may either attempt to conceal or it may endeavor to frame its responses so that they seem to be in accord with what it assumes are HEW's prejudices. When a Welfare agency is found niggardly or exclusionary, HEW is likely to be informed that there are insufficient numbers of trained personnel. Because bureaucracies at all levels seem equally anxious to proliferate themselves, the federal government will then attempt to frame new programs to provide incentives for increasing the size, payment, and training of staff. But not all the problems of the Poorhouse State are remediable by improving personnel standards. When poor and wealthy states alike passed "suitable home laws" to disqualify many thousands of Negro Welfare clients, even HEW was quick to recognize that these acts were political in character; and HEW Secretary Robert Fleming wrote a directive requiring that no agency invoke such laws unless it provided alternative forms of care for the children whose parents were excluded from benefits.

Fundamentally, the effectiveness of HEW as a policing agency is dependent on the information provided to it by the states. The "suitable home law" states openly boasted of their policies; they could be disciplined. When the behavior of local officials is not so well publicized or when an agency has attempted to conceal its practices, HEW's abilities to police Poorhouse State abuses are limited. The U.S. Commissioner of Welfare has lamented, "No state program for the needy is so broad as to permit it to receive all of the federal funds that it could claim if it took advantage of all the public welfare provisions of the Social Security Acts,"[1] which would seem to indicate that the method of offering incentives to rich and poor states is founded on basic political disagreements within these states, although politics will prohibit such an official from drawing that inference. On the pretext of determining compliance with new legislation or to permit it to acquire the information to propose that legislation, HEW will conduct surveys in the field; and here again it will usually be dependent on the local agency to supply it with data, and it will usually go no further down the line than the administrative echelons of that agency. If such legislation is deemed in the interests of the local community, its agencies may respond with appropriate candor. If, however, the ultimate findings of HEW are likely to prove controversial, there may be general collusion among all the interested parties to obscure them, on the theory that public welfare is in such disrepute that it would serve nobody—except perhaps the clients—to publicize reports that reflect to the discredit of the welfare system.

A noteworthy example of this was a recent HEW survey entitled *Operation Big City*, which was published in Oc-

[1] Foreword by Commissioner Ellen Winston to *A Constructive Public Welfare Program*, Department of Health, Education and Welfare, Washington, D.C., revised September, 1965.

tober, 1965, and not released until the following February. It purported to inquire into the typical "effectiveness" of public welfare agencies in urban America in dealing with the special problems of the urban poor. One agency in each of the six major geographical sections of the country was surveyed. After inspecting the activities of the Poorhouse State in Los Angeles, Cleveland, Philadelphia, Atlanta, Minneapolis, and New Orleans, even HEW was forced to conclude that these agencies were somewhat less than effective:

> Federal and State eligibility requirements exclude a substantial portion of needy persons from significant help.

> Certain legal and fiscal limitations handicap city agencies in meeting such emergencies as eviction and lack of food.

> The most serious gap in resources for meeting emergency need in urban communities is that of financial help.

> Determination of the eligibility of public assistance clients accounts for most of the work load of agency workers.

When I telephoned Washington for a copy of *Operation Big City*, after reading a three-inch report buried on the obituary page of the *New York Times*, a rather edgy public information officer insisted that I also have a copy of the HEW pamphlet, *A Constructive Public Welfare Program*, so that I would be able to put the information "in better perspective." The latter is an amusing document. Among other things, we read that federal incentive programs are to be used by states and communities "in dealing with juvenile delinquency, chronic unemployment, family breakdown, neglect and exploitation of children and aged people and other social problems," but also that "the poor are as trustworthy as other people." Less than a week after the issuance of *Operation Big City* some confirmation of its findings for New York were found in an anonymous *New York Times* report of interviews with a group of unnamed Welfare caseworkers in Harlem.[2]

The workers told the *Times*, "My clients are afraid to tell me anything for fear it might affect their eligibility. They are just plain suspicious, and I don't blame them."

At fault was the rigidity of many department rules, they insisted. One said: "When there are delays in checks or clothes allowances, or when I can't get them what they want because of procedure, who do they hate? The Commissioner? My supervisor? No. Me they hate."

Effectiveness is, of course, a rather curious criterion to use in connection with a public assistance program. Effective at what? Effective to do what? The findings released by HEW made it clear to me that somebody thought they were being extremely effective in humiliating and victimizing the poor; *Operation Big City*, of course, tries to paint a fresher complexion on its own blushes. As usual, the report expresses HEW's desire to eliminate stress and alleviate some of the demands on hard-pressed workers as well as HEW's yearning to provide better services for clients; it calls for "rehabilitation" and an examination of the client's "total situation" even as it makes it abundantly clear that the clients' total situation is poverty.

2 *New York Times*, February 22, 1966.

But despite such pettifoggery the report on *Operation Big City* is a revealing document. By observing reception facilities and procedures, policies for the giving of emergency assistance, complaints procedures, and public information policies in these six American cities, the HEW staff could not but stumble on a good deal of curious behavior. No attempt was made to interview clients outside the setting of Welfare offices and the chief form of investigation was a kind of supervised physical inspection, along with a review of agency publications, policies, and case records. It seems clear that the HEW staff relied heavily on interviews with the interested state and local parties and that it did not—considering the delicate relationship that exists among the local, state, and federal governments—make any attempt to inspect Welfare premises or procedures without the knowledge of these functionaries. Despite all this, close study of the neutral bureaucratese in the report of *Operation Big City* reveals a pattern of contempt for people on public assistance that manifests itself in insufficient, inadequate, and grudging services.

Two of the six cities closed their doors to needy clients whenever they felt they had reached a capacity intake, telling people to come back the next day, or perhaps the next.

In four of the cities surveyed a single office served the Welfare population of the entire county, creating "long and expensive" travel for some; and two of these cities had reception rooms described as "bare" and "drab."

In only one city were special facilities provided for women with children waiting to apply for assistance.

And although Welfare workers are uniformly described

in the report as "understanding" and "concerned" about the needs of their clients (by what standards?), the investigators found delays in completing applications in half the cities and "insufficient exploration prior to denial" in half the cities. In half the cities the attitudes of the staff members (described as "good," but again, by what standards?) were "largely found to be focusing on determination of eligibility to the exclusion of adequate consideration of family need and circumstances"; and in some of these cities "applicants were . . . being required to assume too much responsibility for substantiating their own eligibility" by having to prepare lists and collect documents attesting to their lack of resources.

Operation Big City tells of delays of up to half a day for mothers with young children awaiting their preliminary interview for assistance. Only three agencies provided emergency assistance through agency funds, while others generally referred such indigents to shelters or voluntary groups such as the Salvation Army. In most of the cities surveyed general assistance (Home Relief) contained stringent limitations on eligibility and demonstrably lower schedules of benefits than the federal programs. One of the chief conclusions is that "Employables, whether employed or unemployed, and non-residents" as well as "other special groups . . . that vary by locality" are excluded from benefits in every one of these cities.

The staff of HEW caught very few of the dynamics of Welfare intake, application, and referral procedures, but some details impinged upon the consciousness of the observers and, although played down, they were noted.

One office was located in a basement room that could be reached only through a side exit down a flight of thirteen narrow winding steps on which there had been many accidents.

In two offices women were observed attempting to answer intricate eligibility questions while managing several small children at the same time.

Of the untrained receptionists who are given the job of initially screening clients, it is reported that "Generally they do not make decisions," but the report then goes on to state that they were given the leeway to "determine what the person wants . . . to secure identifying information . . . and make routine referrals to other community agencies" (e.g., Salvation Army).

In two of the agencies clients were screened by "contact interviewers," and only then were they given an appointment to apply for assistance. In one agency the applicant had to pass before four different professionals during his processing.

In four of the agencies, the elapsed time between screening and formal application varied from a low of three days to as much as four to six weeks.

In three cities checks were commonly withheld "because the agency was not satisfied with efforts the woman was making to locate her husband from whom she was separated or until an applicant located and got the putative father into the office for an interview."

In one agency it took more than sixty days for an applicant to receive a payment and at least that much time to be notified that he was not to receive payments.

In another agency clients could be denied assistance when they applied if they provided "insufficient information"; or they might be given one-time-only grants, after which their cases would be closed. Assistance at the same agency was routinely denied whenever there was felt to be a "loss of contact" between a client and his investigator.

In one agency, eligibility for relief could be determined only on the basis of proof of physical disability of two months' duration ("makes it extremely hard to help alcoholics," HEW noted). In still another agency, when a case was closed through an allegation of "unreported income," a penalty was applied against the former recipient whereby his "unreported income" would be prorated against his potential assistance payments during the penalty period until such time as he was again deemed eligible. In a third city, AFDC mothers were regularly required to wait six months from the date of separation from their spouses before they were made eligible.

None of the agencies maintained twenty-four-hour service for those in financial need.

In one or more of the agencies (number unspecified by HEW), no legal service for clients was available.

Among the deterrent practices observed by HEW were what I will call the "forty-eight-hour stall" and the "coyness ploy." At some agencies clients were to be deterred by being informed that if found presumptively eligible, they would have to wait forty-eight hours for a grant of emergency assistance. At one agency the receptionist was instructed not to volunteer information about cash assistance. At the close of each contact she was simply to inquire, "Do you have any questions?" or "Is there anything you want to ask?"

HEW found that all the agencies said they were anxious to hear and process complaints. Although in general there were frequent expressions of dissatisfaction about eligibility rulings or the amount of assistance granted (as well as complaints from outsiders that the clients were cheating, neglecting their children, had unpaid bills, or were not eligible), three of the agencies surveyed maintained no records of complaints; others refused to honor any complaints made ten days after a ruling; still another, which maintained a special information officer to deal with complaints, had handled only fifty-one formal interviews of complaining clients in all of 1964. Two of the agencies also reported that they "do not make administrative use" of the complaints received.

Can so many routinized indignities be attributed merely to high turnover and "serious staff shortages," as they are in

Operation Big City? It would seem that HEW has missed the point of its own evidence. It is not because these agencies have insufficient and poorly trained staffs that clients must wait four to six weeks for their initial checks, but because such agencies consistently make sure that personnel will be used for purposes other than making certain that checks are mailed out on time. The fact that clients are not always given emergency assistance is also not a matter of inadequate staffing. It has to do with the way the Poorhouse State administrator has been made to view his function, which is to be responsible to everybody—every special interest group—except that represented by his own caseload. It is because workers are compelled to question clients in extraordinary detail before they will presume need that so much of their time is spent in establishing eligibility. It is because clients fear, distrust, resent, and despise the functionaries, as representatives of an alien and hostile social order, that so few complaints are made through official channels. "Within the modern relatively democratic state," the sociologist George Simmel once aptly pointed out, "public assistance is perhaps the only branch of administration in which the interested parties have no participation."

There are numerous reasons why clients are apathetic about their rights and why discretion is left untrammeled within the Poorhouse State, but the most fundamental reason is simply that it is in nobody's interest that it be otherwise. The professional has an investment in his skills and is not likely to wish to turn himself into a check-writing machine. Only the poor want an effective Welfare program when that comes to mean, as inevitably it must, more dependency. When HEW speaks of effectiveness, it preaches a mealy-mouthed rehabilitation; when local agencies address themselves to the problem, it usually means new devices for deterrence. A recent HEW pamphlet invites the citizen to inquire into the adequacies of his local public welfare program, as if it were in the interests of the man with $6,000 a year to wish to pay more taxes so that Welfare recipients will get larger budgets. But our belief in individual achievement is still so strong that it is next to impossible to convince such people that it is in their interests to do something about Welfare; they are still close enough to poverty themselves to wish to preserve the distinction. Try to tell such a man about the deprivations of the poor and he will tell you about his own deprivations. And with justice! In the richest country in the world, his poverty is likely to seem just as relative as that of the pauper. How else can one explain why no pressure has mounted in any American cities (including New York) to make efforts—in the midst of a War on Poverty—to recruit all those eligible for Welfare who have not yet been enfranchised?

Our dominant assumptions about citizenship in the Poorhouse State is that if a person is "getting along" (whatever that may mean) without assistance, he should continue to get along unassisted. Thus New York City regularly approves Welfare budgets that bear no relationship to the numbers or needs of its paupers because they are merely a series of educated guesses based upon past budgets, which were probably also inadequate; and, as I pointed out earlier, the New York City Welfare Department is not terribly anxious to enfranchise even those people for whom it is already responsible with additional cash benefits. It tends to want to provide them with services that, hopefully, will make them less dependent, and it has received certain incentives from HEW to do precisely these things. Seventy-five percent of the costs of rehabilitation programs are reimbursed by the federal government; up to 75 percent of the share in salaries for trained personnel are also reimbursed. Consequently, Welfare agencies tend to demonstrate their prudence by increasing their number of service programs, for which somebody else is paying the bill, at the expense of their clients' cash needs. Or they plan imaginative reorganizations of their services with those of other public agencies which may make them more efficient but not necessarily more generous. If a given caseload can be diagnosed as 62 percent "mentally disturbed,"[3] it somehow alleviates our guilt that it may also be undernourished. But one sympathetic Welfare official in New York discreetly reported to a friend of mine that as much as 30 percent of the caseload was being underbudgeted—a remarkable rehabilitative device for the emotionally disturbed—and I have reason to believe that this estimate may be low. A private social

[3] On February 23, 1966, the New York Times reported that one New York City hospital, for example, was using registered nurses as amateur psychiatrists; they talked to patients about the causes of their physical complaints and were thereby cutting the number of readmissions by 80 percent, speeding recoveries, and making them last. Although the patients at Montefiore hospital were also being given medical treatment, one official was quoted as saying, "When they learn how to problem-solve on their own, they don't have to get sick." The Montefiore program, as described in the Times, appeared to be an honest attempt to heal and help, but the principle established could lead to some rather bizarre consequences elsewhere. Its underlying theory is that many people "get sick because of their inability to cope with their lives."

worker on the Lower East Side told me that practically every one of his clients was underbudgeted "if you include all the special grants they are not getting . . . If all my clients were to receive adequate winter clothing at the same time," this worker confessed, "there would be havoc at DW."

The budgeting problem is so endemic to the operation of our assistance programs that it has become their most salient feature. Obscurantism and niggardliness create underbudgeting, which creates the dependency that so obsesses Welfare officials that they are prone to characterize their caseload in terms of its squalor. In slum neighborhoods independent social workers find themselves giving handouts to supplement Welfare payments. One agency spends as much as $600 a month at one tiny storefront center, providing a dole of its own to those who are not let on the official dole or who are chronically underbudgeted. In all the slums of New York there are aggressive workers who are forced to spend many hours of every day cajoling and coercing reluctant Welfare officials into giving out petty grants, which the Department refuses to treat as entitlements. Their efforts still affect only a small minority of the caseloads; and it is at least questionable whether such efforts do anything more than transfer the dependency from the public worker to the private worker. But given the obduracy of the Welfare system, such efforts are probably unavoidable. The dominant attitude among taxpayers' alliances seems to be that if people are not getting all they should, it is because they do not know how to ask or have failed to interact successfully with their caseworkers, which, I suspect, may be like saying sometimes that the Southern Negro does not know how to interact with the white sheriff. At the Lower Manhattan Welfare Center I once asked five women in a row, as they left the building, if they had ever received itemized budgets from their workers. Only one had, and that, a veteran Welfare worker assured me after examining it closely, was grossly underscaled.

If the wish to alleviate some of the demands placed on workers were in the interests of those in Welfare administration, they would certainly carry out a more vigorous educational campaign among Welfare recipients. HEW could prepare radio and television spots informing people of their rights to public assistance; local administrators could prepare simplified charts to be displayed in Welfare Centers advising people in dollars and cents about their entitlements. The fact that nobody is advertising among the poor to give them public assistance means that the poor must come and beg for assistance when they are ill-informed and easily exploited. It means, too, that many will be easily deterred by their desire not to be humiliated. The largest single category of recipients is, of course, women with minor dependents, but a not inconsiderable category consists of employed fathers whose earnings are simply insufficient for the needs of their large families, but nobody interrupts the lovely blare of *pachangas* on New York's three Spanish-language radio stations to inform the city's 800,000 Puerto Ricans, for example, who form such a significant portion of the potential recipients, that they can receive assistance; and many who qualify for it still do not get it. These men also seem to evade our scrutiny when we try to characterize dependency, for they are not victims of any misfortune but economic inequality, and their chief ill is that they are employable, but only at the minimum wage, or, if they work in industries that offer part-time, seasonal, or casual employment, at weekly wages that are less than the minimum. These men receive supplementary financial assistance from the Department of Welfare whenever it can be established that their budgetary deficits are larger than $5.00 a month. There are, however, some peculiar disadvantages to such a form of supplementation. The eligibility levels have been scaled so that many do not receive cash but surplus foods. Others may simply get special "one-shot" grants for services they cannot afford to purchase, i.e., clothes and dental care. Even those men who are given cash do not receive their grants as a matter of course. They must be investigated and reinvestigated. Once in three months they are required to produce payroll receipts, and they are budgeted and supplemented on the basis of these receipts. In the meantime they must either learn to make do on their present deficits by credit-buying or seek other means of income, which, if detected, disqualifies them from Supplementation.

When we dream up the next ambitious scheme for rehabilitating the Welfare Poor, it would be chastening to remember that there are such men among them and that their chief disability is only that they work hard and get paid little.

In any Welfare neighborhood the Poorhouse State creates the dependencies it purports to find distressing; its policies generate the numerous Welfare grocers who are also unwitting victims of the dependencies of the clients. Tiny entrepreneurs, whose dusty storefronts echo the deprivations of their surroundings, are such men more or less dependent than their customers? To the Poorhouse State the credit buying of the client is an improvidence not to be countenanced. The victim of such a policy is often not the client but his grocer. Such men can exist only by extending credit to their customers, who have no basis for credit except their Welfare statuses. When the customer defaults, the grocer cannot always be reimbursed by Welfare. In the end, he must place his faith in his customers' good intentions. If he charges too much or becomes too clamorous about all the unpaid bills, he must expect to be deserted for one of his numerous equally hard-pressed competitors. I have seen such men wrangling in the corridors of the Welfare office over the bills of their defaulting customers. Usually they remain solvent by keeping their stores open seven days a week and as much as fourteen hours a day. Even then, some of them barely manage to pay off their jobbers.

This is the backlash of wretchedness imposed by those income-maintenance policies designed to encourage individual initiative and incentive. I know of three such men whose wives must still be supplemented by Welfare. To get by, such grocers must stock a little bit of everything—canned goods, dairy, vegetables, meat, delicatessen—but rarely can they find the cash to keep up adequate inventories of anything. Many are abused and hated by the very people they serve, and in the course of the day's business they will hate and abuse their customers in turn. According to those who uphold the virtues of slum living, such entrepreneurs perform a vital communal function, which, I suppose, they do. But at what expense to themselves and to their lives! Barely above the Welfare level themselves, they compete with the supermarkets by operating a charge account business in a bad-risk neighborhood; and they also have to compete with their neighbors, who are not much bigger than themselves. As they wait to be repaid a few dollars at a time, they continue to be relieved of their merchandise at approximately the same rate of demand, so the shelves grow barer as the due bills increase.

Antonio Ubas has been the owner of one such *bodega* on Clinton Street for the past six years. In all that time he has still not managed to sell off any of the huge pyramid of canisters of kosher salt that were in his store windows the day he gave $150.00 key money to its former occupant, Mr. Alex Colmar. Antonio has a wife and two children. He lives in a project, considers himself a good manager, and is generally well liked in the neighborhood. To his kosher salt display he quickly added the standard array of Puerto Rican delicacies—chick peas, guava shells, nonalcoholic malt beers, and tamarind juice—and then he ran leaders on such items as rat poison and cockroach powders, which are also staples among the urban poor; but he has never yet been able to do as much business on the register as he can usually show in his little black book. Antonio's is that kind of tiny, close establishment, a storefront deep, with shelves going up to the ceiling. The place gives off a deep, rich smell, and you feel you could reach up with his wooden pole hook and pull down exquisite delicacies. Not so! Paying $80.00 a month rent and $20.00 more for his telephone and utilities, Antonio has been in such a tight squeeze over the past six years that most of his top shelves are still crowded with old Mr. Colmar's dusty boxes of Quaker Oats and Oxydol.

As he puts it, "You build up a lot of credit and you hope that people will start repaying you so you can buy more goods and sell more. Sometimes they just don't. It's hard. I'm not complaining. Some of these people have it worse than me, but it's hard...

"When a person comes in and it's not the first time, he don't ask permission," Antonio continued, explaining the rules by which he must do business. "He will take this. He will say he wants something like that. Then he will say, 'Write it down!' Well, Macy's can write it down and the Welfare will say okay, because they have people who make up the bills and it looks good, but all I have is this little book. How do they know whether I am telling the truth? If I say it's not all right to such a person, she will only go to the place down the street, and then maybe when she has a little money she won't come back here. I give people what they want . . . and all month long they give me back a little at a time. It's not so nice because sometimes I can't do that with my jobbers. It just seems like I have to be here for these people, and they are sometimes very inconsiderate. They run up a big bill . . . maybe $25.00 . . . and then they disappear.

"Well, if you go to Welfare about such a person they will say, 'It is your own fault, for being so greedy. We give such people such cash so they should buy with cash. If you want to take risks with people like that it is your own fault.'"

It hardly seems fair to call Antonio Ubas a greedy person.

Once, a few days before Thanksgiving, I was talking to him when Brownleaf came into the store. Brownleaf nodded to me with the blind side of his face and then went over to browse among the shelves, as if in some lending library.

"Watch this," Antonio winked at me.

When Brownleaf showed up at the counter, he unburdened himself of a large can of turkey, two small cans of cranberries, a frozen turkey TV dinner, a loaf of bread, a bottle of hard cider, and four bananas. Antonio wrote up each item on his pad and added up the total, which came to $2.59, but he wouldn't put anything into the bag.

"And two packs of Salems," Brownleaf added then.

Antonio stared down at his fists which were digging into the sticky counter.

"I'd like those cigarettes," Brownleaf said.

Antonio smiled. "I don't even know your name . . ."

"You know me," Brownleaf said. "My wife is here all the time . . ."

"I don't know you," Antonio insisted. "Tell me your name."

"Come on," Brownleaf said. "You know me."

"What's your name, Mister?"

Brownleaf said, "Are you being funny?"

Antonio did not act as if he were being funny. He was putting all the groceries away under his counter.

"Holy shit," Brownleaf said. "You want me to spell it out? It's Brownleaf—B. .r. .o. .w. .n. .l. .e. .a. .f. ."

"I still don't know that name," Antonio said. "Are you sure I know your lady?"

"You know her. She comes in all the time with the kids."

"You got to do better than that. A lot of people do that."
Antonio was smirking as he put the purchases into a bag
and handed them across the counter to Brownleaf.

"What about my Salems?"

"I don't like people to go hungry," Antonio smiled. "But
I don't see why they got to smoke . . . I don't smoke . . ."

Brownleaf said, "Cocksucker," and he went out the door
with the package in his hands.

"So that's what I am," Antonio said. He found a page
marked Brownleaf in his little book and wrote down $3.00
next to the date.

I asked, "What was all that about?"

"What do you want me to do?" Antonio exclaimed.
"Call the police?

"I know that guy. Sure," he added, "he and his wife . . .
they're coming in here all the time just like he says. Look
at this!" He showed me the page in his ledger with a long
column of scribbles on it. Brownleaf seemed to owe at least
$20.00. "He knows I know him. Sure," Antonio said then,
slamming his book shut. "We just play this little game
sometimes. It's just a little thing he's got with me . . ."

"An expensive thing," I said.

"*That?*" Antonio was blushing. "He doesn't mind that.
He's a pretty good guy most of the time and he pays his
bills. It's just that I've got to take care of my customers
and so they've got to pay a little extra for the service."

"So you two knew each other all the time?"

"You don't understand anything," Antonio said, turning
back to his book.

Antonio Ubas is a small, plump, fair-skinned little man
with shiny black curly hair and soft brown eyes. He always

wears a clean white shirt with sleeves rolled up to the elbows, and his arms are firm and thick but hairless. If Antonio were not so plump, he would be handsome, like his fifteen-year-old son Dickie, who is sometimes pressed into helping out in the store. One Jewish holiday, when school was out, I stayed with them from 8:00 A.M. until closing time to keep a log of the day's business. Here are my notes.

7:51 A.M.: I arrive. Store open. Dickie loading milk in fridge. Antonio sweeping.

8:35 A.M.: Antonio sends Dickie for three containers sweet coffee. First customer arrives. Young bohemian girl in slacks. Buys milk, a box of chocolate doughnuts, Kents. Pays cash.

8:40 A.M.: Man buys Luckies, cash.

8:42 A.M.: Woman buys three oranges, a pound of margarine, a pack of frankfurters, and cigarettes. Asks for credit. Dickie comes back with coffee as Antonio is writing down purchases. Woman is reminded that she needs coffee. Antonio grinds a pound of beans. Woman says, "That's a nice smell."

8:51 A.M.: Boy buys toothbrush, chocolate milk. Pays cash.

9:03 A.M.: Bill collector buys cigarettes. Woman with three children gives Antonio a slip of paper with a big order. They seem to know each other well. She asks if he will send Dickie with the packages. Dickie, who is playing with her kids, looks up frowning but agrees to go. Antonio puts slip with order next to register, asks if she will pay. She hands him $5.00, which he pockets. "I owed you this. Now I'll have to owe you some more."

9:35 A.M.: Antonio completes order, sends Dickie with

delivery. Total sale: $6.75. He writes it in the book and then subtracts $4.75. "I want to be able to give Dickie something for his trouble," he explains. Woman comes in, buys sugar. Pays cash.

10:03 A.M.: Antonio is putting away the rest of the milk when Dickie returns. He asks, "Was she all right?"

"I got a dime," Dickie says.

Antonio throws him a quarter. "For school!" He smiles at his son warmly.

Dickie says, "I think that man is back with her—"

"She better watch out," Antonio says. "I can't carry her like that last time."

10:37 A.M.: Antonio has been telling me about his army service in Korea, which he enjoyed, he claimed, because it gave him a chance to see a lot of things.

Dickie is reading *El Diario*, looks up, says, "Tell him about Japan."

Then a customer walks in, Spanish-speaking, asks for Drāno. Antonio hasn't got it. Offers to send Dickie down the block. Woman shrugs, walks out. Antonio writes down Drāno on a pad next to register and then starts adding up due bills. Man in work clothes comes in, obviously a friend. He and Antonio chatter together in Spanish. Dickie asks if he can take a break. Man goes to counter. Orders a half-pound of bacon, bread, eggs, a chocolate bar, and a large bottle of orange soda. Pays cash—$2.15.

"She got her check today. She'll pay what she owes," the man says in English as he leaves.

11:07 A.M.: No business at all. Antonio working on due bills. Beer truck arrives. Dickie goes to unload cases. De-

livery man buys a pack of Camels and some gum, hands
Antonio an invoice, which he signs.

"Tomorrow I will have it," he tells the man, who says,
"I won't be back until next Monday."

11:23 A.M.: Dickie putting away beer. Goes to lunch. No
business for half an hour. Then a sudden flurry: Spanish-
speaking woman buys can of beef stew (charges); boy buys
rice, can of spaghetti, bread, and a jar of peanut butter
(charges $1.39). Boy also wants cigarettes. Antonio says no
because he is under age. Negro man buys a large bottle of
beer. Pays cash. Fast-speaking woman gives large order in
Spanish for bread, milk, rice, beans, fishsticks, condensed
milk, teabags, sugar, half pound of butter, hot chocolate,
three tomato soups, a pound of hamburger, box of Tide; she
says she wants to charge everything, and she adds bananas,
Brillo pads, and another container of milk; but when Antonio says no, she finds $3.00, which he pockets, and then
he lets her charge the rest. Other women waiting. One
wants soap. One wants chocolate doughnuts. Both cash.
Delivery man arrives with soda. Antonio asks, "Where the
hell is Dickie?"

1:00 P.M.: Dickie has returned. Still busy. Mostly school
children. They each buy a different can for lunch . . . corned
beef hash, spaghetti, beef stew, baked beans. One kid insists on Franco-American. Antonio doesn't think he has any.
Too busy to make sure in the back room. Six children, six
different credit sales . . . total $1.46. Antonio sends Dickie
out for more coffee, eats a banana and a Drake's cake. Offers me some.

2:15 P.M.: Very, very slow. Antonio turns on radio. We

listen to news in Spanish, then he switches and we listen to English-language news. Bohemian girl wants Gauloises. Antonio hasn't got any. Woman buys Tampax and toothpaste. Friend of Dickie's drops by. They go for a walk. Creamery truck arrives. Antonio waiting on customer with thick Jewish accent, wants *Yartzeit* candle. Antonio hasn't got. Creamery man presents bill for $25.00. Antonio looks in the register, gives $15.00 on account. Policeman comes by. They chat about a certain Mr. Box, whom I don't know. Maybe Antonio's landlord? Woman buys Ivory soap, a can of chick peas, a roll of toilet paper. Pays cash. Man buys Mars bar, flips dime against counter. Antonio all out of pennies. I volunteer to go next door . . .

2:50 P.M.: I have come back to busy store. Children buying ice cream; women buying potatoes and chopped meat, onions, fishsticks, detergents. Children pay cash— $.60. Women pay cash—$3.05 and $2.55, but one woman realizes she must charge—$4.50. Afterwards Antonio looks in book. He is very angry! Woman now owes $32.00. Dickie comes back.

"Where the hell you been?"

Dickie shows father that he has bought *El Diario*. Antonio smiles, sends Dickie with order to Mrs. Cabeza.

"Be sure you collect!"

He takes a bag of potato chips and offers me some. I buy a bottle of coke for each of us—$.20 cash sale. Antonio waits on Negro man who wants link sausages and half a dozen eggs. Pays cash—$1.02. Dickie comes back with $9.00. Antonio gives him another quarter. Pleased, Dickie starts to sweep up. Antonio yawns. Man buys Winstons. Woman buys English muffins. Antonio grinds coffee and tells Dickie to take it home to wife.

He says, "You got the rest of the day off. Take your sister to a show."

Dickie runs away. Antonio yawns again. Goes to back of store. Calls a number. His wife? They are talking in Spanish.

Antonio comes back. "You think this is interesting?"

I try to duck his question. Customer walks in wearing big heavy coat. Asks for Carbona. Antonio hasn't got. I look at watch. 4:15 . . .

6:03 P.M.: Very slow. One woman wanting fish balls for cash. A man to whom Antonio won't sell. Mrs. Ubas comes with stew for Antonio's dinner in double boiler. She says children all went to movies. She is going to see her sister. Will Antonio stay open late? He shrugs, starts to eat dinner. Wife wishes me good night. Dark outside now. Man comes in to buy milk. Pays cash. Woman wants a lemon and a bottle of Clorox. Antonio won't charge. Woman puts back Clorox but buys lemon with cash.

Antonio says, "She is a terrible woman."

Won't tell me why. Antonio's sister-in-law calls. Could he lend her a few dollars tomorrow? He says he will give it to his wife in the morning, but she mustn't come to the store. Man wants to know if Antonio can cash Welfare check for $39.00. Antonio hasn't got enough in register. Offers to hold the check and lend him $15.00 on account until tomorrow, when he will give him the rest.

Man says, "You give me $20.00 and the rest is for my wife's bill."

Antonio smiles and looks into register. It's a deal. He

hands man $20.00 in singles from register and sticks check in pocket. Only two or three bills now in register. Antonio marks off $19.00 from man's account. Still plenty more on the bill. Man breaks bill to buy Luckies . . .

7:19 P.M.: Very, very slow. Kid wanting correct time. Woman pays for phone call. Buys milk and a square of cream cheese. Antonio's supper cold. Empties out double boiler. Says he has heartburn. Asks if I would go next door for tea. As I leave, he turns on radio again . . .

7:30 P.M.: Antonio too busy to say thank you when I return with tea. Radio blaring. Spanish-speaking man with big order: rice, beans, sardines, anchovies, eggs, bread, canned tomatoes, olive oil, Malamar cookies, Ajax, canned peaches, pineapple cubes, milk, and frankfurters. Also thinks of buying guava shells but decides no when Antonio gives him price. Pays cash—$9.15.

8:05 P.M.: Antonio and I have been talking about all the airplane crashes lately when Drāno woman comes back. She has Welfare check for $55.00. Can Antonio cash? He tells her he hasn't got. She becomes angry. Curses. Leaves store. Antonio picks up *El Diario*. His eyes are a little bloodshot, and it looks as if somebody has just dabbed shoe polish underneath the lower lids. I go to get a sandwich . . .

9:12 P.M.: Come back to Antonio's store. Door open. Lights on. No Antonio. Finally he appears from back carrying heavy case marked "Franco-American."

"I just knew I had some . . ."

Sweating and panting, he tears open the case, puts all the cans on the shelf, and asks me to throw the cardboard box in the can outside.

"Any more business?"

"A woman with a nosebleed," Antonio smiles. "I sold her Kleenex."

9:36 P.M.: I feel as if I have been here forever. Antonio is very silent. I don't think he has much patience with my hanging around, although he seemed pleased at first. He asks me when I intend to leave, and I say whenever he closes down.

Antonio says, "Won't be long now."

He opens up the register and starts to count his money. There is not too much to count, but he knows he has a few dollars in his pocket. Three teenagers come in. Antonio slams register. Boys want cigarettes. Antonio sells a pack of Camels and a pack of Kools for cash. Third boy buys cupcakes. Cash.

Antonio sings *"En mi corazón . . ."* as he goes back to register.

Spanish-speaking man comes in. Very timid. Looks over at me once as he talks, and Antonio finally sells him large box Kotex—man pays cash.

"No me burlas," Antonio starts singing again.

Woman enters store. Buys milk and Easy-Off. Pays cash.

Antonio asks, "You new around here?"

"I just moved in."

She buys cockroach powder and a stick of gum. Goes out and then comes back in. She lives across the street. Her name is Helen Dugan. She needs a bed.

"Where is a good place to buy a bed?"

Welfare gave her the money, but they didn't tell her where to go. Antonio says he doesn't know but he will ask his wife if she will come back tomorrow.

She says, "Why not? I live right across the street."

10:45 P.M.: I am getting very groggy. Antonio also seems to be feeling the strain. Once I catch him dozing against the counter. At 10:15, a phone call. A woman wants him to deliver. Antonio says he can't. At 10:25 teenagers. Cigarettes again. A man buys a pound of coffee. A man in work clothes buys cigarettes and a Mounds bar. Another man comes into store.

Antonio says, "I've been waiting for you."

Man hands him check. Antonio takes out book, crosses out column of figures. Writes down balance: $14.00. Goes to register and gives man five singles.

Man says, "My wife will be in tomorrow for a big order."

Antonio nods sleepily. Man breaks single to buy Kents. Antonio goes to center of store and pulls switch on one light. Starts sweeping up, but won't lock door. Man drops by. Shows Antonio paper.

"No," he adds, "I don't know of such a family."

Man buys cigarettes and leaves.

Antonio says, "I bet he's from the Welfare . . ."

Negro woman comes in. Buys a can of tuna, a jar of mayonnaise, some onions, and a bar of chocolate Halvah. Pays cash—$1.25.

Antonio says, "Don't you want bread?"

When she doesn't answer, he goes to empty out register. Man comes in. Doesn't seem to know what he wants. Walks from shelf to shelf.

"I'm closing," Antonio says.

Man has hands in pockets. Antonio repeats that he is closing, in Spanish. Man comes over to counter. Buys a loaf of bread. Pays cash. Fat man comes in. Has Antonio got fresh ham?

"I'm closing," he says.

Man buys a pound of frankfurters. Wants to charge. Antonio asks for name and address. Man lives right above store. Produces Welfare card. Antonio okays sale but copies down serial number in book. Man then buys cigarettes and orange soda.

When he leaves Antonio says, "Now I'm really closing." Bolts front door.

"I hope you know why you stayed here," he says, "because I don't."

I offer to buy him a beer but he says that he is just too tired. I buy a pack of cigarettes. Antonio wants me to pay wholesale. We argue. I look at my watch. It's 11:27 . . .

By working nearly a hundred hours a week Antonio Ubas is likely to gross in the neighborhood of $1,400 a month, from which he will net about $350 to $400. About one in ten dollars will go directly to his pocket so he won't have to report them to the government. As much as 20 percent more of his business will consist of credit, on which he will charge a small premium, probably no greater than the inflationary trend. Antonio will carry his people just so long as they continue to pay him back every couple of weeks, and his jobbers will endeavor to carry him in the same way. Twice monthly he will need large sums of cash on hand to redeem Welfare checks that will be proffered as partial repayment on bills. In 1964 he filed a federal income tax return showing $4,160 gross income on which he paid $450 in taxes. There were also state taxes and licensing fees amounting to perhaps $100. He sent $10 a month to his mother in Puerto Rico and supported his family on a budget of approximately $55 weekly, which he earned at a rate of less than $1.00 per hour. Antonio has GI life insurance worth $10,000 and a small savings account, which is used to pay taxes and licensing fees, to forestall creditors in a pinch, or to cash Welfare checks. In any week his margin of profit is usually the few extra pennies he can wring out of his clients through credit. This tends to make his attitude toward people on Welfare somewhat ambivalent. On the one hand, he recognizes with a certain bitterness that some people are not working yet are doing nearly as well as he. On the other hand, he sees that his chief *raison d'être* at present is to provide a service that the larger stores refuse to provide. The following morning, after my visit, Antonio was at work by 8:00 A.M. I didn't arrive until 11:00. He looked a little tired but was in good spirits. His sister-in-law's husband had just found work through the State Employment.

"That's a load off my back," he smiled, and began to thumb his way through the pages of his ledger.

It was a school day. Dickie would not be coming to help out. He was going to close early because he wanted to take his wife shopping. How early was early? Antonio scratched his head. He explained that he wasn't quite sure when he would actually be able to close down. This guy owed him a lot of money and he had just gotten his check, but he was in the Bronx and would be there all day. Antonio would just have to wait until the man got downtown after suppertime.

3

MANNY GELDER: SLUMLORD

• Manny Gelder is big in the chest but stands only five feet two inches tall. In elevator shoes he would look as if somebody had sawed off his legs from the knees down. Short and stocky, Manny walks with a stiff-legged strut, and his face is usually tinged with a deep angry blush, but he is a shy man. At the end of World War II he weighed ninety-one pounds. Now he weighs a hundred and fifty, and he looks like he has on too many sweaters. None of Manny's suits look like they quite fit, and he is usually careless about being neatly dressed. At forty-six he has neither wife nor child. Gelder inhabits a residence hotel on Riverside Drive and spends weekends with his uncle in Rockville Center. Within the chivalric order of slumlordship he is a very minor vassal. He owns two buildings on the Lower East Side, both nearly a hundred years old; they are separated by many blocks of slums, which explains why Manny's face is always red as he runs back and forth from one to the other, attending to his business.

Tenements are often sold at approximately five times the rent roll, and Manny has a combined rent roll of nearly $10,000. On paper, then, he is one-twentieth along the way to being a millionaire—if only somebody would buy his buildings. If his tenements were adjoining, Manny could sell them as a "parcel" to a speculator. If they were even on the same block, he might be able to trade with another adjoining landlord, adding on a little cash as a bonus if necessary. But, like so much slum real estate, Manny's two buildings are distinct infestations; they are so desolated by age, decay, misuse, negligence, his own greed, and the shoddiness of their original construction that about all Manny can do with his buildings is milk them regularly for their rents, move the tenants in and let them move out again (hoping that others will come to take their places), keep his overhead down, and wait to be bought out one at a time, picked off, as it were, by one of the larger realms of slumlordship that are constantly amalgamating along the Lower East Side.

This does not mean that Manny could not do a lot more if he were an altruist. But how many of us are altruists? How many of us own slum property? If we did, how many of us would be so altruistic that we would redecorate all the apartments, put toilets in the flats, install copper plumbing, pipe in rock-wool insulation, put up storm sashes, or, even better, "run a bulldozer through the *dreck* and then wait for somebody else to do something with the empty lots?"

"But then," Manny could always point out with solemnity, "where would my tenants live?"

When Manny said this to the judge who gave him a suspended sentence for trying to bribe a buildings inspector, he was perhaps being a bit disingenuous, but there was some truth to his statement. It was not exactly true that Manny felt sorry for the man when he told him to buy himself a suit of clothes—that was not altruism but a combination of fear and greed—but Manny was not far off the mark in insisting that if he could not afford to be an altruist, his tenants could not afford for him to be one either. The fact was that Manny's tenants lived in his buildings because they could not pay the rent anyplace else. So the extent of Manny's altruism was that he and his tenants needed each other: Manny made his living solely from his tenements, and the tenants were given their shelter solely by people like Manny. What kinds of options could either party have under such an arrangement? It was not quite right to call it altruism, but it was true to say that they were as dependent on each other as shoe and foot. If Manny charged the maximum rent for the minimum service the law allowed, most of his tenants could not honestly complain—they did not pay the rent. And Welfare, which did pay the rent, did not care to complain either—so long as none of the money was going to the tenants. Besides, Manny was also prepared to be obliging to his tenants whenever the law insisted that he be; and he was just as happy to pay off a Welfare inspector to insure that a tenant would be allowed to move into one of his buildings as he was to pay off the building inspector to forestall his summons for violations.

"I don't say I'm an angel," Manny told the judge. "What do you think I got for tenants?"

But while it was true that he was spreading it on rather thick, there was fact supporting his fictionalizing. Manny knew that he was the only kind of person fit to do this kind of work. If there were no more poverty and no more tenements, there would be no more Mannys. But what else could a man like him do if he were not a slumlord? In 1946, when he came to this country, it was already too late for Manny to go into any other business. At his Uncle Harry's urging he borrowed $2,000 and bought his first tenement. Living very cheaply, Manny was able to repay the bulk of Harry's loan in less than two years. Then, with another loan of $3,250, Manny bought his second property. (He eventually paid back his uncle with restitution payments from the German government.) But neither tenement proved to be such a good investment that Harry wanted to encourage his nephew to buy still another. He now calls Manny's buildings "crap," and more and more he has urged his nephew "to get out from under that crap" and invest his capital in second mortgages. Manny just will not listen to his uncle. He says he does not want to be dependent on him again and that he doesn't have so much capital that he wouldn't be; but the fact is that Manny is afraid that he would have nothing to do. Nobody makes him offers. He is afraid that some of the bigger slumlords are waiting to starve him out, so he cuts corners and tries all the harder to make his "crap" pay. After taxes Manny is usually able to chisel between $4,500 and $5,000 a year, but he cannot chisel on his mortgages (on which he still owes $3,000), and the judge said that he had no right to chisel on his landlordly obligations and fined him $500. Manny paid the money gladly enough. He was not so badly off that he could not raise $500, but he knew he was not such a "success story" that he deserved "that kind of a fine." After his appearance in court he went back to his tenements and decided he would stick it out a while longer. As he put it, "It's a hard life when you got nothing to do. You don't get nothing for nothing . . . only this way I got a little chance . . . a little something . . ."

Or so Manny thought until his larger building went out

on rent strike.[1] Manny did not like it, but he *shmeared* a little here and a little there and, in the end, grudgingly attended to his violations under a court order. But the strikers only discovered more violations, and Manny had to take out a small second mortgage on his other tenement to pay for the repairs. Since then Manny has been deathly afraid that both of his buildings will strike at the same time, leaving him so destitute that he would have to default to the city. This fear has bred a certain paranoia in Manny and has confused him about who his adversaries really are. Sometimes he claims that the politicians are afraid of the Negroes, and at other times he maintains that they are stirring Negroes up for their own political gains. By Negroes Manny means anybody who lives in his buildings, whether black or white, English- or Spanish-speaking. Manny does not discriminate. He has the class hatred of a radical and the social attitudes of a conservative. He believes that all politicians are whores and all bureaucrats are their tools. He believes that the Negroes have been more sinned against than sinning, but he also believes that he has been sinned against more than anybody else.

"Look at me. I pay taxes just like everybody else. I even pay Welfare . . . Take a good look at me," Manny will insist, "because you are looking at the man who has been twice a victim. All the tenants will say is what they want, and I'm paying income taxes, real estate taxes, sales taxes. I even pay a special tax on the hotel room. So look how I'm treated . . . It's because there is only one of me," Manny insists, "and

[1] In New York City courts have held that tenants may withhold their rent from the landlord and may pay rent either to the court or to an escrow fund pending correction of alleged violations by the landlord.

there are so many of them. Sure, there are just too many of them. They got all the votes."

Manny usually whispers such accusations, but sometimes he does not, and sometimes he will be aware that there is more than a scintilla of truth to what he is saying. Of his sixteen tenants, nine are collecting Welfare. Without Manny's taxes it would be harder for the city to maintain them in Manny's buildings. But it is certainly just as true that without Welfare it would be more difficult for Manny to find tenants. Renting to Welfare tenants is risky because the Department of Welfare will not cosign his leases, so when a tenant defaults, Manny is usually unable to collect his rents. Such a risk is compensated, however, by the fact that few people other than Welfare clients would live in such quarters. Of his seven tenants not on Welfare, two are old ladies on Social Security; the third, an elderly Albanian man, gets his rent free for helping out as super and handy-man. Of the rest Manny says, "I don't want to know their business so long as they pay the rent." And Manny has always refused to allow himself to feel ashamed about such a livelihood. Succinctly, he will point out, "If they want low-income housing, that's what I got. Where else do you find anything like this in the City of New York?"

Where else indeed! Once again, there is a great deal of truth to Manny's flagrant assertions. Some of his tenants are paying less rent than they would pay in a project and much less than they might pay in some of the "renovated" tene-ments. One of Manny's three-room railroad flats recently rented for $36 a month. How much can a landlord be ex-pected to provide for that kind of rent? Manny's tenants get very little of anything; they can expect to be without

heat or hot water at least one week in every month while his
workman struggles over the furnace; there are no lights in
the hallways, the refrigerators are converted iceboxes, and
the pilot lights on the stoves leak gas. When the heat comes
up his houses chatter. In the evening the lights are the color
of American cheese because of the faulty wiring. The flats
are tiny and stifling in summer. The views are appalling, un-
collected garbage heaps that support a population of rats.
The toilets are always backing up; if one does flush, the
whole house groans as if some giant were choking on his
phlegm. When it rains, the plaster sweats. Then it dries and
flakes all over the rooms. In the past Manny's tenants have
committed numerous acts of vandalism. They have passed
out from overdoses of narcotics in his hallways, pawned his
mailboxes, and defecated along his stairs. Manny is no
longer upset by such occurrences.

Manny knows he could get more money if he furnished
the apartments, but he says, "I don't want to tie up my
money in garbage . . . and that's what it would be." Once
he dreamed of a tenement empire, but now, faced with rent
strikes and rising expenses, he has come to accept a more
limited ambition. He would like to be a better landlord to
the tenants "if it would pay," but "blood from a stone is
impossible."

Poor Manny! Poor stone! Listen as he talks about his
tenants.

"It's not that they don't know how to live, they just don't
care. If I were them, maybe I would be that way too, but I'm
not them. Why should I be? You think they are so sweet
and nice? If I ran a different type building people would be
nicer. Who would ever give me for such a building?"

Manny once had an option to buy a better tenement on 3rd Street, but he did not buy it. He put the money in mutual funds and hoped the market would go up. When former Mayor Wagner announced a campaign against rats, Manny's tenants sent him a dead rat in a package. Since John Lindsay took over, Manny is becoming more and more paranoid. He thinks that some of the crusades against slum-lords are anti-Semitic, a possibility that he does not seem to mind, but he is also very bitter about the treatment he receives from building inspectors and social workers. The former hold him up for a lot of money. He claims not to know what the latter want, but he believes that they put the tenants up to sending him the rat.

When Manny is asked how much he must pay off each month in bribes, he will say he is not a rich man; then he will tell how he almost had a chance to get rich once, about ten years ago, when a well-known "action" painter was living on the top floor of his Ridge Street tenement, and Manny had to take forty canvases in lieu of back rent. Then he considered himself lucky in unloading the canvases for $500, but now they sell for more than $10,000 apiece.

Manny says he is not bitter because, "it was never meant that I should be an art collector," but he is not so forgiving about his treatment at the hands of the social workers. "Who the hell they think they are?" Manny will demand just as soon as Mobilization for Youth is mentioned. Then he will say, "They don't like how I run things, let them buy the buildings and see how they like it." But when you ask Manny for a price, he will snap, "Don't be so funny!"

"What I got? What am I going to do?" Manny will

declare, but he will never let you pin him down to a price. "I'm all alone," he'll say. "There is nobody on my side."

Sometimes one gets the feeling that Manny must tell himself these things as he climbs up the dark stairs to collect his rents. Other landlords can get loans to rehabilitate their properties, but nobody wants to rehabilitate Manny's *dreck*. If he gives up now, perhaps some speculator will grab his buildings for a song. Manny knows that under current rent control laws the only way he can raise the rent is to move his tenants out, but he cannot be sure that he will get new tenants. He tells himself that if there were no Welfare, he would have no tenants, but he also hates Welfare every time a check is delayed and he has to go climbing up the stairs to dun one of his sullen, squalid tenants. Manny says, "I make more home visits than the social workers, and you wouldn't want to see some of the things I see."

Not too long ago one of Manny's tenants dropped a garbage can down on him as he came up the stairs, and he had to stay in the hospital overnight; but Manny refused to press charges when the woman swore she thought he was her Welfare worker. "You got to expect such things," Manny said, although he had the woman evicted as soon as he could when she failed to pay her rent the next month. Then the apartment lay vacant a month and a half, and he had to pay $20 to the inspectors before the new woman would move in with her children; but Manny got an increase from the Rent Control Board that pushed the rent up. Even though he is now convinced that his buildings are not worth anything, Manny still likes to multiply his rent rolls.

4

BREAKING THE CIRCLE

● These interviews were conducted at a single-room occupancy hotel on Manhattan's Upper Broadway during the 1965 mayoralty campaign. The area is heavily populated by narcotics addicts, many of whom have been placed there in hotel rooms by the Department of Welfare. Republican Liberal John Lindsay had just promised to initiate programs to "break the dependency circle." His Conservative opponent, William F. Buckley, had announced that he wished to set up quarantine camps for Welfare recipients. When the candidate of the regular Democratic party, Abraham Beame, proposed raising Welfare benefits, I asked some of the residents how they thought they would vote—if they voted.

● PRIMITIVO: "I don't vote. My wife collects, but I don't get any of it. I don't get anything at all for myself. So when I hear this stuff, I say to myself, 'They are all liars!' If they gave me something for myself, I wouldn't have to take from my wife. Why should I complain? My wife lives with her parents, but at least they feed my family when I go away. I have been away like that three times. Three times I come back and there is trouble.

"The man says, 'You must not let your husband have the money to do such things.'

"Then I see she has life inside her, and I am very angry. How can women be such pigs while their husbands are away?

"When a man goes away, maybe they ought to put his wife in a camp like that man says. It would help. But you can't put men in camps like that. It would be like the Tombs [City Jail]. They would only cause trouble.

"On the Welfare there are two kinds of junkies. Many just say it's time to get Welfare, but they only take something once in a while. Others are taking a rest from their habits. You can't support a habit on Welfare, but you have enough for something if you are ever desperate. Of course, many of the children see the grown men and they learn from them, and there isn't much anybody can do. Kids need Welfare. I wouldn't be surprised if there were more junkie kids than adults. Maybe they ought to have camps for them if their parents are on Welfare . . .

"One reason why you don't find more grown men on the Welfare is because of the hospitals. No junkie wants to go to the hospital because it's worse than prison. There is no sentence. So when a man has a habit, he looks for friends or he steals. Everybody knows that. It's only the men taking a rest from their habits who you see on the Welfare. I think people down there know this because they will try to leave you alone . . . if you don't have children. If you got a family, they think they got to worry about your kids. I think they are just two-faced because if they really worried about the kids, they would give the fathers more money. I think people should worry about the single men, too, because they get on and then they're off again . . . just like their habits."

• PHILLY: "I won't vote for the Jew [Beame]. We just had a Jew—Wagner [The former Mayor of New York is a Roman Catholic]—and he didn't do anybody any good. But it really doesn't matter what I say because I don't live here permanent and I can't vote.

"My real name is Marcus. I'm from South Philadelphia, so everybody here calls me Philly. In New York I never collected Welfare except once, during the strike, when they said they would give everybody $2.50, but I did for a long time in LA, and once in Butte, Montana, they gave me a job. Also in Saskatchewan—that's in Canada—I got a little help in between jobs. When they saw I wasn't one of them, they sent me back across the border.

"In Canada everybody gets a little something from the government. Babies . . . old people. It's nice, I think—if you're a Canadian. But it isn't that much. And they don't have the same kind of people in Canada. Here you give everybody a little something, and we would all end up on the nod. How do I know? If you've been around here, you understand, that's all . . . and I also know myself a little. If I thought the Welfare would give me enough to keep me happy, I'd be the first man on the line, and I would know how to handle the social workers because they can't be that bad. But it just doesn't work out that way. So when I got to go to the Welfare next time, I will ask for the bus fare to go to Camden. My mother lives there, and she can't say no to her oldest boy. Don't ask me what I will do now because I will only have to say, 'I don't know.' "

• LENOX: "Once I thought that I would break my habit, so I went to the Welfare, and they were nice as toast. They put me in a rooming house in Harlem, and the man would come to visit me every day. He would see how I was getting on. He told me to keep your door locked and don't go out unless you're hungry. He didn't tell me that place was a junk shop. Everybody there was shooting up. So when it got just too bad for me, I tried to get to know some of my neighbors . . . and that's when I got busted the first time . . .

"This guy who says we should all live together in camps, he really would like to cause a lot of trouble, I think, because that's just the way it was in Harlem when I got busted that time . . . and that's just the way we live now. Don't kid yourself. A man comes to this place, he's in trouble . . ."

• BINDER: "I don't think it's right . . . a Jew for Mayor. There are too many other people in the City of New York. My parents voted Republican, and I will too because Lindsay has a nice face and you feel you can trust him. A politician should have the right image.

"If I would tell you who I was, you would say he's kidding. A man from his background, you would say it couldn't be. I tell you it's not easy for a man like me. You ask somebody to do you a favor, and he looks at you like what kind of business is this. Well, I'm not the first, and I won't be the last. I was born in Hartford, Connecticut, and my father knew Abe Ribicoff, but he never voted for him. I don't see why not. Abe has a nicer face than Beame. But in Hartford you had to watch your step. I had an aunt who went to school with Sophie Tucker . . .

"I am letting you bother me because you look like a nice Jewish boy, but, to tell you the truth, I would let you bother me anyway because you never can tell when it will lead to something. You want to know something? Once Joe Louis the prize fighter gave me $10. It was in front of the Madison Square Garden. He came to see the wrestling, and I recognized him immediately.

" 'You got to help me, champ,' I said.

"He was nicer than a lot of people. He gave me ten dollars. Maybe he was drunk . . .

"Once I was drunk, and I lost all my money, and the man at Welfare sent me to the HIAS [a Jewish charity]. A lot of refugees there . . . it wasn't too nice. So now whenever I go to Welfare and they ask me what I am, I say, 'It's a free country!' I know my rights. If I don't have anything, they have to do something for me.

"Once I went to see Cardinal Spellman, and this young priest gave me some money. I told this Irish friend what happened. He said, 'Spellman is a Jew.' Well, I don't believe that, do you?

"A man on Welfare should get what he needs, and they should put him with a good family who will help him. Likewise with a junkie. You never heard of any Yids who are junkies . . . I think that's because junkies can be terrible anti-Semites. In Chicago we had a guy could only speak Jewish. All his family were dead in Europe. He was the saddest man I ever knew . . . and he took the stuff . . . but nobody liked to make from a connection for him because they said they couldn't trust him. I'm happy I was never that way. A lot of people will help you if you're a decent person, but a junkie is a lost cause. You could lock the door and throw the key away, and who would care? I wouldn't give the junkies anything, but I would give it to the drinkers . . ."

• ROSE: "I don't vote. I don't have time. Down here there are two types of women. Some are busy and some are not. The lazy ones don't mind if a man is on Welfare. Others do because it spoils the rest of their trade. If a woman goes with men from Welfare, she is usually a gypsy or a Puerto Rican who says she is a gypsy. Some Puerto Rican women are also of the higher class, but they are mostly Negroes or people like me. My father was Polish and my mother said she was English. A man once told me he thought I had Irish blood. It's possible. When I was on Welfare, I said I was from Texas. Actually, I was born in Greenpoint. But nobody ever bothered to check up because I would never stay on that long. For a couple weeks maybe it was fine. Then I would run into somebody, and it would seem very stupid. If a woman could stay on Welfare and have a little trade at the same time, it wouldn't be so bad. Nobody is going to let you do a thing like that. All they got to hear is you got men and you are finished. Seems they don't mind you giving it away, but they don't like you to make a profit."

• PHYLLIS: "Why should I care what any of the politicians say? They're not talking about anybody I know. My mother used to get the Welfare, and she raised her children decent. She was a pretty woman. I think she still is. You would really like my mother. Most men do. And she got Welfare all the time we were growing up. She was very high-spirited, and sometimes it could be a drag. I don't think her company liked it one bit. I mean, we would be entertaining people, just for sport, and maybe it would be three in the morning. Then the Welfare would come around. Finally, she got so disgusted that she took a job in this laundry . . . and she's still there. Well, I didn't want that to happen to me, so here I am . . . I have a little sister too. I don't know what will happen with her, but I don't think she will ever take Welfare."

• AWILDA: "If you ask me, Welfare is for women who don't have too much brains. A smart woman knows how to get along. I have been here now sixteen months, and I've never had any trouble, so even if I could get it, I don't think I would take it because I am doing all right just as I am.

"Let me tell you what it was like in PR. If you went to bed with the worker, you took a big chance because how did you know what he would say afterwards? And if you went to bed with just anybody, it was equally bad because how did you know how some of those *jibarros* lived at home?

"Here I am sure it is very different. You get to tell a bird by his droppings and a good date by the way he looks. I don't know Beame, but Buckley is like a woman.

"These monkeys around here, even some of them know how to dress, but when you ask them, they are all on the Welfare, and you just can't trust them. If you fuck one of them, their wives are sure to find out.

"Next thing you know, you are in the hospital. I get a lot of people on Welfare just the same, and I don't give credit. How else will they get what they need?

"Why do you ask me if I am all alone? Here I am, but I got a sister in Queens. Once she helped me. Now I am helping her because she just lost her unemployment. She worked two years in the brassiere factory, and they only let her keep the unemployment ten weeks. Yes. They took it away from her. Her husband says they do it all the time. They don't like you to have more than ten weeks. They give. Then they start asking questions.

"They will say, 'Looking for work?' Or they'll say, 'Step over here a minute.'

"With my sister they took her out of the line and gave her a little book to read. They told her to bring them lists of all the places . . . where she went to look for work.

"My sister didn't think it was such a necessity, so when the man asked her next time, she said, 'I can't remember.'

" 'Why do you tell me such things?' he says.

"He was very angry with her. Now he is holding her check until she brings him those lists. I told her don't be a silly monkey because she should look in the yellow pages and put her finger on some names. The people in the factories don't know one of us from the next. They won't care. My sister's husband says it's a good idea, but my sister says she just can't do a thing like that. A lot of things she can't do . . . my sister. That's why I have to pay her bills."

• PETERS: "Once I knew a man," Peters claimed, "with a ten pound note in his pocket. He kept it there all the time.

Every time we went somewhere Henry Renfrew would say,
'I am terribly sorry that all I have is this ten-pound note.'
Henry never had to pay for anything . . ."

Peters is a West Indian. He is plainly rather impressed
with his putative friend, has a mouthful of gold teeth and is
always eating something. Juicy plums in a paper napkin,
hard boiled eggs, egg rolls in waxed paper, steaming golden
chicken legs, hot Sabrett franks with mustard and sauer-
kraut, chocolate fudgies, orange pop, Skybars. Peters eats
like a bird—he is a perambulatory eater, always on the move.
Up and down Broadway he goes, stopping here for one thing
and there for another. One sometimes gets the feeling from
watching him that by the time he has swallowed a particular
morsel, it has already been consumed, so he has that terribly empty feeling in his stomach and has just got to fill
himself up again. Peters has big white eyes and hair the
color of pencil lead. He is in his early fifties.

For more than five years I have watched Peters every Friday evening when I go to 96th Street and Broadway to buy a
weekly magazine. After a while we began to nod at one another. Then we started to utter sounds.

"What time is it?"

"Have you got the time? Nice out . . ."

"It's very nice . . ."

"Read about the plane crash?"

Peters would be chewing away at some grimy scrap of
food or sipping hot chocolate from a paper cup, breathing
with a fine alimentary mist. Once I asked the news vendor
with the crooked fingers about him, and he said, "Don't
mind him. He's a liar . . . West Indian . . ."

On the night of my visit to the hotel Peters entered the lobby just as I was about to leave. For five dollars he was more than anxious to talk:

"I've been around the world four times, and when I don't like a man I tell him, 'You stink on ice! You even make the ice stink! You stink on ice!' That's just the way I feel about all these people in politics. For the last five years I have had this physical ailment. They say I can still do light office work, which is just fine with me, but they don't say how I am to get light office work. Do they tell Cuban refugees that? They don't tell that to some of the younger men. In this hotel there are Cubans and Hungarians, and there are even two Africans who are getting Welfare from somebody ... maybe the FBI ... because they don't do a stitch of work. Stuck-up! They sit in their rooms all day reading. Nobody ever tells them to do light office work because they're Africans. I think I have as much chance to do light office work as you have of sleeping with the Queen. I was examined by three doctors—one Italian and two Jews—and they all said I have this physical ailment. They said I would feel better if I did light office work, but now they're telling me I'm not totally disabled and they want to train me—at my age. I'm fifty-two or fifty-three. Nobody tells the Africans to do a thing like that, and they are not that much younger than me. I think it's because they're Africans. Politics ... I'm an American citizen, so they can't send me back. They could send back those Africans. Why do I keep mentioning them? Because somebody is keeping them, I don't know who, and we're citizens and look what we get. One of those Africans doesn't even speak English. They read all the best newspapers and they smoke a lot and they have women. I hate Africans. They're stuck up . . .

"When we were in Dakar, Senegal, I saw a man drink a whole bottle of Martinique rum. When he got through, all he did was fart. He was an African. I don't see you can trust those people. They drink a lot of coffee and they don't seem to eat much, and they're always up there talking. That's why I come here. If I were on the Welfare board, I would say take care of your own first. Let the Africans worry about their own. Also I would get rid of restaurant allowances. I can't stand cafeterias. I like a little bit of a lot of different things. Well, that's very hard to do on what I get.

"Another good idea is if we could have charge accounts in some places . . . not just the grocery stores. Another good idea—I would think—is recreational. They ought to have parties. Why do people have to look like death warmed over just because they are on Welfare? I told those people on 31st Street by the time you find something for me, I'll be dead. I told them you stink on dry ice. I don't have faith in anybody. That's my trouble . . .

"When I first got on Welfare I had a dog. A friend give me him because he was being sent to an institution. He said he was a very valuable species. Looked like a terrier. So I was on the restaurant allowance, and there wasn't too much I could do for the dog. Then I met this woman, and she had a cat, and we used to go up to Harlem together once a month, when they gave out the surplus foods. We'd take along a big shopping bag and go from garbage can to garbage can. Pretty soon I would have enough canned meat and cheese to last for the whole month. It was such a waste. Those people wouldn't even bother to open the stuff. It would go right to the garbage can. My dog got to like the rolled oats, which I would make into a mush with powdered milk and water. Then somebody . . . I never knew who . . . fed her some leftovers from a certain cafeteria and she got sick and died . . .

"So, you see, there's an awful lot of wasting going on, and if I were Lindsay I would do something about that. It doesn't seem right that the government should buy from the farmers and give to these people and five minutes later it's in the garbage cans, and when I wanted to get some for my dog so I wouldn't have to go up to Harlem like that they said I couldn't because I was on the restaurant allowance. Maybe people don't like the surplus foods because they don't think it tastes right, but my dog liked them . . . She liked the canned meat. She liked the oats. She liked the cheese. And it was better for her than the stuff at that cafeteria . . ."

5

JORGE

• Whoever designed the Vla-
deck Houses probably had a slightly higher opinion of the
poor than most public housing officials do today. Although
they were one of the first large-scale projects built along the
Lower East Side, they still seem to do honor to the trade
unionist after whom they were named. Located between
Henry and Water Streets, in a section of the Lower East
Side where restored town houses and crumbling tenements
are dwarfed by the sameness of the many new high-rise co-
operatives, Vladeck is a pleasant, parklike place to encounter
in New York's longest-running slum. None of these brown-
ish brick buildings are more than six stories high. They are
laid out among aisles of fine plane trees, so the scale between
the flat land and the rise of the adjacent buildings is not so
bleak and inhuman. Between the various buildings the walks
are terraced in a series of steps leading up and down through
the courtyards of the project. There are stone benches along
these walks and stone tables with chessboards, and you can
walk to the top floors of Vladeck through a glass-windowed
staircase with a fine view of the terraces below, the aisles of
plane trees, the sepia flow of the East River. There are
1,771 apartments in Vladeck, some still occupied by the

original Italian and Jewish site tenants—and even some of their children—who moved in shortly after construction was completed in 1940. In terms of the affluent society they are those who "never made it," but if they were once bitter, they are probably now consoled by their surroundings. On fine days you can see them seated on their benches, squinting up at the weak sun, or perhaps walking singly or in pairs to the community centers nearby, bundled up in their greatcoats like little timid sparrows. Toward the river side of Vladeck there are some new middle-income co-operatives at least three times as high, but there are no trees or bushes around them. I have often wondered what the "upwardly mobile" residents of these new cooperatives must think of their "immobile" Vladeck neighbors, who, from the point of view of shelter at least, occupy much more hos-pitable surroundings.

Considering the prevailing attitudes toward the new poor, who are not believed so deserving as the residents of Vla-deck, it is difficult to imagine New York ever again building such pleasant accommodations as Vladeck was clearly in-tended to be, nearly thirty years ago.[1] For one thing, these low buildings with elegant casement windows do not make maximum use of the space allotted to them. Then, too, one feels that the men who designed Vladeck hoped that some-body they knew, perhaps their parents, would want to live in such humble but pleasant residences; but with our new poor refusing to be humble, Housing Authority officials are be-

[1] At this writing, legislation to ease the chronic shortage of low-income housing with federal subsidies so that our poor can find accommodations in middle-income housing has barely been funded.

coming increasingly concerned about "standards" for "the proper operation of projects." Vladeck is one of the numerous memorials along the Lower East Side to a time when at least some men refused to regard the poor as individual pathologies to be interned in bleak, jail-like structures rising high off the ground and then expelled back into the slums whenever some functionary decided that they seemed to represent a "clear and present danger to their neighbors." But in recent years even Vladeck's serene surroundings have felt the pressures of accommodating a new population. As more and more of the older tenants have moved away or died, many of their replacements have been large, poverty-stricken, somewhat disoriented families of Negroes and Puerto Ricans.

I stopped in front of the Henry Street entrance to Vladeck Houses one day last winter. I was with a social worker friend employed by an uptown agency, who was on the way to see Mrs. Inez Maldonado. Her oldest son, Jorge, had been arrested for fighting. She was being evicted. My friend had known the Maldonados when they lived uptown. He had heard of their trouble and had come downtown to convince Mrs. Maldonado to see a friendly attorney—to argue her case before the Housing Authority's Tenant Review Board; but he told me that the lawyer thought it extremely unlikely that Mrs. Maldonado would win. Housing Authority tenants do not have the rights of ordinary lessees. They live from month to month in their apartments and can be evicted without their landlord ever appearing before a judge. The Tenant Review Board was planning to consider Mrs. Maldonado's case in less than a week. There wasn't much time to frame appropriate responses to such informally presented charges as "flagrant disregard for the rights of others" or "improper and execrable conduct."

After my social worker friend, Hy Solovei, had showed me the complaint letter, he said, "I suppose I should be angry at those clowns down there. They're good people. They're just doing their jobs. I'm angry at Mrs. Maldonado. You never get to see these people until the last possible minute, and then they expect miracles." Hy seemed very bitter.

When Christmas comes to the Lower East Side, it is gloomy by four o'clock in the afternoon. On the day we visited Mrs. Maldonado, it had snowed in the morning. By mid-afternoon the air was a grimy, smoky gray. Walking under the brickwork arches of the Williamsburg Bridge, Hy blew out billows of frost like a chain-smoker, while he told me about a Christmas party held further uptown at one of the well-to-do churches at which all the children were given mittens, toys, and—oddly enough—flashlights.

It was nearly five o'clock when we got to Vladeck, and the air was a deep, smoky blue. Hundreds of dark-skinned children—some dressed in snowsuits—were still racing among the buildings, flashing their puny beams of light up at the sky. A hard gray crust of ice from an earlier snowfall lay along the ground; the occasional gusts of wind off the river were sharp with the cold. But none of the children seemed anxious to go inside their houses. Their flashlight beams traced upwards through the branches of the tall plane trees and into the hard blue darkness overhead. Already batteries were growing faint; one mother yelled down to her child from an open window to save his light for tomorrow, but he laughed at her, waved it about, and ran away from the sound of her voice, as if refusing to believe that his little beam could not last forever. Nearby, two young Negro children were playing a war game with their flashes. Hiding behind the parked cars, they would circle each other silently and then spring out, suddenly clicking on their lights and screaming, "*Bam-bam . . . got you!*" Once they turned their lights blazing into our eyes with a chattering, "*Bam-bam-bam!*"

"What you looking so silly about?" one of the boys exploded at us.

When Hy pretended that he was even more astonished than he really was, they both giggled and raced down through the grounds of the project toward the river, flashing their beams like fireflies at the windows, the trees, the passers-by, until they vanished behind a corner of one of the project buildings; again we heard "*Bam-bam-bam . . . bam-bam-bam!*"

Then, for just a few minutes, it was absolutely dark and still along Henry Street save for the lights and noises of Vladeck Houses, which were all rather pleasantly muted. As I leaned against the fender of a car, I could see the project women in their kitchens preparing dinner. Occasionally I could even hear the sounds of a utensil scraping against a pot. Many of these windows were already decorated with Christmas wreaths or childlike drawings of Mary, Joseph, and the Christ-child. In some living room windows sparks of tinsel caught fire against the high beams of passing cars. A metal object crashed against one of the nearby icy sidewalks.

A boy yelled, "Now you broke it, stupid. Now what you going to do?"

Then Hy looked at his watch, as if awakening from a deep slumber. "I suppose it's all right now," he said. "I like to get there when I say I'm going to get there. You know, otherwise you never can tell what you might see."

Inez Maldonado lived on the fourth floor. When we came to her green metal door I noted that, like Nestor Escobosa's, it had a *mezuzah* pressed flat against the lintel and painted over with that same green enamel. Hy was more interested in what somebody had scribbled across one of the hall tiles: "Spades beware!" When he directed my glance toward the legend, I could see his gloved hand trembling.

"I just hope nobody sees this," he said, "because if they want to they can make it mighty sticky for Jorge . . . defacing public property."

"How do you know he did it?" I asked.

"I can tell . . ."

Removing his glove and wetting his finger, Hy rubbed at the writing. Then he said, "I better leave it until I make sure . . ." He rang the Maldonados' front bell.

Inez Maldonado wore jeans and moccasins, and her black hair was short. She spoke with a rush of words and was lean and haggard; she resembled an angry little Spanish man.

"You," she said, opening her door, "you know I did what you said I should do . . . I went to see the man up on Madison Avenue, and I told him everything is going to be all right with Georgey now because he will be in this training program, but you know what she says then, this woman? She told me you're a stinking housekeeper."

Then she realized that I was a stranger, and although she seemed surprised to see me, her manner became less belligerent. She started to apologize for the mess in the apartment.

"It's crowded here," she said, "and I didn't expect anybody but him."

"That's all right," Hy said.

"That's right," I said. "It doesn't matter."

Mrs. Maldonado nodded. As she started to usher us into her living room, Hy introduced me, but I didn't pay much attention to what he was saying. The air inside the apartment was close and pungent—as if somebody had been using a nasal vaporizer—and the furnishings were extremely Spartan. There were only a small, frayed gray couch and two or three slatted wooden chairs. There was a bridge table against one wall, and there were a number of cardboard cartons half-filled with pieces of cloth, chinaware, pots, and pans. Evidently Mrs. Maldonado had begun to pack, or perhaps she had never really unpacked. Right now she seemed to be the only person at home. After insisting that we sit on her couch, she stood in the entrance to the kitchen with her arms folded across her chest, separated from us by a narrow strip of faded gray carpeting. As the yellow kitchen light turned the windows behind her opaque and then touched her coarse black hair, Mrs. Maldonado started in angrily again.

"You know what I think? It was that business with the windows all along. That's why they're after us. Georgey was a kid in those days. And what about the rest of my family? They never did such things. I bet if I got George to go down there and apologize that still wouldn't change their minds.

What's the difference? I can't get Georgey to apologize. He says, 'They can go to hell.'"

"I ought to have a talk with Jorge," Hy blurted out.

"Yeah," Mrs. Maldonado said, "he respects you . . ."

Hy asked, "How do you know that?"

"I don't know," she said, "and it doesn't matter anyway. Because they want to get us out of here . . ."

Hy asked, "What does Mr. Maldonado say about all this?"

"You know," she said, "he works hard all the time, and when he isn't working he's sleeping . . ."

"So he doesn't have any time?"

"He's like all the men. He doesn't know any better, and he doesn't have any time," she said. "It's up to me, Mr. Solovei . . ."

Hy said, "You're a remarkable woman, Mrs. Maldonado . . ."

"Yeah," she said, "I may be tough, but I'm not tough enough to deal with these people. Suddenly they got a whole new set of complaints against us. We make too much noise. We disturb all the other tenants. I'm a lousy housekeeper. You know how they got that one, don't you? After Georgey got in trouble they came up here to tell me, and they took a good snoop around the place. You think I was in any mood for company?"

"I know," Hy said, "they do those things . . ."

"Yeah," Mrs. Maldonado said, "they do them, all right." But again she had managed to shut off her anger like a water faucet. Then she said, "Maybe I ought to make us some coffee . . ."

"Never mind that," Hy said.

I echoed him. "Never mind . . ."

"Oh, it's all right." She started toward the stove.

Hoping still to deter her, Hy asked, "How are your other children?"

For the first time Mrs. Maldonado smiled. "Rose is at a Christmas party . . ." But she continued toward her stove.

"And *Alejandro?*" Hy asked, with a surprisingly good Spanish intonation.

"*Alexander,*" she corrected him. "I sent him over to get some things. He ought to be back pretty soon . . ."

"Any problems?" Hy asked.

"Why should there be problems?" Unable to control her anger any longer, she added, "There are no problems. It's just this stupid business with the flat. Where do they think we gonna live?"

Hy said, "You shouldn't look at it that way. That isn't the question . . ."

"I don't know of any other questions," Mrs. Maldonado said, as if daring him to point out another to her. She broke a wooden matchstick against her thumbnail, cursing silently. "You sure you want coffee?"

"I already said I didn't want any," Hy said.

"Well, make up your mind already," Mrs. Maldonado said. Returning to the living room, she sat down on the floor in front of us. Then she said, "You think this lawyer will help?"

"Can't hurt," Hy said.

Mrs. Maldonado thought about it a moment and said, "I haven't received a check from Welfare all this month . . ."

"Do you think they closed your case?"

"I think they forgot about us," she smiled.

Then she stared at me. "You think they know all about Georgey?"

"It's none of their business," Hy said, obviously outraged at the thought that one thing might have anything to do with another; but his spoken outrage was less convincing, apparently, than what burned inside him. Sensing this, he added, "Just stop worrying. That won't do any good. Tell me, what else is new?"

"You always ask me that," Mrs. Maldonado said. "What do you think? You think anything good ever happens around here? They were here to see me from MFY. If he don't go to MFY, does he go away? Is there another school? You tell me. He's no longer a kid. I don't know what to tell him to do. You know what he wants to do, don't you?"

"Let's settle one thing at a time," Hy said.

"Yeah . . ." Mrs. Maldonado kicked at a piece of fluff on her carpet, quite ready to assume the role of client whenever Hy suggested it. Then she said, "It just don't work that way. When something happens they come at you from all different sides. I tell you I'm so angry I don't care what you say I just don't think we are going to stand a chance with these people. Georgey knows what I mean. He doesn't lie to his mother. He told me sure he fought, but it was these others who hurt the kid. You think that matters? I'll have to go with him to court just like the last time and the judge will read me a lecture. 'If you don't know how to keep your kids out of trouble, Mrs. Maldonado . . .' Can I tell him I got two other kids who have never been in any trouble? They don't know anything about that. It's like with this woman in the office up on Madison Avenue. Because of Georgey we all got to move away ..."

"One bad apple spoils the bunch."

"He's not a bad apple!"

Hy said, "I was just being funny ..."

"Yeah. Sure," Mrs. Maldonado said. "Sorry, Hy ..."

But it was getting late and he interrupted her apology. "So ... you'll come with me tomorrow to see the lawyer ..."

"Of course," she said. "Should I bring Georgey?"

"I don't think it matters. By the way, where is he now?"

"I gave him money to go to the movies. He'll stay out of trouble that way ..."

"You send him around to see me tomorrow," Hy said. "We better have a talk ..."

Mrs. Maldonado nodded. "What's that lawyer going to do, anyway?"

"He'll write a brief," Hy said. "He'll do the best he can. It's a lady ..."

"Lady lawyers!" she snorted, getting up to show us to the door.

Then Hy asked, "Jorge put that stuff on the tile outside?"

"What stuff?"

"Come on," Hy said, "you know what stuff I mean."

"No," she said, "he didn't do that. Honestly ..."

"Well, you better try to get it off anyway ... with soap ..."

"I guess so," Mrs. Maldonado said, "and I'll send Georgey to see you tomorrow. Don't you worry ..."

"Yeah," Hy said, "keep your spirits up. It could be worse ..."

"For who?" she asked.

"Oh, come on," Hy said.

He had started to close the door, but Mrs. Maldonado said, "Say, wait a second! What about my Welfare? And the school?"

"I'll look into it," Hy said, "but I told you, didn't I, one thing at a time..."

"Yeah. Sure," she said. She didn't mean to, but it just happened. When she let go of the door, it slammed hard in our faces.

Downstairs, in the darkness, all the project children had gone to their suppers. Hy kicked at the curbstone and looked about. Then he grabbed me tightly by the fat of the arm.

"Goddamn, you see what it's like, Dick. It's Christmas in New York, so my clients, they got to get a double kick in the ass. Not only don't they get their money to buy their kids gifts, but their regular checks don't even arrive on time. And then I got to come here. I must have had fifteen people in to see me today because they didn't get their checks. Christmas mails." Hy smirked. "I mail Christmas cards so these people can get it up the ass..."

"Come on," I said. "It isn't that way..."

"Oh, what do you mean," Hy said. "You think anybody down there at Welfare would ever think to mail those checks out early?"

"Well, at least everybody got flashlights."

"*Flashlights?* That's just what these kids need. A flashlight they give out. You know what a kid like Jorge Maldonado needs? He needs a whole fucking social revolution..."

"Come off it, Hy. I'm sure you know it isn't going to happen that way just for Jorge's sake..."

"As if I didn't know that," Hy said. "But Jesus, it's Christmas, and I got two evictions, and the rotten checks from Welfare don't even arrive on time. It's like everything else," he went on. "Bobby Kennedy comes here the other day, and you know what he gives these kids for Christmas—a bunch of balloons on sticks. That's what I call generosity. Balloons on sticks and little sailor hats saying SS INDEPENDENCE —and all those people over at MFY love him for it. Why? Because he stood up there and sang *Jingle Bells* at them. Balloons and *Jingle Bells* from Bobby Kennedy when some of my people still have flush toilets in the halls . . ."

"They have flush toilets," I said. "At least they all have those . . ."

"Yeah. I guess so," Hy said. "But it's damn stupid just the same. Some generosity . . ."

"Which is it you want?" I asked. "You want generosity or do you want a social revolution?"

Hy said, "You know what I mean. Cut it out, will you?"

I could see that Hy was getting about as cross with me as his usually exaggerated grandiloquence would allow him to show, so I said, "Tell me about Mrs. Maldonado. What do you think will happen with that lawyer?"

"Come and see me tomorrow around two o'clock," Hy said. "I don't specialize in crystal balls," and he shoved me in his friendly way before he disappeared into the darkness near Vladeck Houses.

When I got to Hy's office the next day at nearly two-thirty, I could hear him hollering from the other side of the partition.

"Are you kidding? Why don't you get wise, Jorge?

Where do you think you would be without these things? Where will your mother go if she has to move out?"

"I don't want to hear that kind of talk," a young man's voice—somewhat more restrained—came back at him.

Then I heard Hy again, "Listen to him. I could kill him..."

"Aw, cut it out, baby..."

"Cut it out? You get wise. You've got no choice in the matter..."

The door swung open and Hy saw me. "Dick . . . come on in." He pointed to a small, thin, pock-marked fellow wearing duck pants and an expensive-looking blue quilted ski parka. "This is Jorge Maldonado. Jorge, Dick Elman ...He's a writer..."

"Oh, yeah?" he said. "You gonna put me in your book?"

"Should I?" I asked.

"Suit yourself," Jorge said, "only I would because, you know, ask Hy here... I'm a real character..."

"Yeah," Hy flushed, "Jorge here is quite a funny kid. He thinks he knows it all, so as a result he is always screwing himself. He says there are such liars over there at the Project that he don't give a damn what they say about him. Have I got it right, Jorge?"

Jorge replied, "What right you got to go talking about me to other people?"

Poor Hy. He was so taken aback by this bold challenge to his customary garrulousness that he began to stammer, "I'm sorry... sorry, Jorge..."

"Aw, forget it. What difference does it make?" Jorge Maldonado now turned to examine me more closely.

"The only thing is," he said after awhile, "as I was telling Hy here, I don't see why my mother has got to go apologizing for what I did, and if she doesn't you know damn well they are going to throw her out of the place, Hy! You think I don't know what that lawyer is going to tell them? First he'll say give her another chance. Then he'll say it wasn't like you said it was . . . about Georgey here fighting with those other boys. Well, it's true all right, and I still don't see what that has to do with my folks. You know what I mean. They are hard-working people. You want to punish somebody, you can punish me. Leave my parents out of this . . ."

"So? Do you want to be punished?" Hy asked.

"Shit," Jorge said. "Sometimes I don't even understand you at all." Then he spoke to me again. "Half the time Hy here is telling me what a lousy deal it is that we're getting, and the rest of the time he's saying be careful Jorge or you'll get into trouble. You think that makes any sense? If we're getting such a lousy deal, why don't we do something about it? Maybe it's because you don't think we are, Hy. You see," he added, "that's why I don't trust him or his lady lawyer friends . . ."

"But Jorge," Hy said, trying not to respond to the insult to his integrity, "if only you would use your head. Maybe that lawyer will say they haven't got any right to throw you out in the first place . . ."

Jorge's face crimsoned. "Is that really true, Hy?"

"I don't know," he shrugged.

"Shit. What you telling me that if it's not true?"

"Maybe he likes you," I said. Jorge snickered.

Hy said, "I give up. You want your mother and your sister to get thrown out, it's on your conscience, not mine. I give up on you, Jorge, because you're a real character . . ."

"You're a character too, Hy," Jorge smiled.

"I give up! I give up," Hy said in mock anger.

Jorge turned sullen again. "I knew you were a quitter, Hy. I just know the way you think sometimes. Well, maybe you can help my mother and her kids because they still need somebody to feel sorry for them, but I'll take whatever I deserve . . ."

"You don't deserve nothing." Hy slapped himself on the thigh. "Who said you deserved anything?"

Jorge said, "Cut it out, Hy, will you?"

"No," Hy said. "Because I'm not kidding you now. Whoever told you you deserved anything or that you had a right to anything? Did I ever tell you that?"

"You never put it in so many words . . ."

"Did I ever tell you that?" Hy demanded.

"Cut it out. You know you did, Hy."

"Well," he said, "I was kidding. I was just talking through my hat . . . and I don't have a right to anything either . . ."

"You son of a bitch, Hy . . ." Jorge got up as if to leave. "Are you kidding?"

"I am not kidding you."

"You are a son of a bitch, Hy!"

He went storming out through the office door as Hy called after him, "At least I don't go pissing out the windows, Georgey . . ."

It was a cruel, spiteful remark, and Hy knew that it was because he glared at me then for having witnessed it. Then he turned to the wall again. "There ought to be a law against me," Hy said, as if talking to the dirty, scarred, beaverboard itself. "What did I have to say that stuff for? It happened two . . . maybe three years ago. I am a son of a bitch sometimes . . ."

"I guess it's pretty trying," I said.

"Jesus, I just had to put it to him straight. You just wait and see. He'll come back. At least I hope so . . ." But he couldn't quite control his nervous smirking.

Luckily for Hy, the phone rang just then. He had to busy himself because it was Welfare.

"Just a second," Hy said.

He cupped one hand over the mouthpiece of the phone. "You'll love this," he said to me. "Wait till you hear me do my song and dance. One of my people just moved into this apartment, and I told him to use the rent money to pay security. Now he's being evicted because Welfare can't justify paying so much rent. Get a load of this!"

He put his ear to the phone again. "Solovei here."

"Yeah. I told you. This is Mr. Solovei . . . Yes. I know . . . It's about Mr. Otilio . . . yes, Abner Otilio . . . not Fred Otilio. What did you say, sweetie? . . . Look, I'm not interested to know your problems. Let me speak to your supervisor . . . Why do I want to speak to him? . . . Now you think about that a moment . . . I know all that, but my Mr. Otilio is going to have the city marshals on his back unless you come across with his rent . . . You say you inspected the apartment and it's not up to standards . . . You got one that is? Now look, you want to make this an emergency case? . . . Well, what the hell kind of a case do you think it is? Jesus, you people, can't you get something straight once in a while . . ."

Hy clapped his hand over the phone and said, "Now watch me put the knife in and turn it a bit."

"Hello? Are you still there? Yes . . . I'm a social worker . . . Are you a social worker, Miss? What did you say? What's the difference . . . What's that?" Hy exclaimed. "Yes . . . I understand you're just trying to do your job . . . No . . . I don't want to write you any letters . . . I want you to think about it a moment . . . Who did you say your supervisor was? Look Miss, I'm not threatening you . . . I just don't want Mr. Otilio to have to look for another apartment . . .

"What did you say? Is it an emergency? Yes, of course it's an emergency . . . Would I be calling if it weren't an emergency? . . .

"Who's a loudmouth? What do you say? Now listen here, Mrs. . . . what did you say your name was . . . Mrs. Benedictus . . . Well, look here, Mrs. Benedictus, why can't you and I talk this over like two sensible people. You've got the money . . . you can get the money? That's just what I wanted to hear . . . Yeah, I know a professional when I talk to one, Mrs. Benedictus . . . I just knew you could be relied on . . . When can I get it? When? Can I send Otilio over to get it now? . . . Oh, yeah, and Mr. Otilio needs for a winter overcoat too, Mrs. Benedictus . . . Yes, of course, that's an emergency too . . . You ever been without a winter overcoat?"

When Hy hung up he had a big grin spread across his round face. But it was only for a moment. "You see what it's like," he started to say, just as a dark plump woman appeared in the doorway. "Oh, hello, Mrs. Coaley . . ." Hy said. He raised one hand. "Don't tell me. Your check never came."

"I just can't understand," Mrs. Coaley said.

Hy said, "Wait a second . . ." He found a number from among a sheaf of papers on his desk and dialed. It was the post office. Hy asked to speak to Mr. Kay. "Hello. It's Solovei again," he said. "Any word about those Welfare checks? I see . . . Well, let me know when, will you?" As he hung up, Hy stuck his hand into his trouser pocket and took out a roll of bills. He peeled off five singles and handed them to Mrs. Coaley. "Go easy on this," he said. "It's got to come sometime . . ."

"Thanks, Mr. Solovei . . ."

"Don't mention it . . ." Hy winked at me. "Cradle to grave Solovei they call me . . ."

Another woman appeared in his doorway, smaller and older than Mrs. Coaley but obviously on the same kind of mission. Hy said, "Never mind explaining. I know, Mrs. Caballero. Here. This is all I got to spare . . ." And he handed out five more single dollar bills.

When the woman had left, Hy scribbled something on a yellow pad. "I got to remember to be reimbursed," he said. "You may not believe it, but this is what I call routine . . ."

"I'm impressed . . ."

"Impressed?" Hy started up from his chair, spilling papers all over his desk. "You know," he said, "they got a right to these checks. It isn't as if it was charity . . ."

"That's not what you told Jorge."

"Jorge?" Hy seemed genuinely puzzled for a moment. "Oh . . . you mean Georgey," he said. "Come on. You know what I was trying to say to that kid. You can see it, can't you?"

"I guess so," I said.

"I wonder where the hell he is," Hy said. "He should be back by now . . ."

"Does he do this so often?" I asked.

Hy nodded. "He's a tough kid, but he's got some good instincts . . ."

"Yeah," I said. "I'll bet . . ."

"He really does," Hy said. His phone rang again.

"Hello . . . Solovei . . . yes, Mr. Grossman . . . What did you say? Yes . . . She's a client of mine . . . Yes, of course I sent her . . . Why? Because I wanted her to get there, is all . . . Yes. Okay . . . I'll pass it along."

Hy hung up and scratched his head. "Don't you want to know why he called?"

"Why?"

"They wanted us to know that Welfare checks don't get forwarded. If any of our clients have moved recently, they should go to Church Street to get their checks . . . Honestly." Hy drummed his fingers on the top of his desk. Then he suddenly said, "Where the hell is Georgey?"

For the next forty-five minutes Hy Solovei spoke to various functionaries of the Department of Welfare on the telephone and once to the Bellevue psychiatric social worker and once to the Department of Buildings. He also handed out money from his dwindling roll of bills to a procession of women stepping across his threshold. Then there was a lull for about five minutes, during which he went out to the water fountain. Upon returning, he said, "Are you still here?"

I smiled at Hy. "I wonder where Georgey is?"

"Yeah!"

Again I asked, "Does he do this often?"

"He's such a rough kid," Hy said. "He just won't do anything the right way. I tell him I can get his mother off if he joins the training program, he says he wants to enlist in the Marines . . . You ever hear of such a stupid idea? There's a war going on, so this *shmegegy* wants to join the Marines . . . Well, that's one thing I won't help him do . . ."

I asked, "Does he need your help?"

"He won't get in without it," Hy said. Then he looked at his watch and said, "I wonder where the hell he is." Hy was silent a few moments while he gnawed on his lower lip. Then he said, "You want to take a ride?"

"Where to?"

"Let's run over there and see what's going on."

We took a cab downtown, got snarled in traffic and walked the rest of the way.

Hy Solovei is a heavy-set man. When he walks, he is soon short of breath. By the time we had gotten to the Vladeck Houses, a sweat had broken out all over his forehead and upper lip. It was dark outside by now. Hy was breathing heavily. Hy stopped for a moment to survey the walks, jammed once again with children.

"Look," Hy said, "already no flashlights . . ." Two Negro boys brushed past in a terrible hurry, almost knocking me over, and Hy said, "Watch where you're going, kids . . ."

When we came to the Maldonados' door, he said, "Let's just listen a minute." Jorge must have heard him because he opened the door, as if by a prearranged signal.

"I figured you would get here sooner or later," he said. "And you brought the writer."

"Cut it out, Georgey," Hy said. He pushed his way past him and entered the apartment.

"Can I come in too?" I said.

Jorge smiled, "Why not?"

There seemed to be nobody at home, at first. Hy said, "Where is everybody?"

"Keep it down," Jorge said, "my father is sleeping." He pointed back toward the bedrooms.

When Hy collapsed on the sofa without waiting for an invitation, I sat down next to him. "All right," he said then, "where've you been?"

"You know something, Hy," Jorge said, "you're a fucking liar..."

"Nice talk..."

"I can't help it," Jorge said. "You are. What you tell me I can't make the Marines? I went down there. I talked to that man. You know what they said? If I get a letter from you it would be just fine with them..."

Hy winced. "You're only seventeen and one-half," he said, "you want to get yourself killed?"

"Not everybody dies, you know..." Jorge said.

"What kind of life is that, anyway?" Hy asked. "You think it's such a big deal?"

Jorge said, "It isn't so bad. To you it may not be so much. You're old..."

"Aw, cut it out," Hy said.

"What's the matter?" Jorge said. "You think I'm not good enough?"

Hy turned to me. "You tell him . . . I think you're too good, you *shmuck* . . ."

"Cut it out, Hy." Jorge fumbled for his cigarettes and offered them to us. "All I want you to do is write a letter . . ."

"No!"

"And he tells me about rights," Jorge said. "You ever hear of the constitutional right to serve in the militia . . . you know, bear arms?" Hy stared in amazement at his client, articulating like a city councilman. "It's in the Constitution, Hy, that the state shall make no law prohibiting the right to bear arms or to serve in the militia . . ."

"Look," Solovei said then, "I am not the state. Get that out of your head. It's just that nobody has the right to get himself killed . . ."

"Jesus, Hy! . . ." Jorge Maldonado was pacing back and forth now like a caged animal. "Will you stop talking about killing? How do you know I'm going to get killed? I might not even get to Vietnam. Jesus," Jorge added, almost pleading, "If not now, they'll draft me later anyway . . ."

Even Hy Solovei could not help being touched by his client's pleas, but he said, "I'm just not going to do it, Georgey. You better get that out of your head. You think it's a whole glamorous bit? I'm telling you it's dangerous. It's not only you I'm thinking about. You ever stop to think about all the women and children who are dying over there? You want to have them on your conscience?"

"Cut it out, Hy," Jorge said. "I don't know what the hell

you're talking about." He snuffed out his cigarette. "Jesus," he added, "you think I'm like that? You think I'm going to do things like that? All I want to do is get the hell out of here, and you got no right to stop me. Hy . . . come on," he pleaded, "be a good guy . . ."

"And get you killed?"

"I mean it," Jorge said, "I don't like that kind of talk . . ."

"And I don't like to hear you dreaming about the Marines . . ."

"Cut it out, Hy. Come on. What do you say?"

"You could at least wait until you're eighteen . . ."

"Yeah, sure," Jorge said, "and who knows what will happen to Jorge by then? This way I'll be all right. You can see that much, can't you? I know it won't be so nice, but I also know they'll do something for me. What is MFY going to do for me? You think I don't know what I'm talking about? If I hang around here any longer, I'll be in even more trouble in six months. So what are you playing with me? Come on, Hy. You know I'm telling the truth . . ."

"In six months they're maybe going to have a truce," Hy said.

"Cut it out, will you . . ."

Hy frowned. "What do your parents think, Georgey?"

"My mother thinks it will help her keep the apartment . . ."

Hy said, "That's a shitty thing to say . . ."

"Face it," Jorge said. "We're shitty people sometimes, just like you . . ."

Hy rose from the couch. "Well, I'm not gonna do it! . . . I'm just not going to do it! . . ."

"Keep your voice down," Jorge said.

Hy blushed deeply. "I'm not going to do it," he said again.

We heard Mrs. Maldonado's key in the front door. She saw Jorge first before turning and seeing us.

"I got my check," she said, dropping a bunch of grocery bags on the floor.

Hy said, "Good deal . . . why don't you help your mother, Georgey?"

"She's managing . . ."

"So . . . you got your check. I'm glad," Hy said.

"But it isn't the same as last time. It's all wrong," Mrs. Maldonado explained.

Hy said, "Let me see it."

"I cashed it," she said. Inez Maldonado came into the center of the room and nodded at me. Then she said, "Maybe you can tell me why isn't it ever the same two months in a row?"

"Maladministration," I said.

But Hy said, "Sometimes they're giving you more for special reasons . . . We'll take a look next time."

"Yeah," Jorge said bitterly.

She turned to her son. "You eat?"

Jorge nodded.

"What did Hy say?"

"About what?"

Mrs. Maldonado smiled. "You spoke to him, didn't you?"

"About what?" Hy demanded.

"It's nothing," she said. "It's just that I think everything is going to be all right. I called that woman on Madi-

son Avenue. She says if Georgey isn't going to be living at
home . . ."

"Where's he going?" Hy interrupted.

"Didn't he tell you?"

"Tell me what? Where's he going?" Hy was asking, just
a little hoarsely.

Jorge said, "Hy won't write that letter . . ."

"Say," she asked, "what kind of guy are you?"

Hy said, "You want your son to go to Vietnam?"

"Oh, why don't you stop that already," Mrs. Maldonado
said, and Jorge laughed.

I thought Hy's watch would break from the way he kept
winding it, but he said, "Damn. It's getting late. You better
come to see me tomorrow, kid . . ."

"Will you write me that letter?"

Going over to the boy, Hy grabbed him in an awkward
bear hug. "I could kill him," he said, "I could just kill him
sometimes . . ."

"Leave him alone," Mrs. Maldonado said.

Jorge squirmed out of Hy's loosened embrace and said,
"You better write that letter, baby . . ."

Below us on the street a car's brakes screeched before it
careened loudly into the chassis of another passing vehicle.

Inez Maldonado blinked and said, "People don't know
how to drive in this city. Listen to them . . ."

There was the thin, sprinkling sound of glass breaking
against the curbstone.

Jorge said, "See you tomorrow, Hy, baby . . ."

When we got downstairs, Solovei was shrugging his
shoulders. "So I'll write the letter. What's the big deal?"

"I guess you got no choice," I said.

We started crossing Henry Street. Hy said, "I guess they taught me a lesson . . ."

"You do all right," I said.

"Sure," Hy said. "Like with Jorge . . ."

"It's his life," I said. "He's got a right . . ."

"Sure," Hy said. "Some right."

We started up Grand Street toward where a crowd seemed to be forming. "Must be that accident," I said.

"Let's get out of here," Hy replied, and we turned and walked back on Henry Street until we came to Clinton, where we turned to go north again. Hy was talking to me rapidly.

"You know why I went this way. It's not an accident. I know what's happening over there on Grand Street. There's this bum . . . he's colored . . . he's there every night about this time. He's always out there telling the people how there are no Jews on Welfare. According to him, the reason these people are on Welfare is the Jews. I'm not kidding. He stands out there telling people that Hitler was right . . . that if they can get rid of the Jews, they'll be getting rid of their oppressors. Then, sure enough, next morning he comes around to me to get himself reinstated, and—you know what—when he comes in he is as sober as a deacon, and he doesn't seem to have any idea of what he was saying to people last night, so there we go arguing his case with the Welfare Center because, after all, we can't let the guy starve to death . . ."

"Then what would he think of the Jews?"

"It isn't that," Hy said. "It's just that I don't see the point. That's why I don't like walking past him. Why? He might recognize me and then he'll start in about those Jews at Welfare keeping him down, and then tomorrow he could come in really sheepish and I'd have to help him anyway. Besides," Hy added, "it wouldn't do my self-image any good to see him now . . ."

"You mean," I said, "you might not want to help him . . ."

Hy stopped and pulled at his nose. Then he said, "Look. You're getting me all wrong. It's these laws. You got to find out all kinds of things about people which you don't have the right to know, and then when you know you got to do something about them, don't you? Well, I'd rather not know sometimes. The clients come in and they tell you all the things they think you got to know. But you really don't have to know. It's just so unfair once you know. If somebody had to know all those things about me, how would I like it? That's why I figure, what the hell, let him call me a dirty Jew. I'd still want to get him Welfare . . ."

"That's damn white of you," I said.

Hy stopped again. "Don't kid yourself. It isn't easy . . . not the way things are . . ."

"How are they?" I asked.

Hy shoved me again. "Don't kid yourself," he said. "If I had my way that guy wouldn't even get a penny . . ." Then he seemed to take offense at his excessive anger. "Look who's talking! I spend all day on the telephone with that Welfare, and now I'm even beginning to sound like one of those clowns . . ."

I said, "Maybe it's natural . . ."

"Don't kid yourself," he said. "It's the most unnatural thing in the world."

"Well," he smiled, "tomorrow's a red letter day. Jorge

thinks he's going to get signed up in the Marine Corps, and some five percenter will be coming to see me again about their Welfare . . ."

"It could be worse," I said. "You could be putting people off rather than putting them on . . ."

"Don't kid yourself," Hy said. "*I put them on plenty* . . ." He bumped against me, cozily.

But we had turned up Houston Street just in time to hear the voice of Hy's putative client.

"AND LET ME TELL YOU SOMETHIN'! YOU EVER SEE ANY JEWISH BUMS ON THE BOWERY? THEY'S NIGRO BUMS AND PORTO RICAN BUMS —THEY AIN'T NO JEWISH BUMS. THEY ARE EVEN IRISH AND ITALIAN BUMS AND FRENCH BUMS AND SOME MEXICAN BUMS, AND THEY IS PROTESTANT BUMS AND CATHOLIC BUMS. WHY THEY AIN'T NO JEWISH BUMS . . . YOU EVER THINK OF THAT? YOU EVER WONDER WHY? IT'S CAUSE THEY LEARNED HOW TO TAKE CARE OF THEMSELVES . . . THEY KNOW HOW—OVER YOUR DEAD BODY . . ."

"They ought to make him a caseworker." Hy laughed.

"Cut it out," I said.

But he said, "Don't you tell me that. You tell Jorge that!"

The evening traffic skittered by. It was cold and dark on Houston Street, as if it had been that way forever.

6

GUARANTEED ANNUAL POVERTY

• For at least eight million Americans the economy is out of phase. It has been so for quite a while. Whether they are also out of phase with the economy is irrelevant; their method of accommodating has been through dependency. But it has always been our intention to eliminate that dependency along with their poverty. So that the children will not have to beg in the footsteps of their parents, we try to provide higher skills, but we are not prepared to create even more dependency by isolating the young from their embittered and distorted environments, as less affluent countries have done. In the end, our wish to eliminate poverty is matched only by our fervent individualism. Around the poor, therefore, we have erected a Poorhouse State, a system of inadequate payments, grudging services, petty rules tyrannies, and surveillance mechanisms that, though always regarded as a temporary arrangement, has preserved all in their deprivations.

Locked in the bottomless bag of racial poverty, the Negro poor now clamor to escape by all available means, but when the chief asset this group can present to a society of affluence is its deprivation, it is clear that they have little in common with the network of interests and dependencies established between a rapidly vanishing working class and an increasingly self-conscious middle class; and it is the prevailing interests of this latter combination—of General Motors and the UAW, for example—that are reflected in the programs of our liberal democracy. Marx would have despised the Welfare poor as a lumpen proletariat, and those former radicals who have gained a modicum of power and influence seem to feel much the same. So all approve of formulating programs to help the children of these poor escape while their parents rot in apathy and neglect, of encouraging men to seek work even when they are being pauperized at jobs at the minimum wage. Our belief in mobility so dominates our thinking about poverty that the chief mechanism we have used to remove the impediment has been rehabilitation—job training, retraining, and counseling, head-start programs for the preschool children, and work orientation programs for the grown men. The abject poor have reluctantly consented to this diagnosis as if they also thought that their only problem was inability to compete, when, in fact, their problem has also always been what to do with themselves *when* they could not compete. But three decades after the New Deal it has become evident that even the Negro poor are failing to be rehabilitated by such inadequate measures; so the Welfare colonialists are in full retreat. This is said to be the twilight era in our control of the poor. The Poorhouse State, it is now said, must collapse through its own demonstrable inefficiencies. As more people lose their jobs to machines and join the ranks of the unemployables even while the need for skilled labor increases and the number of employables dwindles, it is becoming apparent that the present system of surveillance, scrutiny, and enforced deprivation simply will not work; it is suggested that it be replaced by one that will guarantee minimum incomes—through either direct grants or negative income taxing—with simplified eligibility requirements and, hopefully, higher benefit levels.

Many of those who advocate this change seem to believe that the old incentives and punishments are no longer in the national interest. Nobody now wishes to exploit the poor. Some wish to encourage their leisure. They look forward to the day in the not-too-distant future when the AFDC mother, for example, will merely file an income tax return like everybody else and will be reimbursed in cash for her hitherto unused deductions. Others are lobbying for the right of all Americans to receive a uniform income guarantee (or family grant) with no means test.

"Something is going to happen. It's got to," one highly placed lieutenant in the War on Poverty told me. "Sergeant Shriver wants the program. HEW wants the program. The President's National Automation Commission wants the program . . . and they are businessmen. If there weren't this war in Vietnam, you would have had a negative income tax this session of Congress because everybody now knows that it will be at least a decade before the War on Poverty really provides any income for people. In fact, it was right on Johnson's desk, and then along came the escalation . . ."

Murdering the poor in Vietnam for the next seven to twenty years so that America's poor can eventually have their guaranteed annual income does seem like an odd way to go about it (as does drafting the poor to create shortages in the labor force); but, judging from the fact that Walter

Reuther and the president of IBM are inclined toward some form of direct government-supplied hedge against automation, it also seems likely that if we can ever extract ourselves from Vietnam, there will be an income floor proposed, sooner rather than later. Although this is a hopeful portent, it will alleviate none of the despair of those who are presently living on public assistance except to give them some reason, perhaps, to do all they can to get the United States out of Vietnam. But what kind of income floor will it be? From the comfort of my own middle-class surroundings, it is difficult to pooh-pooh any plan that will put more money into the pockets of Antonio Ortiz and Benny Mosca. And from the flak of newspaper and magazine articles touting such a proposal, how could one deny the efficacy of, say, $3,000 a year per family? It is indicative of the ignominious position of the Welfare poor that the discussion of their proposed guaranteed annual wage has thus far been carried on from the point of view of its administrative rationality, and there has been little attempt made to consider the interests of those for whom poverty is a daily reality.

None of the present proponents of GAI needs to imagine himself living in the future on such an income, for they are of the class whose skills will still be needed when the computer replaces Man; nor will they have to work at any of the dreary new jobs created by automation because it is they who will become the managers. This, then, is social engineering *in flagrante delicto*, made possible, in part, by the enforced individualism of the poor. Barry Goldwater's former economic adviser, Professor Milton Friedman, is for a minimum income tax because he thinks that is one way to curb bureaucracy; but bureaucracy is a major occupational aspiration of the poor. Sergeant Shriver can imagine people living on fixed incomes because he has quite a few thousands more to live on and knows that he will never *need* to. And whether the initial income floor will be approximately $3,000 per year, which is presently defined as the poverty level, or a mere supplement of $500, such as the family allowance system in Canada, England, and the Scandinavian countries, no one seems anxious to enter into debate because none of the potential debaters can engage in it with the least bit of self-interest. The poor do not have leaders who are consulted about their needs, and most liberals— creatures of their own rising expectations—are still too anxious to establish the guaranteed income principle to wish to introduce any element of discord. So the professionals are once again to be allowed to indulge in the marvelous exhilaration of pragmatism, and once again they will set the standards by which others will be obliged to maintain themselves.

The real attraction of the guaranteed annual income is that it is an inexpensive way of giving the poor something without taxing the rest of the population or creating full employment, which can only come about through greater public expenditures on programs other than war. Some of its proponents say they wish to establish government as the employer of last resort, but others say they are against more big government and claim that initially the expense should be no greater than the maintenance of our present paltry public assistance apparatus. If some say they wish to limit discretion, others say grants must be flexible, varying with

circumstances, while still others admire the proposal precisely because it replaces the need to help the poor through
public charity with a new system in which all will be assured
the right that some can be more equal than others. Never
before have the powerless poor been more in need of allies.
Never before have they been more in need of some way to
articulate their interests.

If the initial income base is high enough and sufficiently
flexible, an income guarantee might eliminate a good deal
of public charity (for it could be incremented as earnings
are incremented, as a hedge against inflation), but even at
the $3,000 figure that is presently being proposed, a family
of four might be able to do little more than preserve its
present economic pathology. How will they then get more?
Most proposals now stipulate that if a man earns $500, he
will be able to net only $2,500 from government. It has also
been pointed out that if everybody eligible were given $3,-
000, the national expense would be approximately four
times as great as the estimated $8 billion created in surplus
taxation through economic growth, which it is believed
could subsidize such a program. This suggests that the
initial grants would have to be rather moderate—to forestall increased taxation—which will mean that the recipients, however grateful, will still have to be supplemented in large measure through some kind of public assistance; and they will still have to be ruled by the Poorhouse State.

Even if a $3,000-a-year guarantee could begin to alleviate
some poverty, it seems doubtful that it would eradicate the
dependency that would seem to be one of the targets of the

Triple Revolutionists. There will always be people who will need more than they are guaranteed—either because of their improvidence or because of their increased need—and they will still have to turn to some kind of public assistance program for the difference. If the new post-GAI Welfare program is to be less of a burden on the poor than the present one, reforms will have to be made in Welfare law and we shall have to write new programs for dependent people as well as pass an income floor. If the aim of this guaranteed annual income is to eradicate poverty, more than $3,000 a year will be needed; we shall have to take those steps that insure that families do not pay $120-a-month rent on incomes of $2,600 a year, and that means more low-cost public housing and more dependency. We shall have to peg the minimum wage far above the $1.40 an hour which the Johnson administration hopes to pass and also establish a program of extensive public services of truly excellent quality (i.e., medical care, education, transportation,[1] and credit) to augment even these larger grants. If the poor are still not to remain a class apart, these services —including the income floor—would have to be extended to others who are not yet subsisting on public assistance. Proponents of the guaranteed annual income look forward to the day when the neutral functionaries of the Internal Revenue Service will replace the present agents of the Poorhouse State as watchdogs over the eligibility of the poor; but they seem not to recognize that one reason why IRS of-

---

[1] It usually took me just as long to get from my flat on West 79th Street in Manhattan to Houston Street, a distance of over four miles, as it did to get from the Lower East Side's Houston Street to Gouverneur Slip, a mile.

ficials are likely to be more respectful of rights is because its present constituency is more assertive of those rights and that many of the most flagrantly unlawful acts of the Poorhouse State are consequences of bureaucracy's response to a changing constituency. These same Triple Revolutionists also seem to believe that we must adjust to increased productivity and rewards for some and stabilized incomes for others, but they seem unwilling to realize that this might create an even wider class gap between those who can achieve and those who must content themselves to be subsidized. Can we be so certain that our new meritocracy will treat the relatively affluent poor they help to create with any more compassionate understanding of their interests than did the previous elites of wealth, inheritance, class, color, or achievement?

The most serious failure of our Poorhouse State is not that it fails to rehabilitate people but that it offers to fit them out in outlandish knickers, tries to marry them to an obsolescent thrift, and fails to allow them to consume with integrity. A whole nation is gorging itself, but the Poorhouse State tells the poor that goodness is something other than what they see on their television screens. It talks a great deal about standards, decency, dignity, liberty, and justice but offers only dependency. It not only fails to bestow upon the poor the only value they have been taught to uphold on equal terms with all their fellow citizens, but it also looks up from its martini, winks, and says, "This is a hell of a life."

But thrive and waste we must for a greater America. So now many of our Poorhouse State agencies are talking a great deal about giving things to people, about trusting their clients. It has simply become too unpleasant having that many dark-skinned spinster aunts lying about the house, cursing at you, going out on binges, embarrassing you in front of the company. They are not even to be trusted as baby sitters. So now these poor are to be granted an income floor. At $3,000 a year should one have a Princess telephone? Or take the wife out to dinner once a week? How many suits should our post GAI man own? What kind of car should he drive? Many of the new programs we are now espousing, along with the income floor, demand a self-abnegation that only the very pious, the very strong, or the very rich can afford. They recommend wheat germ and carrot juice for those who wish to chew steak. They offer to teach skills to those who want to be loved for their personalities. They preach transcendence and reserve things for those who show initiative. Either they ask the man on the bottom to aspire to exploitation (to which, of course, the proletariat no longer aspires), or they say, "Take your three grand and we'll try to manage without you." But in the meantime they are likely to be just as insidious in their distrust of the Welfare poor as the old ones.

"A visit to a Public Welfare office will tell you much," a recent HEW pamphlet points out. "At some, you will find long lines of shabby people waiting for service . . . in others, you will find few people in the bright, cheerful waiting rooms because the workers visit regularly in the homes."

Why should the workers visit regularly in the homes? I suppose if I were given a guaranteed annual income, I might consent to such intrusions, but I doubt if I would like them.

Why should anybody like such visits? What would they be seeking? They would seem to carry with them the judgment of presumptive pathology, which the proponent of an income guarantee now claims to detest. Implicit in the idea of the home visit is the forfeiture of privacy. It is our way of asserting that people on public assistance are so trapped inside their own pathology that wholesome elements must be brought to bear on them so that they can be uplifted. Once again, now, the poor are to be rehabilitated or counseled, often by the very same workers who previously served as watchdogs over their eligibilities. In Washington, D.C., for example, applicants for public assistance must be "willing to accept treatment or training" as a condition of eligibility, and one recent social work text I read even recommended a program of "aggressive case finding by workers . . ." to "identify from this discovery incipient problem families early enough to forestall breakdown and disorganization."

It is not necessary to believe that the poor are the repositories of unsullied virtue to find such proposals fraught with possibilities for abuse. When you or I claim our right to vote, we do not expect to be greeted by a social worker who must scrutinize us as something dubious and then, perhaps, make an arrangement to visit us at home. Nor do we hope to establish a "positive relationship"—social work cant for common decency—with the functionary who administers our driving test or certifies our unemployment check, delivers our mail, or administers the oath for our passports. We are repeatedly told by some that under the guaranteed annual income the social service function will be separated from that of income maintenance. Judging, however, from this country's history of its treatment of the poor, this may be just wishful thinking. For those who are thought to be improvident—for whatever reasons—it is clear that they will remain one and the same, making the bestowal of rights or dignity on such persons seem, in the absence of other reforms, like rather high-minded and gratuitous assertions.

"I don't hate them, I'd like not to hate them," one Lower East Side woman told me of the various functionaries who came calling upon her, "but they always seem to have something on me . . ."

Similarly, few of the poor whom I met were oppressed by such well-publicized abuses as the occasional crudely assembled after-midnight eligibility raids, which took place even in New York until recently; but nearly all to whom I spoke felt victimized and oppressed by their relationship to power and expertise as expressed in a social philosophy that constantly measured them against some standard of adequate behavior by which it found their acceptance of a benefit proof that they were prone to the ministrations of a social worker. Confronted by this system of anticipatory remediation (which had little relevance to any actual violations of law), the most typical response of the clients was to play out the pathology it was intended that they represent; they asked for subsistence when they envied wealth, and they confessed shamelessly to mismanagement when they knew it was impossible to manage. The most dreadful reality trapped inside the slogan "Welfare colonialism" has been the creation of this colonial personality, but once in a while Watts and Harlem remind us that the poor are no more grateful for what we give them than we would be.

I remember overhearing one Negro man say to a worker,

"Let's not talk about my kid anymore. Let's talk dollars and cents . . ."

Another time, a woman on Welfare said to me, "I don't know why you so bitter. I wouldn't be if I were you . . ."

In general, though, the Welfare poor have managed to hide themselves behind our image of them as defectives. They have consented to think of themselves as "multi-problem" or "culturally deprived" because they are not so secure in their dependencies that they wish to cause trouble. Besides, they are not fools. They see that their families *are* often likely to be in a turmoil and that their children *are* often doomed to certain pathologies. Why should one expect them to be otherwise? But what is appalling is how they have been cajoled into seeing all their problems as arising from every conceivable factor except inadequate public services and a deprived economic condition. I have seen women acting out tortuous monologs about life at home with their workers or going into intimate and painful details about their affairs—merely to justify a request that pressure be put on Welfare to pay their rent.

In our slums the social worker wishes to strengthen family stability, and the sociologist preaches the new voluntarism of self-help with government spending, but the *otherness* of Michael Harrington's *Other America*, which may be most debilitating for the poor man, is that he has been made into a social problem, worthy of surveillance and study. Always pervasive, even when well meaning, this scrutiny of his home life and child-rearing practices insures that his life will also be obscene with other people's judgments. He alone must consent to such degradations, for to no one else has such scrutiny been presented as the means to a necessary livelihood. Even while the middle class staggers in its disarray, the poor are being told to alleviate their poverty by preserving their families through counseling. While the middle-class youth indulges in LSD and the general *je m'en fous*, the pathologies of the poor man's children are duly noted. It used to be that they were considered improvident if they married before age thirty-five. Now, they are considered pathological when they have children.

In America the poor have been psyched out of their grievances. And understandably so! Nobody wants to fight for a status that assures only poverty and degradation. If only they are forced to live in our Harlems and bring up their children on the insecurities of public assistance, the assumption is all too easily made that such efforts are aberrational to them; and once you have located the aberration, you no longer feel inclined to worry about their poverty. You offer them contraceptives, or you provide them with preschool training, or you encourage them to indulge in self-help. The formulas differ, but the approaches are always decidedly psychic, a debased utilitarianism aimed at deterrence.

"With a little farming, a little public assistance, and much personal attention from the public welfare worker," a recent HEW pamphlet boasts, a sixty-nine-year-old mountaineer and his son, deserted by the wife and mother, "became a part of middle-class America."

This is not some accomplishment to be sneered at by those who would fulfill their radical bent through *épater le bourgeois* (for it is not, of course, sneered upon by most of our poor); but how will we ever know whether it was the money, the farming, or the counseling that made the difference? In the end we claim to believe it was the last out of our own self-hate. If money could really make such a difference, we would all feel diminished in stature. It is as if even those who are only shakily of the middle classes were saying, that can't be all we mean by the middle-class America we inhabit—as if better housing, health care, and nutrition weren't a very great deal indeed!

In failing to make dependency legitimate for those who need it in America, we take a terrible toll on one another and are often blind to our own self-interests. I now work a seventy-five-hour week, trying to hold down a job by day and moonlighting in the evenings to maintain my middle-class perquisites for myself, my wife, and my daughter. Since free-lance writers are not eligible for unemployment insurance, shall I—when there's a dry spell—dun my relatives or go to my local Department of Welfare? Clearly I have solvent relatives, assets, and even a few more skills; I am not precisely in the same fix as the poor man. Is it merely middle-class self-hate that leads me to believe I am in a fix? Or should I delude myself into thinking I am in the same fix as, say, Bobby Kennedy? If, as another recent HEW pamphlet states, "money alone" is "not enough to meet the serious economic and social problems of those in need," shouldn't my middle-class bias lead me to reverse that sentence to read "those in need have not been given enough money"? For how else is the poor man to get the services he needs? Where shall he go to get his teeth fixed? What kind of counseling will he be given at public expense? By whom?

As for all of us, the inevitable need of the poor is for economic and social equality, but while some of us are getting something of that sort (I survive partially on a grant to Columbia University from the National Institute of Mental Health), they are still being offered rehabilitation and handouts, and not all of them are getting these. Proposals for a guaranteed annual income may increase the size of the handouts, but they will not create vitally needed services; they will not redistribute wealth. They can't change the fact that a "well-paid" New York domestic earns $15 a day, a university OEO consultant $50–$100, and a television performer upwards of $1,000. In fact, such proposals, if implemented, may even increase such disparities, with merit or achievement as the new basis for inequality. And with his guaranteed annual income, the poor man may be expected to purchase services, at an inflated price, that were once offered grudgingly (i.e., housing, surplus foods). If the new poor prove improvident or once again fail to achieve, will they once again be deterred and rehabilitated?

How curious it is to compare the tea and sympathy approach of our government with that of Great Britain. Its Welfare State apparatus is far more extensive, although clearly far from perfect, and it seems to operate with an entirely different set of assumptions regarding those who are forced to live on its grants of assistance. Explaining the function of national assistance in the United Kingdom, the Annual Report of the National Assistance Board for 1963 says that its essential task for the majority of its recipients is to "insure that the allowances due to them are paid regularly and promptly, that any special financial needs are met, and that they are treated with courtesy and consideration." Although Britain's public assistance population is greater proportionally than our own, no special missionary efforts are to be made, apparently, for as the report of the National Assistance Board stresses, "more than this [i.e., money] they do not ask and might resent as an intrusion."

In Great Britain, even today, the worker must rely on the person receiving assistance to get in touch with his local branch office for any other forms of social service "quickly and without cost to himself by using a simple franked and addressed form which is left with him for this purpose."[2] But in an affluent America, which continues to spend a smaller percentage of its tax dollars on social welfare than most of the advanced nations of the world, if you want the money you had better accept the counseling; more and more, the person who dispenses money is to be a case finder and therapist, prepared through his "positive relationship" to intrude whenever necessary; and the consequent tendency among administrators is toward translating their formerly lawless punitiveness into acts of lawful professional discretion in the "client's best interest." In New York City, for example, where after-midnight raids are presently forbidden by internal directive of the Welfare Department (because of a fear of litigation arising from some of the capable neighborhood attorneys who are beginning to work among the poor), the Department still feels that it

[2] One of Britain's most profitable exports to this country of late has been the cartoon strip "Andy Capp." Andy lives on the dole, goes to the pub, watches TV, dodges the labor exchange, fights with his wife, and is generally quite lovable. Imagine, if you will, an American version of the same situation in cartoon form. It would be rather grim.

is acting within its legal mandate when a worker makes an
unannounced call on a person after 9 A.M. With those it
deems trustworthy it schedules appointments, but with
those it deems problematical it may arrive at any hour of
the day and demand entrance or forfeiture of Welfare benefits. A New York City policeman used to be dragooned into
accompanying a representative of Welfare's fraud investigation squad, but now these obligations are to be shifted to
the caseworker who, upon entering such a household,
places his client in a peculiar jeopardy that is subject to no
legal redress; if he finds a client's behavior objectionable, he
punishes him in his capacity as his therapist.

Whenever I try to describe this process to liberal intelligent people, they become extremely angry with me and say,
"I'm sure there are decent, ordinary, conscientious people in
Welfare, trying to do the job"; and of course there are. Far
too many! But of what should such a job consist? How
should it be fulfilled? Recently New York City workers in
Harlem refused to go on home visits because they were being
brutalized and robbed, but while the public was justly pro-
voked against the unnamed assailants, nobody bothered to
ask why these workers have to go uninvited into other people's homes. Just what are they doing in these homes? What
advice do they purvey? Would you or I consult such persons if we had a problem? If nobody else in America is
subjected to such intrusions, it is to be expected that
the clamorings of the poor for equality should include
a clamoring for impersonality. You and I can be bothered
about the depersonalization of public services, but the poor
do not yet share in that general alienation. For far too

long all service to them has been extremely personal, and it is as if they were now saying, "Don't talk to us about community because we already have one, and look what it has gotten us." Many know that they will not be getting off Welfare very quickly, and just as many are not so anxious to leave their projects right away, but they insist that they be treated as human beings, which from their vantage point means depersonalization, not intrusions; it means Diner's Club Cards, not budgets.

"They don't want to *do* anything," one woman told me. "They don't have the time to help me with my kids. They don't like to do my housework or my shopping. They would like to tell me what to do . . . but I just don't have the time to listen."

Another Lower East Side woman in a project said she had a great deal of sympathy and respect for workers, but, she pointed out, "They always seem to come around when the floor is dirty and I am not dressed and the kids are carrying on . . . and I feel that maybe they do it personally because I know it isn't always like that. Not all the time. So it doesn't seem right that they get so disgusted with me because we ask them to come and do things for us and then they come and see and they decide it is because of what we are and what we do. It just doesn't seem right that they should have the chance to know so much about us."

I came to the Lower East Side to find out how the Welfare State treated its poor, and I discovered that it still does not even exist for many of them. It does not exist because it is detested, as much by the individualistic allies as by the selfish enemies of the poor. It does not exist because it is such a fervent belief of all that it should someday wither away. Finally, it does not exist because it was generally accepted that the poor would be the last to make good use of a Welfare State. Better, then, to give them the Poorhouse State.

I cannot help but be reminded of how my mother would buy my clothing. "Nothing fancy," she would tell the salesman. "Nothing that will stain or get dirty." The suit we finally selected was always uninspired but costly enough to justify our caution and, of course, it immediately went into my closet so I could do it no harm. Invariably, on those rare occasions when I was allowed to dress up, the very first spoonful of soup or salad dressing, gravy or ice cream spattered its labels, which justified its banishment to my closet once again. But I was not usually too unhappy—I always believed that if I could destroy this suit, the next one might be a little more to my liking.

So now the present state of the poor has convinced some of us that they need a guaranteed annual income because their present dependency is cruel and anachronistic; but are we to assume that dependency is an anachronism? Even as we try to overcome the historic injustices for a minority and to remove the yoke of their unwanted dependency, we must seek out ways to vest dependency with decency, to provide assistance without humiliation. The present generations of the poor may be of little help in this endeavor because they have been so victimized by doctrines of individual achievement that they find all dependency hateful and ignominious. Their immediate need is for sufficient stable sources of income to right their economic statuses so they can begin to aspire to liberty and justice; but if we are not to have new inequalities and indignities perpetrated, we of the rising middle classes must somehow dispel our own myth that we are not dependent and do not wish to become dependent. We must try to create even more agencies of dependency, and we must make it possible for all to make use of them with equality, without being exploited and used by them. But this will happen only if public services are so excellent that it will not be a mark against a man to use them, and that will not happen so long as poverty is relieved through scarcity and tax cuts produce abundance.

"That's very nice," I remember one applicant shouting at the intake desk at 28th Street. "I came here to collect Welfare and you're trying to tell me I came here to collect Welfare. Well, isn't that just what I said? Why else would I be coming here?"

EPILOGUE

• Throughout my research I was continually being asked about this book by the people I met. What would it be like? Who would be publishing it? Who would want to read such a book? What was its title? A few days after I announced to a group of teenagers that it was to be called *The Poorhouse State*, I was greeted by a young Negro named George, who gave me a copy of a poem. It purported to be about his girl friend Hilda. I reprint it here with his permission:

> Hilda goes downtown to Welfare...
> All she wants is a bit of carfare...
> Welfare. Carfare. Wherefore? Whyfore?
> What I got to tell you lies for?
> There's the Welfare at my door...
> Tell him, Hilda, we are poor.
> Tell him, Hilda, go away...
> Visit me another day...
> Tell him, Hilda, he's too late.
> We are living in the Poorhouse State.

We are living in the Poorhouse State.
Pull my weed and masturbate.
Here's your dollar. Don't he touch it.
Put my father on the budget.
Maybe Pop would like to try it.
Mom has got the special diet.
Tell him, Hilda, this is great.
We are living in the Poorhouse State.
Tell him, Hilda, we are poor.
Knock, knock. Welfare's at the door.

Welfare's standing at the door.
Tell, him, Hilda, we are poor.
Tell him, Hilda, it's too late.
We are living in the Poorhouse State.
Welfare? Carfare? Wherefore? Whyfore?
What I got to tell you lie for?
What I got to tell you lie for?
Welfare ain't a thing you die for!
I was born on the ADC.
Ain't nobody gonna make a man out of me . . .

"When did you write that?" I asked. George fumbled with the change in his pockets. "It wasn't me . . . a bunch of us did it together one night. Our social worker helped . . ."

BIBLIOGRAPHICAL NOTE

• A number of books and pamphlets are being published regularly about what public assistance is and what it tries to accomplish, most under official auspices. Very few are informative about who does not get Welfare and why. For my purposes, the most useful documents proved to be the monthly reports of the New York City Department of Welfare. These list intake and disbursements. I also made extensive use of policy manuals from New York and other localities, many of which I have cited in footnotes.

Social Security and Public Policy by Evelyn Burns (McGraw-Hill, 1956) is perhaps the most thorough description of the American welfare system, and Mrs. Burns's writings are truly erudite on policy and statutes, as are those of Elizabeth Wickendon of the National Social Welfare Assembly. The most concise description of the nation's public welfare programs is former New York City Welfare Commissioner James Dumpson's contribution to the *Encyclopedia of Social Work* for 1964. For a somewhat more partisan account of the various legal hazards, may I recommend "Poverty, Injustice and the Welfare State," by Richard A. Cloward and Richard M. Elman, *The Nation*, February 28 and March 7, 1966.

In general, the literature on welfare for specialists and the general public alike lacks a certain candor; often it is wrapped in a thick cloud of professional jargon. Some notable exceptions are the reports of Greenleigh Associates, an independent New York research and public relations firm. See their 1960 study of AFDC in Cook County, Chicago, *Facts, Fallacies, and Future,* and their 1965 "home interview" study of low-income households in Detroit, Michigan. Also of great worth are the writings of Winifred Bell, which I have cited earlier, and Joan Gordon's study, *The Poor of Harlem: Social Functioning in the Underclass,* published in mimeographed form by the Department of Welfare's Interdepartmental Neighborhood Service Center. *The Social Security Bulletin* has printed informative articles on the relationship between welfare and poverty and useful statistical breakdowns on the nationwide Welfare picture; and I have learned a great deal about questions of legal rights from the scholarly papers of Jacobus Ten Broek, Charles Reich, and Edward Sparer, as they have appeared in a variety of legal and social work publications. In general, though, the literature on welfare has shown an administrative bias, and the client's view has been left largely obscure. For some widely disparate views on the so-called Welfare problem, as well as some interesting peripheral works that shed light on this discussion, I recommend the following:

Berle, Beatrice Bishop, *Eight Puerto Rican Families in Sickness and in Health.* New York, Columbia University Press, 1958.

Glazer, Nathan, and Moynihan, Daniel P., *Beyond the Melting Pot,* Harvard-MIT, 1963.

HEW, *Serving People in Need: Public Assistance Under the Social Security Act,* Bureau of Family Services pamphlet, Washington, D.C., 1964.

HEW, *A Constructive Public Welfare Program,* Welfare Administration pamphlet, Washington, D.C. (as revised September, 1965.

Horwitz, Julius, *Welfare—New York City,* a report to Senate Majority Leader Walter J. Mahoney, Albany, March, 1963. (See also the author's first-person narrative, *The Inhabitants,* which is about as able an apology for Welfare investigation as one can probably find.)

May, Edgar, *The Wasted Americans: Cost of Our Welfare Dilemma.* New York, Harper and Row, 1964.

Schneider, David Moses, and Deutsch, Albert, *The History of Public Welfare in New York State.* Chicago, University of Chicago Press, 1941.

Weingarten, Violet, *Life at the Bottom,* Citizens Committee for the Children of New York pamphlet, February, 1966.